I0755851

"Larry McNeny, a man with a strong faith in God, came into our organization at a very pivotal time in our careers. We were young and had just gotten a taste of success. While touring around the world with Larry at the helm, he kept us grounded and focused. We also had great fun at the same time!"

BILL LEVERTY Guitarist of FireHouse (and still rockin' and rollin'!)

"It's rare to encounter someone whose heart, dedication, and expertise in the world of touring shine as brightly as Larry's. Over the years, I've had the privilege of working alongside him, and each experience has been nothing short of extraordinary. Beyond being the best tour manager in the business, Larry is a true friend and collaborator whose commitment to his craft is matched only by his integrity and passion for the people he works with.

"Larry and I share a deep respect for our work, and together we helped shape a program for Teen Cancer America based on my Symphantasy series—a project that has brought us even closer. His knowledge of the history and evolution of the touring industry is unparalleled, and I can think of no one more qualified to share his journey, insights, and wisdom in a memoir.

"Larry's story is not just one of legendary tours and iconic artists, but of the heart and soul that have powered it all. This book is a testament to the dedication and passion that drives the best in the business—the real deal in every sense of the word."

DANIEL FLANNERY Creator, Producer, and Director

"Larry's fascinating memoir fully captures the complex network of relationships behind the rock and pop scene in the 1970s and 1980s. His exciting and energetic narrative provides revealing insights into the hidden ecosystem of support behind the creative music making, tours, performances, and press calls of the time."

DR. JOHN BARNES Visiting Senior Research Fellow at Canterbury Christ Church University and a National Teaching Fellow

"I have known Larry McNeny for over thirty-two years. Larry, along with Neil Aspinall, Richard Cole, and Kelly Kelleher, was one of the early tour managers who paved the way for the rest of us. His nearly forty years on the road with Eric Clapton, the Bee Gees, Jack Bruce, Ozzy Osbourne, Linda Ronstadt, Three Dog Night, and many other acts helped create and build the industry into what it is today.

"Understand that back in the early days, there were no cell phones, luxury buses with bunks, or affordable private jets. No computerized moving lights or huge PAs. They created the business and tech as they went. In addition, every state or city had their own promoter, unlike today where there is a monopoly with only two concert-promotion firms in the world. These guys were visionaries, magicians, and geniuses. I am proud to call Larry my friend."

RICK THOMPSON Tour and Production Management

"Larry McNeny joined us as tour manager for the 1982 Ozzy Osbourne Diary of a Madman tour. This was just after the plane crash that took Randy Rhoads's life, and I have to say, the most challenging period of ours or any tour.

"During that era, there were none of the high-tech communication devices we have at our disposal today, such as cell phones, which made it much more difficult to resolve the daily unexpected predicaments of our tour with Ozzy. Somehow, Larry, along with Ozzy's manager Sharon Osborne, figured everything out on the fly as well as through creative improvisation. Often, it was magical watching them; however, we're still here playing, so somehow it all worked. Thanks, Larry!"

RUDY SARZO Bass Player and Songwriter for Ozzy Osbourne, Quiet Riot (founding member), Whitesnake, and Ronnie James Dio

"It has been my privilege to know Larry McNeny since he first contacted Roger Daltrey over ten years ago to offer his help to our charity, Teen Cancer America. Since then, we have developed a strong bond in our goal to improve the lives of young people with cancer throughout the United States.

"Larry has been there constantly, always willing to step up to the plate to help us. He's used his network to find someone who could get Ed Sheeran to visit a young fan in the hospital; donated his time and money and utilized his industry contacts to help us make a world-class vinyl production of young people's songs; found talent for our events; collected vintage memorabilia and offered his own to our music auctions; and coproduced with Daniel Flannery the most beautiful concept of Symphantasy that will be our evergreen fundraiser for years to come. Larry is a gentleman who always puts the needs of young people with cancer first. He has become a friend as well as a supporter.

"And in all these years, Larry has never bragged about his extraordinary experiences in the music industry. In this excellent book, he illuminates the critical part that he and his contemporaries played in influencing that industry's direction of travel. This book is a fascinating insight into that world. Enjoy!"

SIMON DAVIES Former Executive Director of Teen Cancer America and Chief Executive Officer of Teenage Cancer Trust, UK, the charities of rock legends The Who. Now retired and an Executive Advisor to Teen Cancer America.

"I think it's safe to say that without Mr. McNeny's benign and competent presence as tour manager, our ship during the Jack Bruce USA tour in 1977 would have totally foundered. Talk about a volatile crew! OK, the captain took the prize for being the most volatile while the rest of us tried to keep afloat in the wake of events.

"But Larry was always there on the case as we made our way east to west across the States. From Baltimore to San Francisco, he dealt with canceled gigs, changes of travel arrangements, trouble on stage, and trouble backstage. I'm pretty sure I didn't know the half of it (thankfully!), though I do remember his emotional response on being told he had to stay on with Jack for a week after the rest of us left for home.

"So yes, anything Mr. McNeny would have to write on the subject of touring, in the shape of reminiscence or advice, would surely be invaluable."

TONY HYMAS Solo Recording Artist and Keyboardist for Jack Bruce and Jeff Beck

Blood, Guts, and No Glory!

Blood, Guts, and No Glory!

Forty Years Touring on Rock's Road.

Larry R. McNeny

TCU PRESS
Fort Worth, Texas

Library of Congress Cataloging-in-Publication Data

Names: McNeny, Larry R. author | Fraboni, Rob writer of foreword
Title: Blood, guts, and no glory! : forty years touring on rock's road / Larry R. McNeny.
Description: Fort Worth : TCU Press, [2026] | Includes bibliographical references and index.
Identifiers: LCCN 2026000763 (print) | LCCN 2026000764 (ebook) | ISBN 9780875659596 | ISBN 9780875659602 ebook
Subjects: LCSH: McNeny, Larry R. | Clapton, Eric--Friends and associates | Concert tours--Management | Rock musicians--United States | Teenage musicians--United States | LCGFT: Autobiographies
Classification: LCC ML429.M407 A3 2025 (print) | LCC ML429.M407 (ebook) | DDC 780.68 [B]--dc23/eng/20260129
LC record available at https://lccn.loc.gov/2026000763
LC ebook record available at https://lccn.loc.gov/2026000764

TCU PRESS

TCU Box 298300
Fort Worth, Texas 76129
www.tcupress.com

Design by Bill Brammer

This book is dedicated to my family, especially my parents and brothers who let me grow up chasing a dream.

And to my wife and children for putting up with this dreamer who would not be told it can't be done!

Blood, Guts, and No Glory!

Memories and stories from a career on the road with some of the world's most celebrated entertainers and musicians.

CONTENTS

FOREWORD

Larry McNeny and I met for the first time at Shangri-La Ranch, a recording studio that I helped design and build. It was said the property was a former bordello on a hill overlooking the Malibu, California, beach. Who knows?

I had recorded a number of bands there and liked the sound, and when I was asked by RSO Records and one of their managers to record and coproduce an album for Eric Clapton, I happily agreed. The album became *No Reason to Cry*.

At the time, Larry had not yet begun working for the Robert Stigwood Organization (RSO) or Clapton but was in Los Angeles and knew several members of the band: Carl Radle, Dick Sims, and Jamie Oldaker. He came by one evening with a friend for a listen and to visit and was introduced to Eric and me.

A week later, as we were still recording, Larry returned to the studio with his friend and had a copy of a clever album cover, suggesting we use it for this album. They had made a mock-up of an oversized postcard that featured the Hollywood sign with sand at its base and waves washing up on the sand. It looked as if a big earthquake had happened, and now the ocean was coming all the way up to the Hollywood sign. It was great and very clever. The other side featured the back of a postcard, which lent itself to putting the names of the songs and other details you'd find on most album covers.

Jamie saw it, thought it was cool, and showed it to Eric, who asked who made this. After looking at it and getting the inside joke of the photo, he said, "This is the album cover I want for this record." Eric then asked Larry if they could have it, and he agreed, so Eric handed the artwork to his then-tour manager Richard Cole. Eric told him to send it to London as the album's cover.

It never made it to RSO, and the album came out with another cover. Years later, Larry told me that while he was working for Clapton, he became friends with Richard, who had gone on to Led Zeppelin, and asked him, "What ever happened to the cover? Eric told you to send it to London to use as the album cover for *No Reason to Cry*?" Richard said something to the effect of, "I really can't remember, but I think I just tossed it in the trash bin," which shows what kind of stamina and control Larry had. I am sure his feelings were hurt after all that work, but Larry sucked it up and carried on as if all was fine.

It was a while before we saw each other again, except in passing if I met up with Eric on tour. A couple of years later, when Larry was working for Stigwood and eventually with Clapton, Jack Bruce, and the Bee Gees, I was asked by RSO to record and produce some tracks for a possible album for Clapton backup singer Marcy Levy. She was and is a very talented singer and songwriter.

We gathered in LA, and Larry was the tour manager for these recordings, taking care of the band, which was mostly Marcy's Tulsa friends from Eric's band. We got to know each other better during that time, and they would often come over to my place when I lived just off Santa Monica Boulevard. It was a casual acquaintance that had become a working relationship, and we got along because we were almost always on the same page. Marcy's album was never fully made, for whatever reason the record company had, but I did what I was hired to do and didn't ask questions.

Time went by, and Larry and I would run into each other occasionally since I'd see Eric on tour often with my wife. She and Pattie Boyd had been friends, and after the *No Reason to Cry* record, Eric and I had become friends as well and kept in regular touch.

A year or so later, Pattie showed up at our place after she and Eric had a falling out of sorts. She left the UK and came to Los Angeles to stay with my wife and me for a few days. Unbeknownst to us and Pattie, Eric and his manager were visiting late one afternoon in London, and a placed bet would upend her life. The next day, almost every newspaper across the UK and USA (six hours behind England) announced that Eric Clapton and Pattie Boyd were to be married. Well, everyone was surprised, but Eric's manager won his bet, and now Eric was on the spot.

After a call to Pattie, they decided to marry in Tucson, Arizona, at the beginning of the upcoming American tour. They would try to keep it quiet and low-key. Eric asked me to be his best man, to which I was flattered, and he asked Larry McNeny to take his blood test for him as Eric could not stand needles. At the time, Larry and Eric looked quite similar, and

Larry was often used as a Clapton distraction where fans would follow Larry's car leaving a venue while Eric and his manager would saunter out five minutes later and leave undisturbed. Larry took it all in stride.

Larry, surprised as he was, said he'd do the blood test for Eric but was not fond of the charade. Regardless, with Eric's bodyguard at his side, Larry took the required blood test at a local hospital late one evening. I'd say Larry showed dedication to his boss and to the overall cause.

After learning what he'd done for Eric, I knew he was the type of person I liked and knew I, too, could count on him if needed—not for blood necessarily but as a friend. I even had him come and stay in my home when my children were young because I knew he was one of the good guys.

Over these many years, despite our different locations and careers—mine in LA and New York, Larry's in London and Dallas—we have regularly kept in touch. He or I will phone the other just to catch up or share ideas, concepts, and upcoming plans. We are both hoping a situation presents itself where we can work together again, although we communicate so much it feels inevitable.

Larry's career has been lengthy and varied, having worked with a variety of celebrated musicians, such as Eric Clapton, Jack Bruce, the Bee Gees, Linda Ronstadt, and many others. Likewise, I know he has been around the world many times and has a great deal of interesting stories and unique events to talk about. When I heard he'd written his memoir, I knew it would be one worth reading.

His book addresses some of the stories you have heard about here and fills in some gaps for those who wonder what transpires on the road with rock stars. I know Larry was grateful for his fortunate position in the music industry, and despite not making it as a rock star himself, he has told me that he never regretted his decision, changing his mind from wanting to be a household name and having people ask for his autograph (though he did have to sign for Eric often enough) to being on the business side of the industry. I feel certain you will enjoy these true and historic tales in Larry's memoir *Blood, Guts, and No Glory: Forty Years Touring on Rock's Road!*

Rob Fraboni

Record Producer and Audio Engineer

INTRODUCTION

I stopped dead still for a long moment and thought, *What the hell am I doing?* In the long hallway of a very nice hotel, I glanced down and in my left hand I was carrying a dark green, somewhat-battered leather briefcase full of itineraries, room lists for hotels we'd be visiting, limo companies we'd be using, and promoters we'd be counting on for a great number of things. In my other hand, I had a pilot-style briefcase. You know, one of those that is about eight inches wide and the tops of the two sides fold over each other before locking. Inside was a ten-ounce glass, two bottles of 7UP soda, and two fifths of Courvoisier cognac, all neatly secured in custom-formed foam padding. This was Eric's special briefcase.

What the hell am I doing? I felt like an accomplice to a potential murder—a murder by alcohol poisoning. *Nothing to be proud of* momentarily passed through my mind as well.

Flash-forward approximately thirty-eight years after I'd last seen Eric in person or even spoken to him and I met him for lunch and told him of having experienced that complicit feeling. But with a gracious hug and kindness in his voice, he told me, "Forget it. Don't feel bad about it. You were only doing your job. If not you, then somebody else would have been doing it. It's OK. It was me."

With that, I felt somewhat absolved and was thankful that I had actually reconnected with someone I could now admire as a whole, happy, and fulfilled person.

– January 2020

I AM A DALLAS NATIVE, BORN AND RAISED. A real Texan—not one who "moved here as fast as I could," like the bumper sticker says.

Early in my life, I did all the normal things kids did in the 1950s. I played football, baseball, and basketball through the YMCA and then in grade school. I was not a great player, I'll admit, nor was I ever on a particularly good team. It just never seemed to happen that way.

We also played a lot of sports with all the local kids in our suburban middle-class neighborhood. I distinctly remember a two-hand touch football game with my brother and a bunch of friends in the front yard of our North Dallas home. For some unknown reason, I got the football, and my teammates were screaming, "Head for the driveway!" which served as our goal line. Next thing I remember, I was face down in the dirt of a flowerbed filled with prickly Holly bushes. *Hey*, I thought, *this was two hands below the waist.*

Nevertheless, I clearly remember deciding, right then and there, that there had to be something better than playing sports for a living. Being a sports star, for some odd reason, seemed to be every kid's plan. It wasn't until I discovered the guitar at age thirteen that I knew what path my life would take . . . or so I thought.

At that time, the Beatles were new on the scene, and I could easily see, even preferred, being chased by thousands of screaming girls instead of would-be tacklers. But first I had to learn to play an instrument. Boy Scouts, too, would have to take a backseat to this new discovery. I never saw any girls chasing a Boy Scout. In fact, I left the Boy Scouts despite being just one merit badge shy of an Eagle Scout award.

Kind of stupid, I know. Maybe one day? Oldest Eagle Scout to ever earn the honor? I wonder if they have a merit badge for all the traveling I did. Or suitcase packing?

That Christmas, my very cool parents got me a Sears Silvertone guitar that came in an amplifier case, which today is a collector's item and can command a pretty penny. That was my first guitar and was darned hard to play with the strings an inch above the fret board. Then again, what could you expect for sixty-five dollars? I should have known. Still, after hounding them relentlessly, my parents had granted my wish. It was a good, no, life-changing Christmas. Thanks, Mom and Dad.

Over the course of the next decade, after quite a few guitar changes—each more costly than the last—and a number of instructors, I learned to play fairly well. I never practiced nearly enough, though. Another thing I'll again have to admit was foolish on my part.

I was in several local bands that made a moderate amount of money, including the Corsairs, a Roy Orbison cover band that played, you guessed it, nothing but Roy Orbison material because that was all the lead singer and lead guitarist knew how to play. We performed at parties and other small functions whenever possible, and sometimes we'd even get paid. This went on for a few years.

Finally, in 1967, I started my own and most professional band with three very good friends who were competent musicians. We called ourselves the Bridge, and after growing in popularity early on during the school year, we were soon playing all over Texas and Oklahoma and making a fairly decent living for teenagers. And we were having a lot of fun, thanks in part to the mother of my best friend and drummer, Larry Meletio, and her station wagon.

We played at fraternity and sorority parties, clubs, and even opened concerts for many major acts of the 1960s, such as Them, the Troggs, Mitch Ryder and the Detroit Wheels, the Mamas & the Papas, Iron Butterfly, the Five Americans, the Jeff Beck Group, Sugarloaf, the Who, and a few others whose names escape me now. The time was truly magical.

However, those previous bands were just stepping stones to a new music group that my close friends Larry (drums), Lanny Lander (bass), Jim McClellan (vocals), and I formed in 1968. We called ourselves Big Punks, although we started a few years before punk music was actually celebrated as "the new thing" and made a lot of people famous and wealthy.

We chose the name from the Bowery Boys of early movie fame. They were a gang of sorts but never did anything very bad. The "coppers" in the films just referred to them as those "punks" or "punk kids." It sounded good, and we took it.

This band played only original music because we knew if we were going to make it in the music business, we had to write our own songs. Unfortunately, that made us a bit hard to book in the traditional local party or club scenes. Our contemporaries liked to dance to music they would hear on the radio, not some new, never-before-heard thrashing.

Most local bands who could sufficiently play cover songs stayed booked at the popular clubs and made, I am sure, a great deal more money than we did. But we loved writing our own material. While our songs were good—listening to them now some forty years later, they still hold up—what we played was not what high school or college kids wanted to dance to, and that was a fact. Which in turn meant they didn't have much interest in us either. There are some samples of our music on YouTube, but you'll have to figure out on your own where the songs survive.

My band moved to Los Angeles in 1971 with dreams of stardom, and, were, for all intents and purposes, quasi-successful. But we never landed that elusive recording contract and never made it big time. Mind you, this was the analog era, and there was no such thing as digital recordings, MP3 files, or streaming. Achieving success was done the old-fashioned way: sign with a record company, record an album, get it distributed, and hope it's a hit.

Big Punks won many Battle of the Bands contests while we were living in Southern California, amassing some much-needed cash. There was always a promise of a recording contract as well, although sadly one never materialized. This was just a ruse by the promoter to get more bands to participate, I suspect.

We even wrote a conceptual, anti-satanic rock opera titled *Danny's Inferno* and performed our ambitious work in its entirety several times, the last being in front of about two thousand students at Loyola Marymount University, just north of LAX Airport. That performance was videotaped by the college, but later it was recorded over as Loyola had a limited budget and always reused its tapes after a few days. If our rock opera had not been deleted, things might have been different. Of course, this was the very early days of personal video machines, so tapes were expensive. Still, much of the original show's theatrics were seen a couple of years later by another band who indeed became bigger than big. They wear a lot of makeup.

Ever since I was a young teenager, I had wanted to be a rock star, although no one regularly used that term in the 1960s. But it was not in the cards. After being together and living in each other's pockets for quite a while, the band finally broke up in 1973, and we all went our separate ways.

I was devastated and lost. I had played with these guys in one band or another for most of my musical career and in particular over the last five years as Big Punks. We knew each other so well, and the music was so tight. I didn't see how I could ever recreate that sound or feel again.

I was not the kind of guitar player who could go and jam with any group of musicians; at least I did not feel I could. Although we played some cover material throughout the years as Big Punks, we primarily played only our own songs. I was way out of touch in terms of jamming with other players.

So I sat around for about a year and pondered what to do with myself, and how I could turn this into lemonade. I was fortunate to find some work as a roadie for a band called Jo Jo Gunne, which had produced a few hit singles. My good friend Jimmie Randall, a former bass player in one of my bands, had recently joined the group, and he was kind enough to help me get a job setting up their gear while they toured with acts such as Black Oak Arkansas and the J. Geils Band.

I'll have to admit it was not a very pleasant position as we were usually the first opening act, so we tried to get our gear out of the venue before the second act took the stage. Otherwise, we'd be stuck waiting for them or the headliner to finish. I remember getting into the truck after one speedy exit and seeing my heart pounding through my sweat-soaked shirt. Similar to my experience playing front-yard football, it was then I decided I needed to look for other avenues in the entertainment business.

During this time, both my father and grandfather also died about four months apart, and after the funerals and sufficient time to grieve, I returned to LA to try to find another direction. Giving the performance side one final try, in 1974, I auditioned for a band Iggy Pop was putting together as well as for a new group being formed for singer Ruby Starr, an offshoot of the Black Oak Arkansas organization. I wasn't hired for either of these jobs as I was just not the type of player they were looking for, and I knew why.

Which left me wondering what I could do good enough to make a living in the music industry. It finally dawned on me, though, that I was always the one who booked our band gigs or worked to get the jobs. I found the hotels and rental trucks. I was a hustler.

Even when it wasn't for my band directly, I was always hustling. I remember talking my way backstage at Dick Clark's 1966 Caravan of Stars show featuring Brian Hyland, Sam the Sham & the Pharaohs of "Wooly Bully" fame, Gary Lewis & the Playboys, and, of all oddities and to my great joy, the Yardbirds with both Jeff Beck *and* Jimmy Page. I was all of sixteen and I ended up sitting in their dressing room chatting to them for quite a while, just because of my moxie and gift for gab. Page told me that night he'd sell me a Fender Esquire guitar, which was similar to a Telecaster, but it never came about.

In the summer of 1974, I found out keyboardist Dick Sims had recorded the album *461 Ocean Boulevard* with Eric Clapton in Miami and was joining Eric's new band permanently. By an odd turn of events, Dick and his girlfriend came and stayed for about a week at the home I shared with my then girlfriend, which we were renting in Glendale, California. Though Dick was holed up in his room recuperating most of the time (medicinally, I suspect), we did get to know each other a bit.

Little did I know that my simple kindness to Dick, letting him crash at my house, would be repaid by him one day. And in a way that would impact the rest of my life.

In truth, I owe a lot of thanks to a great deal of people, especially those who gave me opportunities to prove myself. I feel I've had a career that was incredibly special and unique. When people ask what I did for a living, I tell them I traveled around the world numerous times in the best private buses and jets, and I even toured Europe in a private train twice. I would add that I got to eat at the finest restaurants and listened to the greatest live music night after night. And to add icing to that cake, someone paid me to do it. It would be very difficult to beat that kind of job.

Finally, I must say that as the years have passed—way too quickly, I might add—many friends, celebrities, crew, staff, and business associates I was fortunate enough to work with are beginning to depart this earthly plane. No names here, but every one of them is missed, and I am a better person for having known and worked with them all.

I hope you enjoy my story and some quips and understand that I am aware of how incredibly lucky I have been.

CHAPTER 1

Someone Opened the Door

Going to Work for Eric Clapton

The year was 1976, and once again I was sitting at my small, ridiculously cheap, often-painted desk one morning in the Ricky Hill Agency, the office of well-known musician Carl Radle's personal assistant, Ricky Hill. I have to admit I was getting bored of sitting there every day trying to hustle up some sort of business or career that could carry me through life or even the next few years, but I was grateful for the opportunity he allowed me.

I had been showing up at this desk for a while by then, the space having been offered to me for free as long as I paid my own bills for things such as long-distance telephone calls. Having taken my last shot at being a performing musician, I'd decided that since nothing was really happening in LA, moving to Tulsa and somehow working my way into Eric Clapton's organization might be a good idea. I knew the odds were long, but the city had a good music scene, and four of the six members of Eric's band were based there. So I loaded up my truck and moved to Beverly, er, Tulsa, that is.

I would show up early every weekday morning, often long before Ricky or his assistant, Julie Chapman Spears, and do my best to come up with new ideas for jobs. I'd read trade magazines like *Billboard, Rolling Stone,* and *Amusement Business* for clues that might light a spark. I could have done this from my apartment on the opposite side of town near Oral Roberts University, but going into an office seemed more productive. In addition, the person Ricky worked for was at least in the music business and coincidently played bass for Eric.

Tulsa was a nice town but not my hometown. I was a former-aspiring-rock-star transplant from Dallas, and although I had a girlfriend who grew up near Tulsa and a few friends, I still felt a bit isolated. The situation was difficult because being in a band was like being in an exclusive club. We did not need anyone else to make us feel whole. We entertained each other, relied on each other completely, and made our own rules, which for the most part were legal. And I most definitely was not in with the local Tulsa music crowd as they were very insular and cliquey. I knew some of them enough to say hello at a club or bar, but that was about as far as it went. At least hanging around the office helped me feel a bit more in touch with the music industry outside of Tulsa, which I wanted to get back involved with.

The office was a purpose-built space at the back of a construction-business warehouse near Eleventh Street and Yale Avenue. We accessed a dusty back parking lot through an alleyway before then entering the building from a loading dock. While it wasn't plush, the place was comfortable and eclectic. At least I was not sitting at home watching soap operas.

Ricky took care of the business affairs, in a manner of speaking, and kept the home fires burning for Carl, who was originally the bass player for Gary Lewis & the Playboys. They had several hits in the late 1960s, most notably "This Diamond Ring," which for my first real girlfriend and me was "our song." Carl had also played with Leon Russell, Joe Cocker, Delaney & Bonnie & Friends, Derek and the Dominos, and now again with Eric. He was a highly respected musician of the era and a very nice guy, so very calm.

Julie was a British transplant and former employee of Robert Stigwood, who himself was a former employee of Beatles manager Brian Epstein and later founded the famed RSO Records. As told to me, she had moved to Tulsa after deciding not to invest in Robert's third or fourth go-around to stave off bankruptcy, which involved him offering his employees a chance to buy stock in his company. This was a decision I wondered if she ever seriously regretted as those who stayed and invested became very wealthy. Instead, Julie, who I liked very much, answered the phone, paid both the office and Carl's personal bills, and handled all the things Ricky was supposed to do but was too busy to deal with because of his own mini-celebrity life of sorts.

Ricky had allowed me to share the office knowing they had plenty of unused space available. It was really no skin off his nose, and having more people around made the office look like things were "happening" for him.

I had little interaction with Carl's business, but Julie and I were friends. Sitting twenty feet apart all day with not a whole lot going on, we had a lot of time to chat.

One morning shortly after Julie arrived, the office phone rang—the one I did not answer unless she or Ricky were out. As usual, he was not there. It was early in the day, about 11 a.m. on a Friday, if I remember correctly, and she said in her fading British accent, "Call for you. It's Carl."

How odd, I thought. Here I was, having worked in the office Carl paid for the last two years of my living in Tulsa, and though we'd spoken a few times and were friendly, there was nothing I could think of that would give him a reason to phone me.

Not knowing how answering this call would ultimately change my life in, oh, so many ways, I casually punched the extension button and greeted Carl. "How's everything going?"

Carl and the rest of Clapton's Tulsa-based band—keyboardist Dick Sims, drummer Jamie Oldaker, and backup singer Marcy Levy—had only recently left the city and were currently in rehearsals prior to the start of a tour across the southern US. Carl asked what I was doing, knowing quite well that I was doing what I always did, hustling to make something, anything happen to bring in income and justify my being seated at this silly desk. To be honest, he probably didn't know what I was doing as he had better things to do than think about me.

"Just the same as always," I responded.

"Would you be interested in coming down to Dallas and helping Eric's manager, Roger Forrester, with some things on the tour?" he asked.

Despite him having all of my attention from the outset, I wasn't sure if I had heard him correctly. I think I said, "What does that mean?"

"You'd be Roger's assistant on the tour," Carl said, "and do whatever he needs you to do."

Roger worked for the Robert Stigwood Organization (RSO) in London and handled Clapton's business affairs exclusively. Stigwood not only managed Eric but also the Bee Gees, Jack Bruce, and several more celebrities, and his company had its hands in other aspects of the entertainment industry. In 1967, Stigwood purchased Associated London Scripts and brought on board Beryl Vertue. As a producer for *Steptoe and Son* and *Till Death Do Us Part,* she helped bring those two famous British television comedies to the US as *Sanford and Son* and *All in the Family*, which became major hits in their own rights. Likewise, RSO was involved in producing stage shows and films such as *Godspell* and *Jesus Christ Superstar*.

At that time, Roger was fairly unknown in music-industry bigwig circles. He had previously been a booking agent in the basement of the Stigwood office, trying to get gigs and tours for any of the agency's acts. Now he managed one of the greatest guitarists in the world who, if Roger had his way, would be back on top of the charts on short notice.

I asked when I would be needed, knowing full well I was going to say yes to anything. Carl said that Roger wanted me to fly down to my hometown of Dallas, meet him at the hotel, and he'd fill me in. I agreed. I was no idiot!

They arranged a ticket for me to pick up at the Tulsa Airport that afternoon. I was to take a taxi, which they asked if they could reimburse me for later, and then once in Dallas I was to check into my hotel room, already arranged, and call Roger upon my arrival.

Oh shit! I only had four hours. I was off and running. I told Julie and Ricky, as he'd come in during the call, that I was headed to Dallas to work for Roger, gathered up my few things from the office, and headed home. I don't think Ricky was too happy as it was me, not him, who got the call. I barely remember getting ready to leave—for how long I didn't even know—and having to tell my girlfriend I had been asked to go to work for Eric Clapton, which I knew she'd have no problem with.

Within a couple of hours, I'd packed my brown Samsonite suitcase and was seated in the waiting lounge at the Tulsa International Airport, thrilled for the adventure that awaited me and thankful for my God-given good fortune. I was extremely pleased, especially because, at least for a while, I would not have to sit in that office hustling for work.

The flight was short, and the taxi ride to West Dallas wasn't very long. The hotel was located in an industrial area off Interstate 35 and Regal Row but seemed fairly new and pretty upscale. It was just up the street from Showco, which is where we purchased our sound equipment. After a smooth check-in, I found that my room was a single, meaning no one but me (an important perk). I laid a few of my things out, such as my Dopp kit in the bathroom, and then I sat staring at the phone for a good fifteen minutes, wondering what lay ahead.

Finally, I summoned up enough courage—this was before I knew everyone, celebrity or not, was cut from the same cloth—to phone Roger's room. He answered fairly quickly in a drowsy, nonchalant demeanor, "Yes?" He never said hello, only "yes" or "what is it?" In fact, Roger always acted drowsy and nonchalant, and it wasn't until later that I realized why.

"Mr. Forrester, this is Larry McNeny from Tulsa," I began. "I was told to phone you as soon as I arrived."

"Yes," he said before telling me to come to his room immediately. Well, step one was complete. Now for the big meet.

I knocked on his door. He was a floor above me, and since all the hallways and doorways looked alike, I assumed it would be identical to my room. No! It was a suite, although I'd later learn it was just a cheap suite in a second-class hotel compared to some of the places we'd eventually stay. Still, it was a suite, nonetheless.

He invited me in and asked if I'd like a drink. Too nervous to drink anything, I took a seat in a chair across from Roger with the sun behind him glaring into my eyes, almost blinding me.

The room permeated with smoke as Roger, among others with the band and crew, chain-smoked Rothmans. They'd bring enough of the British cigarettes, packed in the equipment road cases, to last them an entire tour, since they could not buy them outside of the UK. That could mean fifty to one hundred cartons. Obviously, this was before the campaigns to stop smoking really took off, not that these guys would have paid any attention to what they were saying anyway.

He proceeded to tell me how I came to be there, and I remember being surprised. The tour was planned and rehearsals in Dallas were booked, but when everyone arrived, Roger realized the band totaled eight people, and each would likely bring along at least three pieces of luggage. Already having to manage a renowned artist who was exploding on the scene again, he knew he could not do this tour as the only person responsible for keeping order, hauling suitcases, and handling advance work. So get an assistant, he imagined. OK, here I was.

He also said that when he asked the band at dinner the previous evening if they knew anyone he could hire to help out for this tour, Dick immediately spoke up and said he thought I was the guy for the job. I knew Dick somewhat better than I did Carl as my girlfriend and Dick's girlfriend were best friends. We had spent more time in each other's company. Regardless, I will be forever grateful for him injecting my name into the conversation.

Roger told me he had come on the tour thinking he would take care of all the affairs on a daily basis, but once everyone arrived and rehearsals began, he determined he didn't want to handle it all on his own. He wanted someone he could count on to help him out.

My jobs would include advancing the upcoming travel arrangements and hotel reservations, confirming all was as it needed to be, and making sure the band was in the lobby ready for departure, whether that be to our private plane for the next tour stop or the limousines heading to that night's show. I was also to arrange the venue departure with security and police and hustle the band straight off the stage into the waiting limos, so we'd beat the crowd out of the arena.

Another aspect of my job on this first tour would be to arrange for everyone's luggage to be set outside their hotel room doors an hour before departure. With the help of porters and some "readies" (money), I would then gather all the bags into a waiting van or truck I'd reserved, head to the private airport where our Vickers Viscount four-engine turboprop was waiting, load the suitcases into the hold, and wait beside the plane as a signal that all was right for a timely takeoff. This was also so Roger could see me at the earliest possible moment.

Roger hated surprises, and he took it as his responsibility to keep Eric happy and comfortable. So the sooner Roger knew about any hiccup from what was considered the norm, the easier it would be to concoct an alternative plan. This care from the outset seemed like such a kind and respectful thing for him to do, but that attention to detail would one day become a burden in a variety of ways.

Roger made me a salary offer that I felt was very generous and told me all my expenses would be covered: meals, drinks, laundry, etc. I could not believe my good fortune. I was to spend the next month or so on the road with one of the most famous guitarists in the world . . . and get paid as well.

Having been an aspiring rock star myself, playing guitar and writing and performing songs with my band throughout my teenage years and early twenties, I knew who Eric Clapton was from the Yardbirds, Cream,

Delaney & Bonnie & Friends, and Derek and the Dominos. I'd seen Cream play at the Dallas Memorial Auditorium, and the band's innovation was startling. I knew firsthand that Eric, who we also called EC, was an incredible guitarist, so when we did the first show of the tour, I felt a real sense of accomplishment, career-wise. I had to work hard not to smile from ear to ear and look like the Joker.

In addition, everyone in the band welcomed my help, and they treated me as one of them from the outset. That made everything even more enjoyable.

The job itself turned out to not be too challenging, especially after Roger told me one day that when he did luggage, he never touched a bag. He paid the bellmen to do all the lifting. Say no more. I was in complete agreement.

Advancing the dates, hotels, and travel pickup was not difficult either; it only required time spent on the phone daily, and I could do all of that in my hotel room within an hour. Prior to the tour, Roger had made a very thorough itinerary with all the dates and contacts for the hotels, limo services, and private airstrips. My job entailed calling, introducing myself, and coordinating the exact times and details of every movement during our stay in their city. I was always warmly welcomed because of Eric's name and the money they would be paid for performing their service.

The hotels were instructed to have the band's rooms preregistered with envelopes containing keys and a copy of the room list ready for each member upon our arrival. That way the band would not be standing around in the hotel lobby waiting to check in, a problem compounded if there was a line of guests waiting to do the same thing or fans on hand who'd found out ahead of time where we'd be.

Fortunately, the process worked well and made the experience even more magical. I'd walk in the hotel, ask the bellman for the envelopes, and wham, bam, everyone was on their way to their rooms. The luggage was then usually delivered to the rooms within thirty minutes after our arrival.

While both Eric and Roger had suites in the hotel, Roger's room was the one with a revolving door. When anyone was bored or wanted something to do, they'd congregate in Roger's suite and chat, watch TV, or drink. It was either there, or we'd meet up in the hotel's coffee shop or restaurant, where many meals were consumed and Rothmans smoked. There were a lot of slow times when there was not much to do but relax and enjoy the hotel life or drink. No one was much of a sightseer, at least then.

But Roger and others still considered Eric to be in a delicate place, psychologically and addictively, as he had only been clean of his drug habit for a brief time. Because of this, Roger was determined to keep Eric's interest, mood, and activity up. However, Eric drank, often heavily and occasionally all day, with his choice of drink being Courvoisier and lemonade, the UK's equivalent to 7UP. Despite everyone knowing this was not a great way to pass the time, nobody, except maybe Roger, ever questioned Eric's drinking—well, not out loud. This, too, would eventually lead to larger and more serious repercussions down the road.

With rehearsals done, we left our base in Dallas and headed to Florida. The first concert would be in St. Petersburg, with the second show occurring in Miami at the Hollywood Sportatorium. At the speed and altitude the Viscount flew, Roger realized it would take the plane five or six hours to get to Miami, our first touring home base. Thinking that was too long for EC and the band this early in the tour, he decided they'd travel via a commercial airline, which only took two-and-a-half hours. I was to accompany the luggage in the Viscount, leaving early enough so all of their gear was at the hotel when they arrived. Me alone on a cool private plane? OK!

So here I was, my first travel date on the tour. It's me, two pilots, a stewardess, and forty-five pieces of luggage tucked neatly into the hold, toddling casually from Dallas to Miami a few thousand feet in the air in a very comfortable sofa-and-recliner-style private plane. *I can handle this,* I thought.

The Miami area was home to the second guitarist in the band, George Terry, who was a great player as well and did a lot of musical covering, which I am told was sometimes needed during those early days on the road. After the second show, George said there was a party at a nearby friend's house in Hollywood, a suburb just north of Miami, and that some other musicians were going to be there. He arranged it with Roger to use the limos, although Roger himself would not be going. Roger wasn't very social and tended to avoid parties and extracurricular social gatherings, so he told me to make sure everyone got home. I am not positive who in the band went, but we had enough to commandeer two limos.

After a short drive, we pulled up in front of a normal looking one-story house in a residential neighborhood. It was fairly dark, but there were a number of cars and a few other limousines randomly parked on the street, obviously having already delivered guests to the party. Inside the house, music was blaring, and people were chattering everywhere. To my surprise, I saw that several members of the Eagles band were in attendance along with about seventy-five other guests. I had no clue who anyone else was.

One of the first things I noticed upon entering the house was a large baseball-sized rock of cocaine in a bowl on the front room's coffee table. People were drinking, some sniffing, and everyone was having a very good time. Needless to say, the people who came in my two limos joined right into the party.

I am not sure whether I drank, smoked, or sniffed, but I do remember thinking, and very seriously, *Here I am on my first tour with a major rock star, the second date of the tour, the first after-party, and surely some drowsy neighbor being kept awake by the pounding bass and loud party is going to call the police and complain. We'll all be busted.* I could even imagine the headline on the front page of the *Miami Herald* the next day, "The Eagles and Clapton in Miami Drug Bust."

It's not real clear how long we stayed, although I don't think it was too late because a couple of the others in my group felt the same vibe I had and wanted to leave. I suspected it would not be the last time I'd be in such a position, having serious concerns about the safety or legality of the situation I found myself in. Thank goodness the neighbors were sound sleepers that night. Or were they at the party as well?

After making it out of Miami without getting arrested, we worked our way across Georgia, Alabama, and Louisiana into Texas, where we based ourselves again in Dallas. We'd fly off in the late afternoon to San Antonio on our private plane, which was waiting at Love Field, and then after the show fly right back to Dallas. The next day, it was Houston and then back. That way, we got to stay at the same hotel for five days and unpack, which was very comfortable, I must say. You got to know the staff and local people if you cared to.

Since we had so much time at the hotel, Roger came up with the idea of bringing in a pool table, so we could have something to do. But renting a pool table for five days was so expensive that he just bought one and had it set up in his suite. It was great.

There was always something going on there. If you were hungry or thirsty, just pick up the phone in his suite and order room service. Not bad. We played pool—lots of pool. And when we left, we gave the hotel the pool table as a gift. They were very surprised and pleased.

We did a show in Dallas, and I got to invite many of my friends, which was a nice way to show off a bit. Then we played a concert at the University of Oklahoma, only a couple of hours away from my current home in Tulsa, and several friends from there came out as well. Thank goodness we left straight after the show, though, and flew back to Dallas. It was nice not having dozens of hangers-on milling around wanting to get drunk or stoned with the band. That just made my job harder. I preferred to go back to our fancy hotel and have a drink at our bar. However, not everyone felt as I did, I eventually learned.

After we departed Dallas, we flew to Las Cruces and did a show at New Mexico State University. We then came straight off the stage, flew to LA's Hollywood-Burbank Airport, and were ushered in limos to the Century Plaza Hotel, where we'd base for the next week. Once again, we had a pool table in Roger's suite.

I did my job well. I took care of business and joined in the spirit of things. I was having a blast and could not think of any better job on the planet at that moment. Roger, it seemed, also felt I was doing a good job as I was given a raise.

We flew off to Tempe, Arizona, and back the same evening and then went to San Diego for another show. At Roger's instruction, I had arranged for a police escort to help get us promptly from the airport to the venue. We were following a briskly moving motorcycle patrolman on the way to the Sports Arena in San Diego when he took a corner, hit a slick spot, and went down on his bike. Although we stopped to make sure he was not hurt, he waved us on, not wanting to be the reason for us being late. I remember seeing Eric both concerned and impressed by this dedicated officer who was working on Eric's behalf.

At that time, Eric was not doing sound checks, as is the norm now. The band would just show up as the opening act was halfway through its set. After intermission and a stage changeover, the house lights went down, and the screaming began. Eric and the band would then walk on stage, confident that the sound would be the best it could be. They had hired the most talented crew money could buy, and they relied on them heavily. Keith Bradley did the out-front sound, and he did a great job making sure the lack of a sound check with EC's band was not obvious to the fans.

It was about that time that we noticed a strange occurrence every time I walked by or on the stage prior to the house lights going down. People in the audience were mistaking me for Eric. They would call his name but be waving at me. Mind you, I was twenty-six years old and thinner with dark, longish hair and a full, dark beard. On those counts, Eric and I were similar, although he is five and a half years older.

Not only did I notice this, but the crew, Roger, and the band became aware of it as well, and I had to stop going to the stage to check if all was on schedule prior to the lights going down. Roger tried to keep the timing right, so Eric would not have too many drinks beforehand and play an unsatisfactory show, which had been known to happen. Unfortunately, this looks-alike revelation would come back to haunt me and turn into a benefit for Eric and Roger. In fact, I even took Eric's blood test for him when he married Pattie. That's how easily we were mistaken for one another, but I'll get to that later.

Back in the LA hotel, I remember Roger saying he wished he'd booked us to stay in Tempe as being in LA was a pain in the ass. There were all sorts of "well-meaning" friends just wanting to say hello to Eric, or people asking for free tickets to the Forum show. Roger did not trust Eric's old friends nor his new ones for that matter, as in reality most of them were sharing drugs or wanting to sponge them off Eric or his bandmates. Roger said if we were in Tempe, the distance would be too far for them to harass us. Nevertheless, we were in LA, and it was too late to move.

In fact, the day before the concert at the Forum, Roger took his phone off the hook so no one could get through, no matter how important they thought they were. And no one on the outside could reach Eric's room as he was registered under an alias, a Mr. W. B. Albion. His favorite English football team was West Bromwich Albion, thus W. B. Albion. He used that alias for several years all around the world.

It was then that Roger announced an additional date in San Francisco had been added after what was supposed to be the final show in LA. No problem. I was not ready for the tour to end anyway.

One afternoon I popped into Roger's room to visit, and Eric was playing pool with an old friend, Jeff Beck. It was cool enough I had known Jeff briefly in 1968 and 1969. My band opened up for some of his Dallas shows when he was touring as the Jeff Beck Group with Ronnie Wood, Rod Stewart, and Mickey Waller (I have a live tape of Jeff's gig at a club called Louann's). But even better, here were two of the greatest guitar players in the world casually playing pool while shooting the breeze, and I was able to just sit around, enjoy the game, and relax, albeit in good company.

Not too much stands out from the Forum show except the guest list was as long as you'd expect. Roger, as usual, had his way of unhinging any potential situations by having the cars ready (my job) when the band came off stage. We'd direct them to the waiting limos and off we'd go, back to the hotel before the house lights had even come up—voilà, Elvis has left the building. I'm sure a few people made it back to the hotel for a visit in the bar, but not nearly as many as if we'd waited around backstage.

I do remember some of the band complaining about running out after every show because they didn't have a chance to see friends. Roger's worst fears were in fact the reason we did this because in a number of instances the band wanted to see their guests for some extracurricular partying.

Before our last official show on the tour, Roger presented a gift to the band and me. It was a solid-gold version of the broken guitar pick that can be seen on the album *No Reason to Cry*. It was a very nice present as it included a gold chain and each person's name engraved on the back. I still have mine and wonder what happened to all the others, especially to the ones given to those who have since left us.

After the LA show and a couple of days off, we flew to San Francisco for the last show, which I'd found out would be a tribute concert for the Band, Bob Dylan's former backing band and celebrities in their own right. It was their final show together as they were breaking up to pursue other avenues in music. The event was to be filmed for a documentary titled *The Last Waltz,* which was being directed by Martin Scorsese and recorded by my now longtime friend and record producer Rob Fraboni.

As if that weren't enough to make it a memorable night, famed promoter Bill Graham was serving as master of ceremonies, and performing with the Band on stage would be dozens of celebrity musicians, including

Eric, Paul Butterfield, Bobby Charles, Neil Diamond, Dr. John, Bob Dylan, Ronnie Hawkins, Joni Mitchell, Van Morrison, Ringo Starr, Stephen Stills, Muddy Waters, Ronnie Wood, and Neil Young, among others. All that in one show on one day was amazing. I was in for a treat.

When we arrived at Hotel Nikko, I had to check us in because this was not our traditional Clapton operation. We were doing as all the guests did. I was standing at the crowded counter patiently waiting my turn and heard the receptionist ask the fellow in front of me for some identification, so he could let him have his room key. The gentleman said he did not have anything on him currently and apologized. I realized the front-desk man was not going to give Muddy Waters his room, so I stepped forward, not knowing Mr. Waters personally but recognizing him. I vouched for him with enough gusto that the fellow behind the desk apologized, gave Muddy his room key, and directed him to the nearest elevator. The hotel was nice. I even had a hot tub in my room.

We then went with Eric to the Winterland Ballroom for rehearsal. All went well, and I was just thrilled to be there. After all, the venue alone was famous.

The next day was the concert. Everyone was asked to be there early and to plan on staying until it was over in case extra footage was needed or there were technical problems. We were situated in a large green room in the backstage area that required special passes. There was a bar and an abundance of food, as well as places where we could go watch the show. However, backstage was a show in and of itself.

In the middle of the larger green room, there was another room—mind you, it was 1976—that was painted all white on both the outside and inside. Inside this room was a white coffee table with white pillows scattered around, and a constant sound of sniffing could be heard through speakers hung in the corners. It was called the Cockatoo Room and was used for, well, the sniffing sound through the speakers was not the only sniffing sound in the room. I told myself, "We're not in Kansas anymore, Toto! Where are the police?"

Also backstage were a few film and TV celebrities. It was a wonderful day for a young novice in the world of big-time rock and roll. I remember being in the wings and looking at everything going on around me and thinking, *What a fortunate position I'm in.*

The Band backed all the artists, which often had some of their own band members joining in. Eric's performance went down well, and the audience loved it. Roger asked me if I would take his wife, Annette, who had flown in from England, out front to see one of her favorite singers, Neil Diamond. I was not only happy to do this for them, but I also liked Neil somewhat and thoroughly enjoyed his performance.

The day was special and one I will never forget, but it was over much too quickly. Back at the hotel, a few of the band members and I had dinner and ended up, not surprisingly, at the bar. Before too long, the bar became crowded with all sorts of celebrities, friends, and crew. After only a few drinks, the bar was ready to close, but someone said there was an informal gathering of sorts going on downstairs in the hotel ballroom for people from *The Last Waltz*.

A couple of the guys from EC's band and I ventured down, and sure enough, there was a bar set up and a few musicians drunkenly playing on a small setup. I didn't stay too long as it was loud and sort of dull, but some celebrity names were jamming. I saw the drummer from Santana, Michael Shrieve, and he appeared as if he'd been imbibing for a while at this point. I'd never seen a drummer play so well while wobbling at such an odd angle.

We took this as a sign that it had been a great but long day, and it was best we turn in and stay out of trouble. Upstairs to bed it was.

The next day, it was time for this all to come to an end. Roger, Eric, and the British contingency would head back to England while myself and Eric's band, except George Terry and singer Yvonne Elliman, would head back to Tulsa. We split up at the airport and went to our different terminals. But before I left, Roger asked me if I'd ever been to England. I hadn't.

Then he capped off an already wonderful experience by asking if I'd like to come over there and work. I said I'd enjoy that, not letting on that going to London had been one of my biggest dreams since I was fifteen years old. He said he'd be in touch to set it up.

I arrived back in Tulsa, and for the first time, I had this feeling like I'd been away from planet Earth. No one understood me or seemed to care for anything I had to say, except those people who I'd been on tour with. It was like we'd lived in this very special and privileged cocoon away from friends and family, and now that we had returned, we had to fit in with the real world again—when it wasn't what we, or at least me, wanted to do. Just the opposite, I wanted the tour to never end. It was magic.

Eric Clapton 1976 No Reason to Cry US Tour Dates

November 5, 1976: Bayfront Center (St. Petersburg, Florida)

November 6, 1976: Hollywood Sportatorium (Pembroke Pines, Florida)

November 7, 1976: Jacksonville Coliseum (Jacksonville, Florida)

November 9, 1976: Omni Coliseum (Atlanta, Georgia)

November 10, 1976: Mobile Municipal Auditorium (Mobile, Alabama)

November 11, 1976: LSU Assembly Center, Louisiana State University (Baton Rouge, Louisiana)

November 12, 1976: HemisFair Arena (San Antonio, Texas)

November 14, 1976: Sam Houston Coliseum (Houston, Texas)

November 15, 1976: Dallas Memorial Auditorium (Dallas, Texas)

November 16, 1976: Lloyd Noble Center, University of Oklahoma (Norman, Oklahoma)

November 17, 1976: Pan American Center, New Mexico State University (Las Cruces, New Mexico)

November 19, 1976: Activity Center, Arizona State University (Tempe, Arizona)

November 20, 1976: San Diego Sports Arena (San Diego, California)

November 22, 1976: The Forum (Inglewood, California)

November 25, 1976: Winterland Ballroom, filmed for the Band concert documentary *The Last Waltz,* which was released on April 26, 1978 (San Francisco, California)

CHAPTER 2

It Just Gets Better

England, Europe, and Jack Bruce.

My ticket to London was booked for mid-February 1977, and I was raring to go. I had been off the road since December after returning home from my first foray into the professional world of one-night stands, a tour with Clapton and his band that ended spectacularly with *The Last Waltz*. If you haven't seen it, put it on your list!

The time home in Tulsa was definitely made more enjoyable knowing I had another adventure to look forward to in the form of a trip abroad. Plus, I had some decent money in the bank, a better outlook for my future, and a bit of prestige in my local community of new friends and acquaintances. And I had great memories from the previous tour to see me through the downtime. During the break, I was even paid a retainer—about half the salary, but I'm not complaining.

I splurged and invested in a Zero Halliburton aluminum suitcase that at the time was an extravagance as it was one of the most expensive pieces of luggage on the market. Most of the band had one or two of these rugged suitcases, and my old Samsonite looked out of place (or so I imagined). I also bought a similar briefcase since I had to carry contracts and paperwork.

Ahead of my trip, all I knew was that I was going to work with Jack Bruce and his new band. They had an album coming out and would be doing a tour of Europe and the UK. Not only had I never been overseas, but I was also ecstatic to be working with another member of Cream. Bruce had been the bass player and principal lead singer for the super group.

Waiting until February was somewhat difficult because I was so looking forward to getting back into the seemingly privileged lifestyle I had enjoyed with Eric. Then, too, I was a bit nervous since no one from the

Tulsa-based Clapton band was going with me on this excursion. I was on my own.

Finally, the day arrived, and I flew from Tulsa to Dallas, where I switched planes and boarded a Braniff Airlines flight to London Gatwick Airport. I knew I was going to be gone for several months, possibly longer, and not being a seasoned world traveler yet, I carried a full suitcase, a suit bag loaded and heavy, my grip bag, and my trusty new locking briefcase. No traveling light for me. That came later when I got tired of lugging all that crap with me.

The flight was the longest I'd been on up to that point in my life, and though I was flying coach, I enjoyed the food and drinks. I arrived at Gatwick and followed the throng of people from our plane to passport control, having been told to say I was coming to England on a vacation when taking my ridiculous mound of luggage through customs. After deciding I wanted to go to London some twelve years earlier, I had made it.

On the other side of the customs door, I met a fellow named Harry, who was holding up a sign with my name on it and drove for a chauffeur company that did a lot of work for the Stigwood agency. Harry took me into the center of London to a flat in Dorset Square that Roger had rented for me. I must say I was not too impressed with his choice of accommodations as the apartment was on the basement level and had no windows. There was only a dingy skylight in the hallway that looked into a dirty, paper-strewn alcove between the flats above. My one-room studio included a kitchenette, small fridge, bed, tiny bathroom, and a blurry television, although there was nothing I could ever find worth watching.

Having arrived on a Friday, I remember it being a long first weekend. I didn't know anyone around, nor did I really know where anything was. Of course, these were the days before cell phones, or "mobiles" as they are called in the UK, and even using a pay phone took some practice. You had to dial the number, the phone rang, and when (or if) the person answered, the phone beeped. Only then did you insert the proper coinage. After speaking for a while, all of a sudden a fast beeping would interrupt, signaling time was running out. You'd have to scramble for more change, usually finding it a moment too late.

Regardless, I had made it to England, home of the Who, my favorite band. In fact, while there, I remembered Roger Daltrey, the Who's lead singer, still owed me for a dobro I had acquired for him and then mailed to his house in Sussex. Some members of the band were working in their private Ramport Studios, which was in the Battersea district of London. I got in touch, and Roger apologized for forgetting to pay me. He told me to drop by, and he'd have the money. This was going to be a dream come true.

The studio was, at least to me, a magical place where one of my favorite Who albums, *Quadrophenia,* had been recorded. Damn it, I was there in person! I was able to hang out for a bit and visit with some of the crew I'd met when my band opened for the Who in my younger years. Roger paid me in cash for the dobro and the cost of shipping it to the UK. In the taxi on the way back to my "Hole of Doom" flat, I thought about what a great evening it had been. And now I had a pocket full of unexpected pounds.

Following my handy *A–Z Visitors' Atlas & Guide*, I made my way down Baker Street early Monday morning, crossed busy Oxford Street, and meandered to Grosvenor Square, where the American Embassy was formerly located. On the northeast corner of the square, I found Brook Street. I was close. Just halfway down, I came to 67 Brook Street W1, the headquarters for the Robert Stigwood Organization and my home office for a while. This was worlds apart from the back of a construction warehouse.

It was an unassuming building, four stories tall, although dating back to the 1700s. It looked similar to the other buildings on the street, except behind these white doors was the office that ran the careers of several musicians whose work I respected and admired, as well as one I knew personally and had already toured with, Eric.

Inside was a smallish hallway with doors off to either side and a steep stairway leading to the levels above. Situated prominently was a security desk to check those who were coming and going. This wasn't anything too official like in the skyscrapers of New York but rather was more for answering questions and giving directions. I announced myself to the guard, and he pointed me to the first door on the right, telling me to, "Go on in. They're expecting you."

I thanked him and pushed the door open, not knowing what I was going to find or who I'd see. It turned out to be a rather large space with four small desks situated around the walls. *Not too dissimilar from the Ricky Hill Agency offices*, I mused. Sitting behind a rather cluttered desk, where work was obviously getting done, sat a friendly lady, not much older than me, who introduced herself as Diana Snelling, Roger Forrester's secretary. She punched a button on the phone to notify the boss I was there and, with a sly smirk on her face, motioned me to a larger white door.

Roger was behind his desk—also cluttered with papers, files, and a few phones—with his back to the sidewalk on Brook Street. I could see passersby through the net curtains. England loves net curtains. It's not like the Marmite food spread, which is an acquired taste, but more of a national trait everyone has to comply with—net curtains!

He didn't get up to greet me or shake my hand, but he did ask if I wanted a coffee or tea. I declined, so he ordered Di to bring him a coffee. He then asked how my flat was. Funny.

At the time, Roger drank large quantities of coffee and smoked regularly, although he did not drink alcohol. I later learned he was a former alcoholic and had successfully given it up. We visited casually for a while, just catching up on things, and then he shared his plans for me.

I was going to be the tour manager for the Jack Bruce Band. Jack had been a major voice with Cream, which many of the bands in Dallas were heavily influenced by, including mine. And now I was to meet the band at rehearsals and get to know them, work in the office with Di on their European and UK itineraries, and eventually take them on tour. *Wow! Another score for me,* I thought.

Then Roger sprung another bonus on me, this one even more exciting than going to San Francisco for *The Last Waltz*. He told me that after Jack's tour finished, I could stay in London and meet up with Eric's band, who'd be flying in to record an album with him (which became the hit *Slowhand*). I'd then go on tour with them across Europe. Was there any question what my answer would be? What a great way to start 1977.

Pleased I had a longer job to look forward to, pleased to have been good enough to be asked, and pleased to get the chance to do a Clapton tour again, I smiled all the way while Roger drove me to a rehearsal hall somewhere on the outskirts of London to meet Jack and his band.

The band consisted of Jack and three other excellent players who were as young as me and fairly respected musicians in the industry: Simon Phillips on drums, Hugh Burns on guitar, and Tony Hymas on keyboards. If you're not familiar with these fellows and their music, it would be well worth your time to get on your computer and Google them. You won't be sorry.

Upon entering the rehearsal facility, I could tell the band was great, and Jack's playing and voice were in top form. Most of the songs were new to me, except for a couple of blues pieces and some Cream songs that Jack could not get away without playing. Overall, the set was solid.

Jack and the band members seemed nice, and the crew was as friendly as they had to be, given a new tour manager was being thrust on them. I was an American outsider, but they never once made me feel that way, at least to my face, and I was to work with many of the same guys for years to come.

Later that first day, Roger said he was heading home since he was already part way there, and that I could hop a ride after rehearsals with two of the crew, Bobby Richardson and Peter "Rocky" Morley. I was fine with that, and Bobby drove me back to my dark flat in an old Mini Cooper, the likes of which I had never been in before. This was not the Minis of today, but the bare bones sort. We're talking a 1960s Mini, and believe me, they were pretty basic vehicles.

As we chatted on the way back, I could tell I'd get along with them, especially Rocky, who was hilarious and one of the most unique people I'd ever met. He kept me laughing and entertained with his outrageous stories for the next several years while on tour together.

Despite losing touch with Rocky for over thirty years, I recently reconnected with him only to find out he had suffered three heart attacks, five angioplasty surgeries, and numerous other heart ailments. He is now living in Houston with his fourth or fifth wife and has a small dog-sitting business. Obviously, he doesn't need anything too stressful. But through all those years on the road, Rocky was a highlight. I always looked forward to a tour he was on—he and my soon-to-be-good friend Alphi O'Leary, who was Eric's long-time personal assistant.

With the finalized itinerary and advance work done, the band and I hit the road in March. On this first leg of the tour, we were driven in a small, tourist-type bus, not a fancy tour bus as those were not common yet. The transportation was arranged by Roger through Stigwood's, and in this case, money was an object not to be wasted. Jack had not experienced the success enjoyed by Eric since Cream broke up, so although the management and record company, also owned by Stigwood, advanced money to fund the tour, they were watching their pennies.

The first round of shows would be in the UK, leading off at Leeds University where the Who had recorded one of my favorite live albums, *Live at Leeds*. This was a fitting place to start and another memorable evening.

The venue was not at all what I had imagined while listening to *Live at Leeds*. This was a traditional college function hall with a stage at one end. The band was great, and the audience loved seeing Jack in such fine form. I enjoyed the whole show, not only because they were accepted well but also from just remembering the Who's version of "Shakin' All Over" from the album recorded there, which my band had done its best to replicate whenever we played the song.

This part of the tour was neither very difficult nor outrageously fun as we were in England, and most of the band and crew knew people all over. Of course, there was a lot of drinking in bars after the shows, but I think everyone was on their best behavior because we were so close to their homes. The hotels were all right, although not quite the standard I had experienced on the Clapton tour in the US. Then again, this was a different tour altogether with its own personality. Still, I was seeing new British cities and experiencing new things dozens of times every day, so I had no complaints.

Another exciting experience came on the overnight train ride from Glasgow to London. Train trips aren't common in the US, so this was a treat. After the last show, the band and I hightailed it to the station, where we boarded the train and quickly tucked into our own private cabins for the journey back to the city. I fell asleep fairly soon after we left the station. I had hoped to stay up and enjoy the ride as much as I could, but it was just too comfortable. I was awakened by a porter knocking on my door calling, "Next stop London! End of the line!" I must have slept well because I missed the whole trip, which was OK as it was dark outside anyway.

There were not many drugs going on during this time—just the occasional spliff with cigarette tobacco and crumbled-up hashish, as far as I saw. I did not imbibe as I knew if I got high, I could easily blow this opportunity. And there were not many of the often-promoted groupies. Jack seemed to have a lot of music and musician purists as fans. That's not to say girls weren't around. The scene just wasn't like the stories would have you believe, at least not with this band. Mostly, it was alcohol that was the numbing agent of choice.

The Jack Bruce Band 1977 How's Tricks UK Tour Dates (First Leg)

March 5, 1977: University of Leeds (Leeds, England)

March 7, 1977: Aston University (Birmingham, England)

March 8, 1977: Lancaster University (Lancaster, England

March 10, 1977: Oxford Polytechnic (Oxford, England)

March 11, 1977: University of East Anglia (Norwich, England)

March 12, 1977: University of Sheffield (Sheffield, England)

March 14, 1977: University of Salford (Salford, England)

March 15, 1977: University of Strathclyde (Glasgow, Scotland)

I stayed back in London for a week or so in my Dorset Square burrow. Though I now had friends in the UK, most were enjoying being home with their families, so I was on my own. I visited the office several times, prepping with Di and Roger for the upcoming European leg of the tour, and I took the opportunity to do some touristy things, such as Madame Tussauds Wax Museum. I also wandered by Buckingham Palace, Piccadilly Circus, and Leicester Square. They are a must if you're ever in London.

I did get an invitation from Eric, via Roger, to come out to his house in Surrey, where he lived with Pattie Boyd, George Harrison's ex-wife. It would be for dinner and to stay the night. Roger arranged a car to take me as it was about an hour's drive outside London.

Even though I knew Eric and Pattie a bit, I was nervous. But there was plenty of gin, and after enjoying a gin and tonic, I relaxed. Following dinner, we went to the upstairs room and drank and played pool, talking until the wee hours. I was glad to get to bed. Trying to keep up with Eric was impossible. Plus, he played a good game of pool.

I awoke about eight thirty or nine o'clock the next morning and made my way downstairs, finding the house quiet and still. I picked up a newspaper to occupy myself until Eric or Pattie got up, and it wasn't long until Eric came bounding through the back door. Seems he'd been down to the pub at the end of his drive for a bit of morning cheer. He was in a jocular mood already.

Soon after, Jack's band departed the UK on a ferry to Sweden with the crew having gone ahead a couple of days earlier. London was great, and now my first place to set foot on continental Europe was going to be Sweden. I felt I truly had won a lottery.

The hotel in Stockholm stands out because it was an old classic in style and had one elevator in the center of the lobby that had metal, scissor-type doors. You could watch people rise up through the ceiling or past your floor. The rooms were not large, by any means, but I had a private one all to myself. I knew the crew, on the rare occasions they even got hotel rooms, had to double up.

The shows were going well so far, and I was becoming friendlier with the band and crew. Things had begun to feel comfortable, although I knew I was lugging too many belongings with me. I doubt I wore a third of what I was carrying, but I always tried to look nice and professional—no scruffy jeans and T-shirts. Still, there was no way I was going to wear all the clothes I'd brought, especially staying in a different city every day.

After a show in Sweden and two more in Denmark—a country that seemed pretty similar to Sweden to me—I clearly remember our landing in Berlin. We came in near the city center with apartment buildings close on both sides of the plane. If the pilot sneezed, we'd have easily flown right into someone's living room.

The promoter met us as planned on the other side of custom, and the cars were there to take us to the hotel. These were new Mercedes, not limos, but then everywhere I looked there were Mercedes and BMWs.

The hotel was, so far, the most luxurious one I'd seen on this tour, and since I did not speak German, it was soothing to find that many people spoke or at least understood enough English to communicate easily. In Scandinavia, they did not speak as much English, or when they did, understanding them was a bit more difficult.

I'll admit being in charge of this tour was both thrilling and a bit of a challenge, mainly because this was my first time in Europe. I was learning a lot every day, and when I did not know something or have an answer, I just winged it. Somehow, we survived. While Jack was about six or seven years older than me and more experienced as far as the music industry, life, and most things in general, he allowed me to be the tour manager, as was my job.

The tour through Germany, Holland, Belgium, France, and Austria went smoothly despite having to keep up with the finances through so many different currencies. I was not a seasoned bookkeeper, but I did my best and did not lose any money—at least not yet. Likewise, there had been no particular incidents to cause alarm, and no trouble within the ranks or with the public, for that matter.

It wasn't until we got to Zürich, Switzerland, on the last date of this European leg, that an incident causing me slight concern cropped up. Little did I know that it was just a small glimpse of what would later be some rather nasty and turbulent experiences.

Jack, a few of the band members, and I were sitting in the lobby bar of the hotel, having a drink. Not many other hotel guests were imbibing at that time since it was still in the afternoon, but it was our day off. I never drank during the day while working.

There was an Italian couple speaking their native tongue near us, and eventually the man excused himself and left. The lady he was with, an attractive and elegant "older" woman (at least thirty-five years of age to my twenty-six) was left sitting at the bar alone. Surprisingly, Jack spoke something in Italian to her, and they communicated briefly until Jack begged off the Italian and asked if she spoke English. She moved seats closer to us around the semicircular bar and introduced herself, as we did to her.

Drinks and conversation in her broken English continued, and we all chatted to her and each other, small talk really. Suddenly, with Jack listening to her speak in Italian again, he turned to me and slammed down his drink, obviously drunk.

"She bloody thinks your handsome!" he shouted and then stormed off toward the elevator. Having seen her mafioso-looking friend earlier, I was going nowhere near her.

Up until that point, I had not seen the angry side of Jack. No one, not even Roger, had warned me. I was aware Jack was unhappy that he was not as successful and popular in the public's eye as Eric, his former band mate, but I also recognized that Jack was probably the most naturally gifted musician, talent-wise, in Cream. His vocals and playing were truly impressive. Regardless, he felt slighted by not only fickle music fans but by Stigwood and RSO records, who he felt were giving him the short end of the stick. And he was supposed to be grateful for the opportunity?

I am sure he was, but that did not stop his underlying, seething anger, which was only compounded by alcohol and drugs. He never let me forget that when I was not out with him on tour, I worked for *"Eric,"* saying his name with spite. I remember thinking, *Well, if that's the only thing I did that you didn't like, great.*

The tour through Europe finished well, though it was a struggle to keep the krones, marks, francs, and pounds all in order and not lose track of anything.

We returned to the UK (and me to my dungeon) with only two more performances before Eric's band arrived, the first in Hemel Hempstead outside of London. I would ride in a chauffeured car to pick up Jack at his house in the country, and then we'd go to the gig. Unfortunately, the driver got lost on the way to Jack's place, and we were startlingly late. When we finally arrived, Jack bounded out the door and climbed into the backseat of the car. It was obvious he was angry. He said he had wanted to show me his home, but now, because we were so late, we didn't have time to go in, not even to relieve ourselves. He did not speak again during the rest of the trip to Hemel Hempstead.

Next, we recorded a radio broadcast for the BBC's *In Concert* series at the Paris Theatre in London, and then it was time for the last show of this tour, which would be at the Apollo Victoria Theatre, also in London. This was going to be a big show for Jack and the band, as it was their hometown. All were excited.

Roger came and even Harvey Goldsmith, to this day a renowned UK promoter of many concerts and tours. The show was sold out, and everyone seemed a bit nervous. The backstage dressing room downstairs was filled with some ratty furniture and offered a platter of cheese and fruit. People were gathered and visiting.

The band asked me to hold their car keys and a few wallets as my three-hundred-dollar Halliburton briefcase seemed the safest place. Harvey paid Roger some money due, which amounted to £6,000, about $15,000 at that time, and he gave that to me as well for safekeeping during the show. In addition, Roger had given me the work permits for Eric's band, who were due in town the following morning from America. I was scheduled to meet them at the airport in passport control with the documents.

I locked all these possessions in my briefcase and slid it against a wall behind one of the two slumped sofas, figuring it would be safe and well hidden. When it was time, the band took the stage to thunderous applause and launched into their set. Jack hadn't played London in a while, and the fans were ready. The band was tight after the long tour, and all was well.

I took my leave and retreated to the dressing room to grab a drink and something to snack on. Once downstairs, I noticed the security guard who'd been seated outside our door was gone. I didn't give it a second thought until I went into the dressing room, where I immediately noticed that Harvey's and Roger's briefcases were open. I knew they had not been when we left to head upstairs to the stage.

I dove to the floor in back of the sofa, and upon reaching behind the dusty furniture, I realized my briefcase was gone! I upended the sofa thinking, praying, it had accidently slid underneath. It was not there. I quickly scoured the room, but my aluminum briefcase was nowhere to be found.

I exited the dressing room in a panic and looked down the corridor for anyone suspicious . . . or just anyone. I even went to the other side of the underground dressing-room area and saw an exit door at the top of some stairs, but it was closed. My heart sank. *Well, great,* I thought, *now I've been robbed!*

While the band was booming away to the jam-packed theater, I ran up to the stage area to find a police officer and was greeted by two gentlemen in suits who asked me if I was the one in charge. I responded yes, and they proceeded to tell me there had been a call to the police station saying there was a bomb in the building, and that I needed to get the band off stage so they could clear the venue.

Perfect. Not only had I been robbed, but the building was going to explode.

About that time, Roger and Harvey, who'd been backstage enjoying the show from the wings, came over after noticing something was wrong. I explained to them and the men in suits—police officers of some sort, maybe MI5—that there had been a theft, and they agreed it was all part of this bomb threat. But I still had to get the band off and clear the facility just to be safe.

I went behind a curtain at the side of the stage to signal Jack and the band, drawing my hand across my throat in a "cut" sign to indicate they needed to stop. Jack just smiled, thinking I was simply saying how good they sounded, that they were killing it, and kept right on playing.

Once the song ended, I guess I had made enough racket to get one band member's attention, and they finally left the stage. Harvey, as promoter of the show, then went to the mike with one of the suits and explained to the crowd that they had to leave the building. This was a time when there were more worries about Irish Republican Army bombings in London, so vacating the premises did not take long.

I don't remember much after that. I can't even recall if Jack went back and finished the show or if that was it for that night. However, I do remember the band, Roger, Harvey, and I went downstairs to the scene of the crime with one of the suits while police and dogs scoured the building.

Nothing from Roger's or Harvey's briefcases was missing or anything else in the dressing room, except for my briefcase. The fellows in the suits figured the security guard was in on the robbery and possibly thought my briefcase, looking similar to what many photographers used to carry expensive equipment, was loaded with cameras and lenses, making for a nice haul. Little did they know that when they pried the case open, they'd find keys from a couple of cars that band members had driven to the show, wallets, my passport, miscellaneous paperwork, and an envelope with a lot of cash—much better than camera gear, no matter how you look at it.

A few weeks later, it was reported to me that the police had found the briefcase and a few credit cards floating in the River Thames.

There was an after-show party scheduled that night at a high-end club in Mayfair, a ritzy part of London, and I was going to ride with Roger to the party. He said for me to wait outside the theater while he pulled his car around to pick me up. As cars passed by me on the street, I clearly remember standing there waiting in the cool night air, feeling angry and guilty about the course of the evening, when I saw Roger in his red Jaguar speed past me, heading toward the party.

Once I finally arrived at the party via a cab, Roger claimed he didn't see me standing outside the theater and figured I'd gotten another ride. I suspect he drove off on purpose, leaving me to my own devices as a way of letting me know that he, too, was not pleased with the evening's events.

The party was not much fun either, at least for me, as I didn't really know anyone, although that usually wouldn't stop me from having a decent time. I make friends and acquaintances easily. Instead, I left early and went to my new accommodations. I was to live with Clapton's band while they were in London recording, a mansion of a rental house just off Hyde Park's north side.

That brought about a dark ending to an otherwise eye-opening and enjoyable first time in Europe and the UK for me as well as for Jack and the band.

The Jack Bruce Band 1977 *How's Tricks* Europe and UK Tour Dates (Second Leg)

March 21, 1977: Jarlateatern (Stockholm, Sweden)

March 22, 1977: Tivolis Koncertsal (Copenhagen, Denmark)

March 23, 1977: Stakladen, Aarhus University (Aarhus, Denmark)

March 25, 1977: Hochschule der Künste (Berlin, Germany)

March 26, 1977: Musikhalle (Hamburg, Germany)

March 27, 1977: Philipshalle (Düsseldorf, Germany)

March 29, 1977: Nederlands Congresgebouw (The Hague, Holland)

March 30, 1977: Cultuurcentrum Hasselt (Hasselt, Belgium)

April 1, 1977: Pavillon des Paris (Paris, France)

April 2, 1977: Stadthalle Offenbach (Offenbach am Main, Germany)

April 3, 1977: Deutsches Museum (Munich, Germany)

April 4, 1977: Konzerthaus (Vienna, Austria)

April 6, 1977: Volkshaus (Zürich, Switzerland)

April 12, 1977: Dacorum Pavilion (Hemel Hempstead, England)

April 14, 1977: Paris Theatre (London, England)

April 15, 1977: Apollo Victoria Theatre (London, England)

April 30, 1977: BBC *In Concert* radio broadcast

CHAPTER 3

Slowhand

New Album? New Tour? OK by Me!

On the heels of a rather dastardly evening at Jack's last show, I had spent a late evening sitting up with Roger and Alphi at Clapton's rented house after the end-of-tour party. The next morning, April 16, I was awake very early and on my way to Gatwick Airport to see what could be done to get Eric's US-based band in the country without their work permits, which had been stolen. I was tired, had a self-induced headache, and was not looking forward to trying to talk to the officials about why there were no documents for these Americans.

I arrived at the airport in one of the chauffeured cars, checked the arrivals board, and noticed I had only a short while before their plane landed, so I set about determining who would be the best person to begin with. I went to the Braniff Airways counter, and they helped me get to a passport control officer, who came to meet me. I was escorted behind the scenes through several doors and into an official area of passport control, where I was told to sit and wait. I waited as the clocked ticked by, knowing the flight was landing soon.

Finally, the first man I met and a couple of others came out from somewhere back in the depths of the office and asked to hear the story. I went through the entire tale of who I was, why I was there, what had happened the night before, and the predicament I was now facing not having the appropriately issued work permits. I also stressed the importance of getting these people through and into the country.

They were not going to make this particularly easy for me, but after some grilling on their part—more who, what, when, where, and why questions—and me producing the police document about the theft, they then made phone calls to some authorities to confirm I was not making this up. Once assured they would receive copies of the reissued work permits very shortly, the passport control officers agreed I was telling the truth.

They did say several times that allowing the band into the country without the proper papers was a very rare circumstance, but they agreed to assist me, especially as they were all Eric Clapton fans. That certainly helped.

The original fellow took me back through another door where I suddenly was in the passport control area for arriving passengers. He asked me to identify the band members as I saw them approach the inspectors' kiosks.

I pointed them out one by one, and he made the necessary overtures to the agents about the situation. Finally, everyone was allowed entry into the UK. I was extremely happy it worked out and that I could see my friends once again. After collecting all the suitcases, we loaded up the black Daimler limousines and departed for the drive back into the city.

While getting the band into the country was a priority and my first duty for this new adventure, I still had residual problems from the previous day's troubles, which would haunt me for a while to come. I would have to notify my credit card companies, get new cards, a driver's license, and the most difficult part, a passport.

Despite all that, we immediately hit the ground running. Two days later, the band began rehearsing, with the first show of the UK tour taking place on April 20 in Leicester. Clapton's tour was noticeably different than Jack's. Not any better, just different in that the hotels were a scale or two higher, and the crowds and venues were bigger. The music was good and enjoyable, but then so was Jack's.

We played the Glasgow Apollo on April 23, and it was pointed out to me that when the crowd got to its feet and was into the music, you could see the balcony bouncing up and down. They were right.

Following a show the next night in Newcastle, we returned to London for four more concerts and stayed in a hotel. We performed on the BBC TV series *The Old Grey Whistle Test*, which can be seen in its entirety on YouTube. That was an interesting experience for this novice, watching a television show being filmed. The band then played two concerts at the famous Hammersmith Odeon, an old theater in West London, and the place was packed both nights with many of Eric's celebrity friends on hand.

The last show of the UK swing was at the Rainbow Theatre in North London on April 29. Everything started out all right, and the night was made even more enjoyable by an old friend of mine and Eric's, Pete Townshend, being there backstage.

Eric and the band took the stage to thunderous applause and launched into their set. About a third of the way into the concert, though, EC came over to Roger, who was standing stage left. That was where Roger always viewed the show, ping-pong paddles at the ready (find out more about those later). Eric told him he felt ill and could not continue, but Roger gave him some encouraging words and ushered him back out on stage, where Eric did another song or two. However, he then walked off again, handing his guitar to Willie, his guitar tech.

Seems Eric had taken something before the gig that someone had given him, and he was disoriented and not well. It appeared Roger would have to stop the show and apologize to the audience when suddenly Pete, who'd been listening, piped up and said that Eric had to shake it off, get back on stage, and finish the concert. Eric said he couldn't, and this went back and forth for several minutes. Finally, Pete said he'd join the band on stage if Eric would get back out there. He did and Pete did for what essentially became the encore. Seeing Pete play "Layla" was odd, but the audience enjoyed a great show and had a great time.

Following the end of the UK tour, we settled into the rented house in London and sorted out bedrooms for the ten of us. Since this was a five-story home, we each had our own room. Yvonne Elliman, who along with Marcy Levy was one of the backup singers in Eric's band, was married to Bill Oakes, an executive with Stigwood, so she lived at their place in the city. There had been a cook hired to prepare meals for us, and a maid or two would come in a few times a week to clean. Not too shabby a setup.

I went to the store with the cook, a Filipina lady, to help stock the pantry and fridge. I had not really had the opportunity to grocery shop—well, in any quantity of note—since I'd been in England, but this was different. I had to provide food and snacks for everyone. In the 1970s, the British supermarkets were not as advanced as they are now, not by a long shot. Nor were they anywhere near as customer-oriented as American stores. An example of this would be me spending nearly $2,000 to purchase numerous carts of groceries but then getting to the counter only to find they would not bag them for me or carry them to a taxi. I was dumbfounded at the arrogance of the checkers and their attitudes.

So I took matters into my own hands. I calmly escorted the cook to the supermarket door, and while waving my arm toward the six carts overflowing with groceries, said to the checker, "Well, have your manager put all those back on the shelves because I am not going to spend this kind of money and bag my own groceries." The cook was shocked by my stance, not knowing what to expect. Standing with her mouth agape, the checker was speechless, as were the dozens of other customers who'd heard.

I was no more than five steps out the door when the manager called out, "Please come back! No problem. We'll sack the groceries and help you get them in a car." Now that was more like it. Though I would never imagine using money inappropriately, I was learning that it did have some advantages. Nevertheless, I didn't think spending that much and expecting my groceries to be sacked for me was too much to ask.

After a couple of days to rest, the band and Eric began meeting in the evenings at Olympic Studios in London, which was quite famous for having produced many top rock-and-roll albums. Working with famed producer Glyn Johns, they started to put together songs and record tracks for a new yet unnamed Clapton album. Cars would show up at the house late in the afternoon, usually the Daimlers, and transport the band to the studio.

While I'd often stop by the recording sessions, I was also going to the office regularly, running the house, including helping the cook make menus and working to finalize the ledgers from Jack's tour to turn into the company accountants. In addition, I had to get a new passport, which entailed me filling out both a lost passport form and an application for a new one. The paperwork was the easy part of the problem. The process didn't become a nightmare until I had to go a block west of the Stigwood building to the US Embassy in Grosvenor Square.

I had the forms, fee, and photos, all according to specifications, and waited in line like everyone else. After a long time snaking my way through the velvet ropes and stanchions, I was signaled to a window, where I presented my papers.

The lady, an American, looked at the papers and asked me what I needed. I explained my passport had been stolen as part of a bigger robbery that had taken place. She asked me to elaborate and explain further, which I did. When she then asked for the police report of the robbery, I pointed out it was already included in my paperwork. She rummaged through my neatly stacked papers, found it, and read it quietly. For some reason, I did not get a comfortable "this is the American Embassy, and I am an American" feeling. She told me to have a seat and that she would be with me shortly.

Now I knew I was in for a more difficult time than I'd expected. I sat there for a short while until the lady behind the window and another official man came through a door and approached me. They had me repeat everything I'd previously said to the lady, and once I had done that, she opened her mouth and made a statement that floored me. She said, "Frankly, I don't believe a single word you've told me." Through my anger and frustration, I realized this was not going well at all.

I was told to sit back down as they disappeared through the door and back into the depths of the decision-making offices. Much later, long after I had begun seething, I was signaled to the window by the same non-believer. This time she told me that my passport would be processed and available to be picked up the following day. I don't know what went on behind those doors, but evidently the fellow believed me. Or perhaps that was just a scare tactic to hustle away criminals and scoundrels who try to obtain fraudulent documents.

With that task finally completed, I could focus on other pressing matters, like finishing the accounts from Jack's tour. I will say this: what transpired from my first UK and European tour in regard to bookkeeping, as messy as it turned out to be, taught me a very valuable lesson—never go to bed without closing the day's books and double-checking them.

Thankfully, my room on the third floor of the house had plenty of space and a desk. Mind you, this was before the computerized accounting programs that are widely used today in this industry. No QuickBooks then. I spread all my receipts and notepads out and, having acquired some graph paper from the office, set about reconstructing the spending and income stream of the last month.

I sorted the receipts by currency, date, and city and put them in piles with their respective tour dates. I had copious notes of all details relating to the money as well. Basically, I had to invent my own accounting system because we'd receive money in one currency, and then after relocating to another country, some of this currency would have to be changed into the necessary local currency. This went on throughout the tour.

By the time I got back to London, I not only had receipts and accounting trails in different currencies, but I also had money remaining from those various countries. And as anyone who has traveled internationally knows, the exchange rates fluctuate daily. This, too, was not looking like an easy job. At least I had some time and the peace and quiet of my own room in a nice house to do the task.

It took a good week of head-down effort, but I finally came up with a system that worked and allowed me to account for all the money in question—or so I thought. I'd even asked Roger how he wanted me to reflect the missing £6,000, which was taken in the briefcase robbery. His answer was, "Just say lost in action." And that is exactly what I did. I wrote *Lost In Action* next to the red £6,000 on the ledger. Who was I to question my boss? I happily turned in the file of my receipts and accounts as well as the remaining cash to the accounting department in the basement of the Stigwood offices.

It wasn't until a couple of years later that Roger told me how much difficulty my accounting caused when the Inland Revenue Service, the UK's version of America's IRS, audited the company, a regular occurrence. He said that when they saw *Lost In Action* next to a negative £6,000, that raised a big red skull-and-crossbones flag. They were sure there was something criminal going on. Roger wasn't angry, probably because it had been so long since it happened, but then I imagine his response might have been something to the effect of, "Well, it will give the bean counters something to do."

Regardless, after a week in my room sorting all that out, I vowed to never let my accounts go a day without being settled, at least in my own ledger. And I kept that vow.

The band was a couple of weeks into the album, and recording sessions were coming along nicely. Though I did not spend much time at the studio, as it was sort of boring not being a player or having anything in particular to do, I did pop in once in a while. The studio was large but had a causal atmosphere, except when Glyn was in a mood.

I would have the cook fix dinner for the band and two crew members, Willie Spears and Jeff "Bombs" Bradley, before they left for the studio. Once they returned well after midnight, everyone was on their own if they were hungry or wanted a drink. During this time, Eric was staying at his house in Cranleigh, a village in Surrey, and traveled in each day. The band took the weekends off from recording, but I still had to run the house.

There was a good deal of drinking and illicit things going on at our little manor, especially late at night after recording and during the weekends. There was a dartboard in the TV lounge on the second floor, and I learned to play English darts, both sober and with a little slant on.

Then there was the time a package from the US came to the house. It wasn't anything too large, but I'd never seen so many people so happy to see a box arrive—until I discovered what was hidden inside. Beneath the brown wrapping paper and some colorful birthday paper was your average department-store woman's bath set, complete with bubble bath, a brush, an after-bath splash, and dusting powder.

I watched as one of my housemates opened the package and took hold of the dusting powder. He unsealed the cellophane and tossed it aside. He then carefully opened the decorative cardboard box containing the powder. So far, all looked normal. Then, pulling a trash can close, he proceeded to slowly scoop the pressed powder out and into the receptacle. When all that good dusting powder was out of the box, he took a sharp knife and slowly ran it around the perimeter of the box's inside lip, revealing a rather large baggie of white powder. *Yes,* I thought, *so that's one way it's done.*

Needless to say, I knew why this was such an anticipated package. For the next couple of weeks, everyone was eating less and sniffling a lot more. And it gave me some of those same thoughts I'd had back at the party in Hollywood, Florida, except this time I could not point the finger at anyone else outside our group, and I couldn't really vacate the premises. Or maybe I didn't want to.

There was an incident on one Sunday when we had no heat or hot water, and of course, nobody wanted to take a cold shower. The house and hot water were heated by fuel oil. Not having dealt with this before, I found a company who came on an emergency call. They found the oil tank within an outside cinder block structure at the back of the house.

We could not figure out a way inside it, but we were able to look through a vent gap in the brick. The fellow shined his light in toward the tank and suddenly retreated.

He discovered the tank was empty because the fuel oil had somehow leaked and was now surrounding the tank a foot or two deep—not a good scenario at all. An explosion would have most likely taken out the whole block.

Not only were we going to be without heat and warm showers, we were basically living next to a bomb. The heating fellow assured me we'd be all right until he could return the next day to drain the outbuilding and repair the tank. We ate out that night and drank a bit more than usual in an attempt to forget the precarious situation.

There was a lot of fun had in that house. Not only was Clapton's landmark *Slowhand* album recorded during that time, but it was also Queen Elizabeth's Silver Jubilee celebrating her twenty-five years on the throne. There were red, white, and blue Union Jack flags all over London. I had never seen such a public celebration, except perhaps the United States' 1976 Bicentennial the previous summer.

The whole year was a buildup of festivities and celebrations. On the day of one observance in May, London's West End was packed, although most of us stayed close to home and watched it all happen on television, which was a lot less stressful. Percussionist Sergio Pastora did venture out for a while and brought home a young lady who we all thought was way too young to be with him or in our house. She probably couldn't even spell consent.

Another incident with Sergio soon after proved to be his undoing. It seems he'd brought to London two cattle prods, a long one and a shorter, more easily disguised one. These were normally used to shock cows into moving along, but what was Sergio doing with these? There were no live cattle in London. While he was a talented conga player, being from Brazil, his outlook on things was a bit different than the others in the band. Everyone liked him but almost always anticipated him doing something odd or out of the ordinary.

When it got back to Roger about Sergio's shocking devices and his lurking in Hyde Park doing goodness knows what, and with ladies way too young, word came from Eric via Roger that I was to tell Sergio his services in the band were no longer needed. Great, here I was the most recent newcomer, and I had to fire one of Eric's band members.

Sergio's bedroom was on the ground floor. My job was to wake him early on Monday morning and give him the bad news while everyone else slept upstairs. I was not looking forward to this. At least Alphi, who was known as a gentle giant, would be there to pull him off me if he went bananas or took his cattle prod to my Texas butt.

Before the operation started, Alphi and I had a cup of coffee and discussed our strategy, which was really just me trying to gain the strength to finish what I'd been challenged to do. I think Roger loved giving me things of this nature to push me, to see if I'd rise to the occasion.

Finally, I'd built up enough courage and banged on his door, waking a drowsy Sergio. I had him come into the den and asked him to sit. Without mincing words, I then told him he was being let go from the band, and I was to have him on the 11 a.m. flight back to America. Well, let me just say he did not get up on the right side of the bed.

Sergio immediately turned red and exclaimed, "You can't do that, only Eric can fire me!" That's when Alphi intervened and tried to explain that Eric and Roger had asked me to simply break the news. The decision was theirs.

We kept him from getting to the phone so he couldn't call Eric, the Stigwood offices were not open this early, and Alphi's muscular physique at the bottom of the staircase prevented him from going upstairs to disturb any of the other band members. I suspect, though, at least some of them knew what was happening as a few were awake, listening at their slightly opened doors.

Sergio screamed and shouted all sorts of abuse, threats, and pleadings in both English and Portuguese, but the die had been cast. Despite eventually realizing he was leaving one way or another, he refused to pack his belongings, so that, too, became my job while Alphi kept a watchful eye out. I remember Sergio wanting to know what he had done, and while I knew a few of the reasons, I did not have an answer for him. I could only say I didn't know and that I was just doing my job.

After his bags were packed and in the car, he yelled upstairs one last time to Joe, his nickname for Dick Sims, to come help him. Sergio then got in the car, and we departed for Heathrow Airport. Once we'd left the house, he became resigned to the situation and was sorry all this had happened. He even apologized to me and Alphi, saying he knew we were only the messengers and that it was Roger and Eric's doing, calling them cowards and a few other choice names.

By the time we reached Heathrow, Sergio had calmed down. We helped him check in and escorted him to exiting passport control, where we waved goodbye to the emotional conga man.

Things seemed to settle down for a while after that, perhaps due to the help supplied by a doctor who was purported to be an associate of the infamous "Doctor Robert" referenced in the Beatles song. This was a Harley Street doctor who would, after a few general questions were answered and his office fees paid, prescribe just about anything one could ask for, including some very strong barbiturates.

I did not smoke pot with any regularity, but I did try, or at least sample, some other extracurricular activities. Pot had the reverse effect on me. It always made me paranoid, providing me no relaxation at all unless I was alone, safely locked in my home, and did not have to interact with anyone else. Heck, I could be a genius all by myself. Instead, I got a prescription similar to what several others in the band received, a synthetic downer of exceptional additive strength.

Mind you, I look back and am not exactly proud of doing what I did, but what's done is done. I survived and am grateful to God I was not seduced as others I know were, many of whom are dead today because of their addictions. Addiction and talent do not mix despite often going hand in hand.

One incident especially stands out as an eye-opener. In early June, we were preparing to depart the house in London for the last time to begin the European leg of the tour. Everyone was gathering their belongings, which after six weeks had become somewhat scattered, and packing them back into the cases they came from. There was much for me to do as well since I had now been in the UK for over three months.

I decided to take a tablet the doctor had given me, but the dosage did not seem to be having much of an effect. Of course, maybe that was because most of the band was cruising on the same pill, so I took one or two more. That did the trick. Between the joking, frivolity, and musings of the others in the same condition as me, preparing for the upcoming trip took me most of the night. It's not that the drugs made packing difficult. They just made it seem as if there was no hurry.

I did get my things put away and managed a small amount of sleep, but the next day on the plane with everyone, I can clearly remember feeling ill and thinking that if I had another tablet, I'd feel better.

Beep, beep, beep. Danger, Will Robinson, danger!

Luckily, before I'd gone to bed the previous evening—or rather just a couple of hours earlier—I realized how addictive and damaging these tablets were after taking only three or four of them, so my better self flushed the remaining pills down the toilet. Let the sewer rats get stoned. I'd had enough.

Eric Clapton 1977 UK Tour Dates

April 20, 1977: De Montfort Hall (Leicester, England)

April 21, 1977: The Kings Hall, Belle Vue (Manchester, England)

April 22, 1977: Victoria Hall (Stoke-on-Trent, England)

April 23, 1977: The Apollo (Glasgow, Scotland)

April 24, 1977: Newcastle City Hall (Newcastle, England)

April 26, 1977: The BBC Television Theatre (London, England)

BBC *The Old Grey Whistle Test* TV broadcast on June 7, 1977

April 27, 1977: Hammersmith Odeon (London, England)

April 28, 1977: Hammersmith Odeon (London, England)

April 29, 1977: Rainbow Theatre (London, England)

June 7, 1977: BBC *The Old Grey Whistle Test* TV broadcast

CHAPTER 4

Train Time on Our Time

Private Train, Private Chefs, What a Life!

With the arrival of June and the next leg of shows about to begin, we were informed by Roger that he'd arranged for us to do the European tour on a semiprivate train. By that, he meant we'd have our own German DSG sleeper, a dining car with chefs from the Orient Express, and the lounge car that once belonged to notorious Nazi Hermann Göring. We did not have our own engine but instead would time our travel so we could hook on behind scheduled trains heading to the same cities where we were scheduled to perform. This, I am sure, took some detailed organization.

First, before heading to the continent, we had two dates to play in Ireland. Things in Dublin had been fairly quiet as far as turmoil and fighting, but while the feeling was a bit tense, especially for some of us Americans, the Brits assured us it was not as worrisome as we were making it out to be.

Still, everything looked gray, and there was barbed-wire fencing and official military vehicles around. There did not seem to be many people on the streets milling about, but I am sure that was all in my own worrisome mind. The scene was similar to looking over the Berlin Wall into East Germany when I had recently toured there with Jack—gray and still. Years later, after the wall had come down, I went back to Berlin with a different band. We even stayed in a grand old Eastern European hotel straight out of the 1930s.

In England and Europe, we did not bring in pool tables because usually the hotel suites were too small, and we didn't often stay at a hotel for more than one night anyway, except for when we had a day off. That meant more time spent in the bar.

Days off could be expensive. During our time in Dublin, we were invited to a party at the Ashford Castle, which was once owned by the

Guinness family (yes, makers of the wonderful stout). We arrived late after the second show date, and we did not really know anyone. After meeting one of the Guinness heirs, we were shown around, and to my surprise as well others I'm sure, there was no Guinness in the house. They were serving Heineken straight from the fridge using a bottle opener!

After a quick stop back in London, we were then off to Continental Europe for a concert in Denmark, where we would also meet up with the semiprivate train. The accommodations felt very opulent as I had my own sleeper cabin that slept two. I opted to keep the lower bunk in the seated configuration and used the top pull-down as my bed. There was a small sink and mirror, a closet, and not a lot else; however, it was all mine for the next couple of months.

The dining car was great—half lounge and half dining with the Orient Express chef and his assistant in the kitchen. There were white linen tablecloths and napkins, and the food was excellent.

Göring's lounge was similar to a beautiful wood-lined library and featured easy chairs and a bar. Some members of the band spent most of their free time in this car, listening to music and, well, otherwise having a good time. On the other hand, I did not spend much time there.

That was one thing about touring. For musicians, there is a lot of free time spent without their instruments. Those traveled with the trucks and crew. Because of that, boredom easily set in, meaning drinks, drugs, and trouble usually weren't far behind. Unfortunately, this was a frequent occurrence.

The train tour was magical, though. The Who had their "Magic Bus." The Beatles had their *Magical Mystery Tour*. Eric had his magical train.

This mode of transportation was a peaceful way to travel. We'd often arrive near a town early and have to be moved to a rail siding outside the train station. While the views were not exactly magnificent on these sidings, use of this time was made resting, eating, and getting ready for the gig.

When concert time came closer, we'd be hooked back up to an engine and moved to a platform at the station. Exiting the train, we'd then load into awaiting Mercedes limos and be ushered off to the venue. Again, once there, the opening act was usually already on stage, and the band would either catch a glimpse of their performance or head to the dressing room until showtime.

The mistaken identity between Eric and me also happened in Europe and the UK, so I had to be careful where I went for fear of causing a scene. I knew the adoration wasn't for me, but I still didn't want people thinking Eric was being a jerk when I didn't wave back or sign autographs. I also didn't want to distract from the other band's set.

At the appropriate time, Eric and his band would then take the stage, and the screaming and wonderful songs would start. I can remember being in the back one night and thinking how lucky I was and how thousands of people would love to be where I was about to go stand and listen.

There was a bar set up behind EC's amps, and I'd hand him his drinks when he needed a fresh one, although I had been instructed to make them weak when he was performing. I also served Carl Radle, the bass player. Drummer Jamie Oldaker drank water, and keyboardist Dick Sims was into other things, so he didn't drink much during shows. The crew took care of the other side of the stage and the needs of those band members.

Roger always sat stage left behind the PA system, just out of the audience's view, with a chair or two beside him for me or other guests. The shows passed uneventfully with Roger and me watching the band and the always interesting people in the crowd.

Sometimes we'd spy a fan recording the show. This was before smartphones and digital recording devices, so spotting them was easier when they tried. Alphi and I would often grab their tapes and give them later to Roger or Eric. One time, Eric and some of the band suggested we wait and confiscate the recordings toward the end of the show, so they could have a nearly complete concert bootleg tape.

In Switzerland, we saw a fellow halfway back who was recording the show using a rather elaborate setup hidden under his seat with microphones in his jacket. We waited until the encore before Alphi reached over the fellow's shoulder, pushed the eject button, and took the tape. That evening, we played it on the train during our journey to the next town, and it turns out the recording was fantastic for a live show. Not only was the band pleased to have it, but everyone actually felt a bit sad for the guy who had lost such a good bootleg. Unfortunately, we had no contact information for him and couldn't send him a copy, but to this day I still have my copy of that concert tape.

When the shows were over, we'd go back to our train cars and often have to wait until our scheduled time to depart. The chefs were always at the ready, though, with dinner or snacks and plenty to drink. Sometime during the night, we'd feel a bump as another train hooked us up, and off we'd go to the next town.

Let me tell you, lying in a bunk on a gently rocking train through the Alps is a wonderful—no, magical—way to sleep. Well, what little sleep was had. Admittedly, a number of the band members and I saw the sun come up almost every night we were on that particular train tour. I probably lost a number of brain cells along the way, but the memories will always remain.

Since then, to my knowledge, no other rock band has ever toured Europe by private train. However, we would travel in such a way again, except the next time we had our own engine . . . and a film crew. Now that's class.

Eric Clapton 1977 European Tour Dates

June 4, 1977: National Stadium (Dublin, Ireland)

June 6, 1977: National Stadium (Dublin, Ireland)

June 9, 1977: Falkoner Teatret (Copenhagen, Denmark)

June 10, 1977: Stadthalle Bremen (Bremen, Germany)

June 11. 1977: Groenoordhallen (Leiden, Netherlands)

June 13, 1977: Forest National (Brussels, Belgium)

June 14, 1977: Pavillon de Paris (Paris, France)

June 15, 1977: Philipshalle (Düsseldorf, Germany)

June 17, 1977: Rhein-Neckar-Halle (Eppelheim, Germany)

June 19, 1977: Mehrzweckhalle (Wetzikon, Switzerland)

June. 20, 1977: Olympiahalle München (Munich, Germany)

CHAPTER 5

Jack's Back

Step Up to a Step Down in the USA.

After a fabulous string of shows in the UK and the unforgettable train tour through Europe with Eric, I returned to Tulsa and that "getting used to it" feeling of being out of place in my own home.

It wasn't long, though, until I received a call from Roger Forrester, which was usually preceded by his secretary, Diana Snelling, saying, "I have Roger for you. Do you have time to talk?" Of course, I would always make time to speak to my boss as I was confident something work-related and fun would come from it.

When he got on the phone after making me wait for a couple of minutes—he always kept the upper hand—he asked if I had any interest in taking Jack Bruce back out on tour. Roger knew how rough the last one had turned out to be, but this time Jack would be playing shows in the US. I don't think he expected me to decline, and I didn't disappoint him, telling him I'd be happy to. I imagined planes, possibly bigger venues, and a more enjoyable time, but who was I fooling?

It turns out we would begin the tour in the Northeast, and the band and crew would travel by two rented station wagons. There would also be a box truck and a driver to transport the equipment. We would do shows across the eastern US before eventually dumping the station wagons toward the end of the tour to fly distances that were too far to comfortably drive. We'd be staying in the same "quality" hotels as in Europe, but at least I still got my single room, as did all the band members. The crew would once again have to share accommodations.

The itinerary was made up primarily of large clubs that held 250 to 500 or more people. Some were concert style, meaning there were chairs where the audience could sit and watch, which neither Jack nor the band preferred. Other venues, though, required fans to stand, lending to a more exciting reaction of the band's performance. Jack was definitely fonder of this arrangement. Oh, well. That was my challenge, to keep him happy.

After we all met at the Philadelphia International Airport and picked up the station wagons on October 25, the tour opened two days later in Wilmington, Delaware. I drove one car and Alphi O'Leary, who was now a close friend, steered the other. We usually traveled in tandem, keeping an eye on each other. These were new station wagons and nice to drive, but I hated driving in general as I had motored across the US with my own band and Jo Jo Gunne way too often. It was not an ideal way to travel.

After a handful of uneventful shows, including two nights in Roslyn, New York, we went to the Agora Theatre in Cleveland, which had a good reputation as a performance club. We also stayed downtown at the Swingos hotel, where all the touring bands of the 1970s slept and admittedly partied. Swingos had become famous for antics such as Elvis booking one hundred rooms on three floors, which raised the then failing enterprise into hotel stardom. Then there were other publicity-making events like the Who's Keith Moon handcuffing two strangers together while dressed as a policeman. Ian Hunter, the lead singer of Mott the Hoople, once described Swingos as "a place you remember checking in and checking out of, but you remember nothing in between."

However, my experience at Swingos was a bit different. We played a fairly satisfactory show on November 7 but stayed in Cleveland for a couple of more days. As always, much of that time was spent at the bar. We were happily drinking one night when in walked Donald O'Conner, the renowned Hollywood actor, singer, and dancer. He must have been in town for a theater show somewhere, and by the state of his condition, he'd enjoyed quite a few cocktails already. I admired Mr. O'Conner from the movies and his dance routines with Gene Kelly.

Then in came Billy Joel and some of his band members, who'd done a concert at the Cleveland Music Hall that night. As usual, this didn't sit too well with Jack, and he pounded down a couple of somethings and went to his room. All I remember from the remainder of the evening was that guitarist Hugh Burns, Billy Joel, and I ended up in my hotel room finishing off the minibar and telling stories.

As it got later, and as we got drunker, Billy asked Hugh to join his band. He was dead serious, not just drunk talking. He really wanted Hugh for his band. I don't remember how he knew Hugh was as good as he was, but I sensed he was not too fond of his current guitar player. Regardless, Hugh respectfully declined the offer and eventually left my room, as did Billy, and I finally got some sleep. The bridges were burning, and we were only seven dates into the tour.

From Cleveland, the Rock and Roll Capital of the World, we headed to Boston for one show at Paul's Mall on November 13. We were then scheduled to play the next two nights in Philadelphia, but unfortunately we had to cancel both as the Bijou Café's stage was just way too small. The worst part was the crew had already driven there ahead of us and called to tell us not to come. We had to rely on them to know what was best for the band. Our sound man, Rob Cowlyn, went on to become one of the top production managers in the industry. We became longtime friends, but sadly we have lost touch.

So instead, it was on to the Big Apple for a couple of dates at the Bottom Line, which was a famous club in Greenwich Village. Most of the great artists played there at one time or another. We arrived for the November 16 show, and Jack was supposed to have been delivered a special bass amp from the Sam Ash music store on Forty-Eighth Street, but it had not arrived. We were on a fairly tight schedule, so I sent the truck driver in one of the station wagons to pick up the amp since the store was having trouble bringing it to us.

Time (way too much time) went by, and Jack was getting peevish. We wouldn't have a sound check if we didn't get a move on. Then we got notice that the driver, a young kid who was maybe twenty-one years old or so, had gotten the amp in the car—while double-parked in the street, mind you—and then decided he needed a slice of pizza from a place next to Sam Ash. The driver dashed inside to grab one, and the purchase only took a couple of minutes. When he returned to the station wagon, the car had been towed away. That fast! In less than two minutes!

Instead of calling me, the driver then took it upon himself to go to the police impound to get the car and amp back himself. No going—because his name was not on the car title or lease agreement, and he did not have enough cash. So come to find out, he casually reached into the officer's cage while the officer wasn't looking, took a release slip, filled it out, forged the officer's name, and tried to get the car out of the pound. Yep, they caught him and took him straight to the overnight lockup in Manhattan. Nowhere I'd want to visit.

We didn't have a clue what happened until he used his one phone call from jail to finally contact me. The show somehow went on without the special bass amp while the driver cooled his heels in the New York City hoosegow.

The next morning, after he was released and we'd retrieved the car with one of my crew members and cash, the driver came to my room, sad and apologetic. We had a long talk, and I was sorry for him, but that was the first time I had to fire someone—at least out in the real world. I told him I could not afford to trust a truckload of band gear to someone making that kind of stupid decision. Not a good day for either of us. I felt terrible, but I did give him a good recommendation letter.

Obviously, I had to replace him right away. I made quick arrangements with the Egotrips trucking company, which was owned by Jim Bodenheimer. He had a driver close by, so off we went to the next gig, a long drive for two shows in Atlanta, November 21–22. The station-wagon train was the least favorite method of travel I ever experienced. Yes, we chatted a lot, laughed, and got to know each other really well, but it was an arduous journey at best.

As we arrived in Georgia, we got word that the second single to be released off Jack's *How's Tricks* album was not going to be the song keyboardist Tony Hymas had written, as he had been led to believe. "Something to Live For" was a great ballad that would have undoubtedly been a hit, but the record company chose some other song to promote. Tony was crushed.

Following our second night in Atlanta, he and I went out after everyone else had gone to their rooms. We headed to a bar away from the hotel and really tied one on. It took a day or two to recover from that experience. Tony and I have spoken about that night a few times, and we both have similar memories—way too much excess.

The next stop was Chicago, where we played two shows in one night at the Ivanhoe Theater on November 28. All went smoothly. That is until later, after everyone had been to the hotel bar and then on to bed. I, too, was in my room dozing off when my phone rang. It seems Jack had gotten up and gone back to the bar, where he ended up in an argument with a customer or two. To avoid any further problems or a fistfight, the bartender called security. They, in turn, had taken Jack downstairs to the hotel's basement lockup. Must have been expecting him.

I dressed and went to the lobby, and Jack was brought up for me to retrieve. He was somewhat apologetic, although he was extremely drunk and being a bit arrogant. I said to the security guard that I'd take responsibility and get him to bed. He left, and I pushed the elevator button.

As the elevator door opened, Jack went in and I followed. There were several floors to this Holiday Inn, so once we were alone in the elevator, Jack proceeded to take off his valuable Rolex watch, rings, a bracelet, and even a gold necklace and throw them at me as hard as he could. He screamed, "Why don't you take all this and go back to Eric! You'd rather be working for him anyway!"

I was on the receiving end of all this pent-up anger and incoming jewelry, but I felt sadly sorry for him. I knew he didn't know what he was doing, and if he did, he probably didn't even care at that point. To this day, I still feel sad he felt so hard done by.

I remember his statement, "You'd rather be working for him (Eric) anyway!" That was not exactly true. Sure, EC's tours were a bit more casual (probably due to more cash floating around), but I thought Jack was a tremendous artist, and I felt lucky to be working for him. He just had this terrible jealous streak when it came to Eric and his seemingly more popular career.

I finally got Jack back to his room and into bed. As I left, I put all his jewelry by his shaving kit in the bathroom. Every bit of it. He never mentioned that incident again or even said thanks for keeping his gold safe.

A booking agent had filled in a date for us in Colorado, a show on November 30, so we had to leave the cars in Chicago, fly to Denver, and then drive up to Boulder. Two crew fellows drove the truck with the gear to Colorado to meet us. That's a tough job no matter how you look at it. Road shows wouldn't go on if it wasn't for a capable and invaluable crew making it all happen.

We were booked into a Holiday Inn, a two-level building with a big courtyard in the middle. They had a restaurant and, even more importantly, a bar. On the night of the show, which I remember going well, especially after Chicago, we went to grab a drink as usual. But after having only a couple, all of us decided to turn in, probably due to the altitude making us tired.

Most of us were on the second level, and I was sound asleep. I don't know how long it had been, but suddenly I heard screaming coming from outside along with someone banging on my door. I jumped up a bit bleary-eyed, and it was—guess who—Jack. He ran into my room yelling, "He's going to kill me! Shut the door! Call the police!"

I asked Jack what happened, and he said some guy was after him and wanted to beat him up. He was scared. I looked outside my door to the right, and sure enough, some guy—not especially large but bigger than Jack—was coming up the stairs, looking to see where he'd gone.

About that time, one of our roadies staying two rooms down from mine opened his door in his boxers and saw this fellow headed toward my room. He glanced around and saw me, and I said, "He's after Jack!"

The roadie, casually as you please, reached behind him, grabbed a trash can lid, and when the pursuer was about to pass by him on the hunt for Jack, he slammed the guy in the face with the lid, knocking him out. Just then, a couple of police officers, who'd been called by the receptionist, arrived. They took him away in their patrol car to cool off and sober up, as it had been reported that someone was drunk and disorderly. Of course, I knew the offender was Jack, but the police believed it to be this other drunk and disorderly gentleman.

I asked Jack what happened because the last time I'd seen him he was on his way to bed as well. He didn't want to explain the story, though. He just wanted to get back to his room.

After putting Jack to bed yet another time, I went down to the bar to get the details and to maybe grab another drink. Evidently, Jack had gotten back up, gone to the bar, and begun drinking again. He made acquaintances with a guy who was chopping out STP or some other drug, and soon thereafter, Jack was snorting and drinking with him.

According to the bartender, this went on for a while, but the conversation grew louder and louder. Jack then told the guy to fuck off and got up to leave, but before he opened the glass door to the courtyard, Jack kicked it very hard, shattering the glass. The door was completely ruined. That's when the fellow got up and popped Jack in the mouth, and Jack took off running toward my room.

The bartender, manager, and the other stupefied patrons were all being nice, and I offered to pay for the door repair. I also bought a round of drinks for everyone, which theoretically closed the books on the Boulder visit. We never saw the guy who chased Jack again, and I didn't have to pay for the door after all as the hotel said it was insured. Still, I've always wondered what the stranger said. Did he ask Jack an inappropriate question?

The next day, we were off to Los Angeles, where we were playing two shows a night for three nights at the Roxy Theatre, a well-known LA club. Joe Cocker even came the first night. Having him on hand was nice, except back then he was a big drinker like Jack. Fortunately, Joe was escorted home after the show before anything got out of hand. I could see a fight breaking out between Jack and Joe, which would wind up in all the LA newspapers. Not if I could help it.

After performing at the Golden Bear in Huntington Beach and the Catalyst Club in Santa Cruz on consecutive nights, we were back in the two station wagons, headed to San Francisco to wrap up the tour. We played two nights at the Old Waldorf, and they, too, went really well. No major upsets. I even got a great bootleg recording, which I still have.

In the meantime, I had received a call from Roger saying that after this final performance, Jack and I were to catch a shuttle to LA and check in at the Beverly Hilton, a hotel I'd grow to know very well later in my career. The rest of the band would fly back to London with Alphi.

Jack was to be a part of the finale scene for the movie *Sgt. Pepper's Lonely Hearts Club Band,* which starred Peter Frampton and the Bee Gees. In addition, Robert Stigwood, Jack's manager and my employer, was producing the film. Little did I know this would be one of the most spectacular and memorable days of my career so far.

Another memorable time, though, came back in 1974 when I got to do some cool things with Roger Daltrey when he called and asked me to come to LA while he was doing a promo tour. He liked having a friend or two along. I accompanied him to Dick Clark's first annual American Music Award's television show, which was held at the Earl Carroll Theatre in Hollywood. The filming was fun, but the after-party in the Beverly Hilton's ballroom was even more fun. Lots of celebrity stars were there, and I ended up spending most of the evening getting cross-eyed with Joe Walsh. This was before he joined the Eagles. For some odd reason, the next morning Roger and I had breakfast with Lucie Arnaz, the daughter of Lucille Ball and Desi Arnaz. I don't remember why we did, but she was really sweet.

Back in Sgt. Pepper's Land, Jack and I checked into the spacious Beverly Hilton. Jack said he had some friends coming by and that I was on my own for the evening as filming was not until the next day.

While Jack got up to who knows what, I wanted to treat myself to a nice meal—we were now on Stigwood's movie expenses—so I went to one of my favorite restaurants, Trader Vic's, there in the hotel. They had good food and great Mai Tais, and I thoroughly enjoyed myself. Afterward, I went to my room. I was very familiar with LA since my own band, when we were aspiring rock stars, lived there for nearly three years. But with no car, I just headed to bed, hoping I wouldn't hear from Jack.

Bingo! Los Angeles has a magic about it because I awoke the next morning well-rested, having not had to deal with a drunk or crazed Jack during the night. I left a message for him with the operator—if he needed me, I'd be in the restaurant having breakfast.

As I was at the counter paying my bill, I noticed I was standing next to actor Jack Palance. Since the producer had asked me to invite any celebrities I met to the Metro-Goldwyn-Mayer Studios for the filming of the last scene that day, I introduced myself and asked Mr. Palance if he would like to participate in this special finale.

"What are they going to pay me?" he responded.

"Well, I am not sure," I replied.

"Well, I'm not interested," he said as he turned to walk away after having paid his bill.

That was that, but at least I tried.

Shortly after that exchange, Jack and I met in the lobby, and a limousine took us to MGM, where we were led to a huge soundstage to meet Dick Ashby, who managed the Bee Gees for the Stigwood Organization. He told us what was going on and led us to our private tent to wait until Jack was called. We both knew Dick from the 67 Brook Street offices in London.

The scene to be filmed would be a live version of the Beatles' *Sgt. Pepper's* album cover with celebrities of all kinds singing the title song. Sir George Martin, the Beatles producer, was conducting the scene. How cool is that?

Not only would that alone be great, but as other guests arrived to the soundstage and their awaiting tents, I was staggered. Dozens of actors and musicians, old and new, were there, and everyone had a director's chair with his or her name embroidered across the back. Very posh. We sat in our tent for a few minutes before realizing that people were mingling, so out we went to mingle as well. There was food and drinks everywhere, just about anything you could want.

Jack went his own way, and I sat down with Dr. John, Etta James, and a few others. Not knowing any of these stars to begin with, don't ask me why I sat with them, but it turned out to be a wonderful experience. They welcomed me, and we chatted for the next hour. I'd see Jack every once in a while, as he passed by. I think I even stopped him to introduce him to my new friends.

Suddenly, a voice came over the speaker system asking everyone to head to the soundstage for the rehearsal and then the filming of the finale. I found Jack and off all two hundred people went. Like myself, not everyone was a celebrity. Many were artists or tour managers.

We entered the soundstage where there were risers and a backdrop identical to the Beatles' album cover. We saw the Bee Gees and Frampton, and although at that time I did not know the brothers or Peter, I would eventually.

We were placed on the risers—yes, somehow, I was included—and I stood next to a young Brooke Shields among many other people of note. It was amazing, and I was thrilled to be there. Jack was placed somewhere down the line.

Martin was introduced, and he gave directions on what to do when the director said, "Action!" We were supposed to sing along to the "Sgt. Pepper's Lonely Hearts Club Band" song and then at the end just stand still until the director yelled, "Cut!"

We did two or so rehearsals as cameramen looked at angles and people. It was pretty cool being surrounded by all that was going on. In fact, everyone was having a good time.

But some of the people on the risers were asked to step down to allow late-coming celebrities to take those places, and yes, my position was filled by a more well-known face. I can't say I wasn't disappointed, but I really was not supposed to be up there anyway—someone mistook me for a rock star.

They ran through the song again before finally shooting the scene for real. This was what was seen at the conclusion of the film, but I was there in the background watching and singing right along.

We were then told to go to our tents, and certain celebrities would be called back for close-ups. This process went on for about an hour or so. Everyone was now tired, mostly from just hanging around as you can chit-chat for only so long.

A voice finally came over the PA system, thanking everyone for participating and expressing how grateful the producers, George, and the director were. As this was happening, these two airplane-hangar-sized doors slowly opened, and everyone was invited into the neighboring soundstage, which had been set up to serve dinner to the guests who had been a part of the filming.

I have never seen anything like this before or since in my life. There were large round tables with red tablecloths and complete settings for about twelve people each. Decorations hung from the ceiling, and there were musicians playing in one corner. They even had cigarettes in open-glass containers for people to smoke, just like in the old movies.

Jack and I chose a table, but I don't remember who was sitting with us. Salads had already been placed, and waiters and waitresses were serving hot meals to everyone. There were dozens of bars as well as tea and water available. No one wanted for anything.

With all the celebrities, managers, and extras eating, mingling, and having fun, it felt like I was in a movie. What a great way to end a rather wonderful day . . . or so I thought. Remember who my date was.

Sure enough, Jack circled back around after a couple of hours chatting and drinking, or maybe just drinking and drinking. Falling down drunk is about the only way I could describe him. I realized I had to get him out of there and back to the hotel because he was scheduled to catch a flight back to London the next morning. I was grateful for that, but I did not know what was awaiting me once we left MGM.

We got back to the hotel in a limo with Jack hurling abuse at me along the way. Because of his jealous nature, this had happened often during this tour. He was drunk, obnoxious, and angry, but I ushered him into the hotel and up to his room. He'd lie on the bed, and I'd think he was asleep, but then he'd be at it again, yelling at me and saying he was not going back to London. Great.

In his shaving kit, I found some prescription Valium, which I did not know he had, and I got him to take one while I tried to pack his suitcase. Soon enough, he was up again, hurling abuse my way. *Another Valium,* I thought since he was becoming angrier and increasingly more violent. He settled down for a while, and although he was still in the clothes he'd worn all day, I had almost finished his packing.

You guessed it, up again, Jack started pulling things out of the suitcases and dumping them over. I was tired and angry myself. I'd had enough. I hoped that one more of the little blue tablets would calm him enough to get him to sleep, and after convincing him to swallow, it wasn't long before he began snoring.

After speedily packing his clothes and readying his cases to be picked up for the airport run, I turned out the light to a sleeping lion and shut the door. I still had to pack myself, but that last event had shattered me beyond all comprehension. I will never forget how sad and horrible that experience was, having to subdue him that way, but he had given me no choice. The only other option was an arrest, and that was not in the cards.

Jack was a great talent, but he could not control his addiction—at least at that time. I pray the rest of his life was easier, and that when he died in 2014 due to liver disease, he passed in peace.

Shaking, the next morning I phoned him, only to find him already awake and waiting to go to the airport. With the help of a porter, I retrieved his luggage, and then Jack and I went to LAX. I escorted him to his departure gate (you could do that back then), and we chatted briefly. I knew he had a terrible hangover but would be all right since he'd be flying home first class, not coach like me—at least this time. There were no apologies offered, just a quick, "See you some other time," and he was gone.

I returned to the hotel in the limo and spent the rest of the morning getting my gear together. Despite still feeling like I had been run over by a herd of rhinos, I grabbed a bite to eat and took a taxi to the airport, making it to my plane on time for the flight home to Tulsa. I did take two director chairs that a couple of people left behind, Chuck Berry and Dr.

John. They looked nice in my home and made good conversation pieces for a while.

I never saw or spoke to Jack again, although I tried once when he came to Dallas in 1990. I'd moved back to my original home city, and he, drummer Ginger Baker, and a young, very good guitar player named Blues Saraceno were touring and playing Cream songs. It was at the Arcadia Theatre, which held around one thousand people. I sent a note to Jack that I'd like to say hello but never got a response. As usual, the band was great, but then I saw Ginger, and I knew his reputation for being difficult was equal to that of Jack's or more so. I believe that was when I decided I'd heard enough. Too many memories.

That last night with Jack in his hotel room, just the two of us, after what could have been a spectacular day instead turned out to be one of the worst days of my life. Sad, exhausting, embarrassing, heart-wrenching, deflating, I guess I could go on and on with adjectives, but I never wanted to see or do anything like that ever again.

As the genie Baronni says in *The 7th Voyage of Sinbad* (a movie that I love), "Don't be so confident, oh Sinbad. There are other worlds to be conquered and monsters to be tamed. This isn't the end!"

The Jack Bruce Band 1977 How's Tricks US Tour Dates

October 27, 1977: The Other Side (Wilmington, Delaware)

October 28, 1977: The Shaboo Inn (Willimantic, Connecticut)

October 29, 1977: The Shaboo Inn (Willimantic, Connecticut)

October 30, 1977: The Show Place (Dover, New Jersey)

November 1, 1977: My Father's Place—two shows (Roslyn, New York)

November 2, 1977: My Father's Place—two shows (Roslyn, New York)

November 7, 1977: The Agora Theatre (Cleveland, Ohio)

November 13, 1977: Paul's Mall (Boston, Massachusetts)

November 14, 1977: Bijou Café—canceled (Philadelphia, Pennsylvania)

November 15, 1977: Bijou Café—canceled (Philadelphia, Pennsylvania)

November 16, 1977: The Bottom Line—two shows (New York, New York)

November 17, 1977: The Bottom Line—two shows (New York, New York)

November 21, 1977: Great Southeast Music Hall (Atlanta, Georgia)

November 22, 1977: Great Southeast Music Hall (Atlanta, Georgia)

November 28, 1977: Ivanhoe Theater (Chicago, Illinois)

November 30, 1977: Blue Note (Boulder, Colorado)

December 2, 1977: The Roxy Theatre—two shows (West Hollywood, California)

December 3, 1977: The Roxy Theatre—two shows, second show canceled (West Hollywood, California)

December 4, 1977: The Roxy Theatre—two shows canceled (West Hollywood, California)

December 7, 1977: Golden Bear (Huntington Beach, California)

December 8, 1977: The Catalyst (Santa Cruz, California)

December 9, 1977: Old Waldorf—two shows (San Francisco, California)

December 10, 1977: Old Waldorf—two shows (San Francisco, California)

December 16, 1977: Sgt. Pepper's Finale, Metro-Goldwyn-Mayer Studios (Culver City, California)

Bee Gees tour personnel, crew, and band—end-of-tour photo!
Courtesy of the Bee Gees and the Bob Sherman estate.

Most of the Bee Gees family on the beach in Florida. From top, left to right: Andy Gibb, Barbara Gibb (mom), Hugh Gibb (dad), Linda Gibb (Barry's wife), Maurice Gibb, Barry Gibb, Robin Gibb. Courtesy of the Bee Gees and the Bob Sherman estate.

On board the ship is Alphi O'Leary, a former bouncer at London's Speakeasy Club in the 1960s, who would later serve as bodyguard to Eric Clapton and Jack Bruce. Courtesy of Mary Oldaker and the Oldaker Estate.

Bee Gees 1979 tour program. Cover: Maurice, Barry, Robin. Courtesy of the Bee Gees and the Bob Sherman estate.

Bee Gees with Andy Gibb and Robert Stigwood circa 1979. Courtesy of the Bee Gees and the Bob Sherman estate.

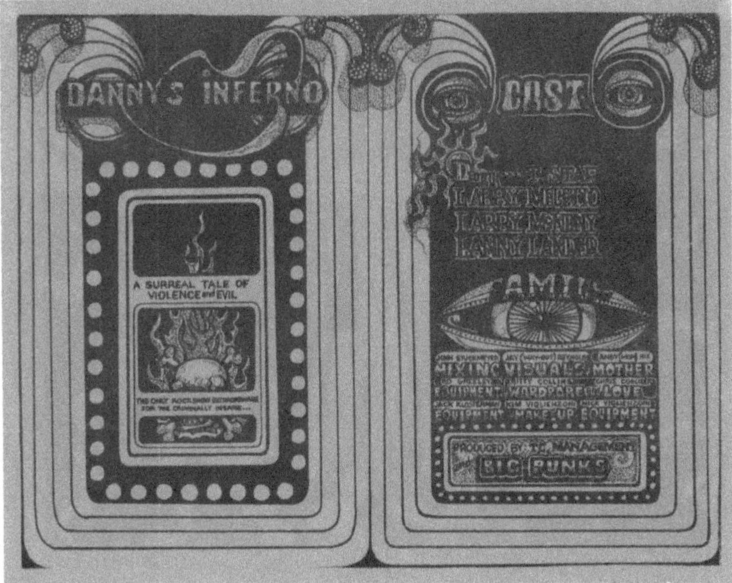

Big Punks show program for original rock opera "Danny's Inferno," (1970). Courtesy of the Big Punks Archives.

Big Punks circa 1969. Courtesy of the Big Punks Archives.

My band Big Punks, circa 1969.
Courtesy of the Big Punks Archives.

Jack Bruce, Bobby Richardson,
and friend circa 1968.

Bee Gees manager Dick Ashby
with one of the Gibb little ones.
Courtesy of the Bee Gees and
the Bob Sherman estate.

Eric Clapton and Nigel Carroll on our camping/fishing trip in Minnesota. Courtesy of L. McNeny.

Copy of Bus Gazette, Bee Gees tour. Courtesy of L. McNeny.

Laminated pass for Eric Clapton 1979 World Tour with Muddy Waters as the opening act. Courtesy of L. McNeny.

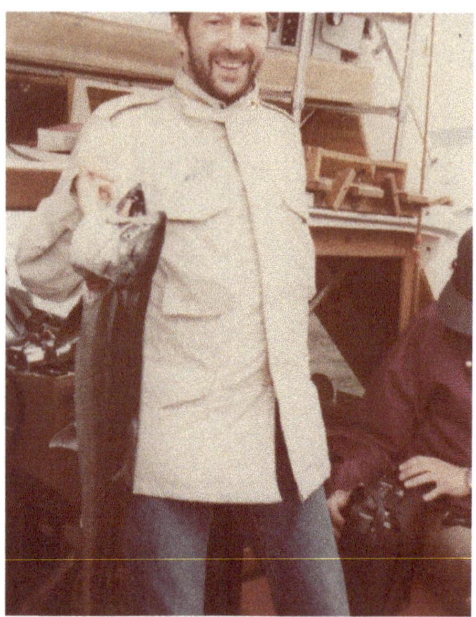

Eric Clapton with the biggest catch of the day on our fishing trip—nice salmon! Courtesy of L. McNeny.

Hugh Burns, guitarist for Jack Bruce (*How's Tricks*), Gerry Rafferty, and Wham. Courtesy of L. McNeny.

One of Eric Clapton's Duck Brothers Bombay guitar picks. Courtesy of L. McNeny.

Eric Clapton tour program cover. Courtesy of R. Forrester.

Pullman Editions train poster from our train tour with Clapton. Courtesy of L. McNeny.

Entrance to Shangri-La Ranch Recording Studio circa 1971. Courtesy of R. Fraboni.

A Les Paul Fretless Wonder like I used to own, except mine has a Bigsby tailpiece! Courtesy of Gibson.

Jack Bruce onstage performing.
Courtesy of the Bruce Estate and Family.

Jack Bruce on a ramp while on tour.
Courtesy of T. Hymas.

The Who, 1960s promo photo signed by Pete to Larry. Courtesy of The Who Archives.

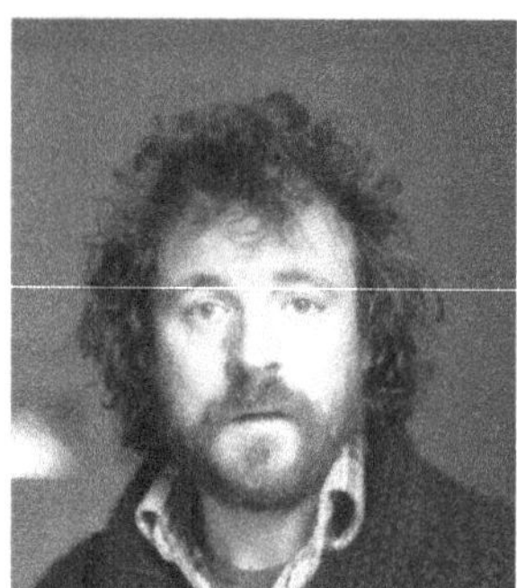

Jack Bruce with beard.
Courtesy of the Bruce Estate and Family.

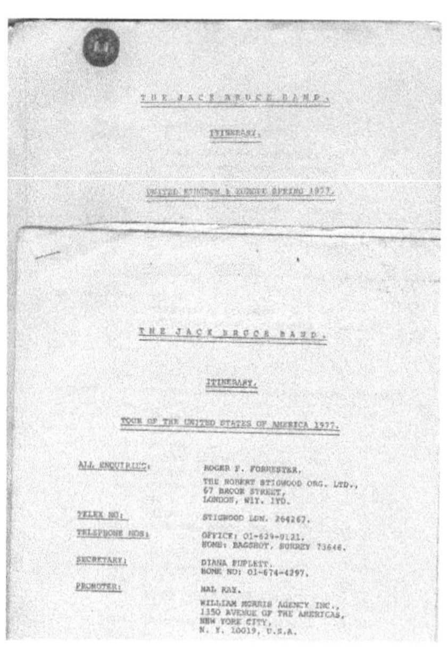

THE JACK BRUCE BAND.

ITINERARY.

UNITED KINGDOM & EUROPE SPRING 1977.

THE JACK BRUCE BAND.

ITINERARY.

TOUR OF THE UNITED STATES OF AMERICA 1977.

ALL ENQUIRIES:	ROGER F. FORRESTER. THE ROBERT STIGWOOD ORG. LTD., 67 BROOK STREET, LONDON, W1Y. 1YD.
TELEX NO:	STIGWOOD LDN. 264267.
TELEPHONE NOS:	OFFICE: 01-629-9121. HOME: BAGSHOT, SURREY 73646.
SECRETARY:	DIANA PUPLETT. HOME NO: 01-674-4297.
PROMOTER:	HAL RAY. WILLIAM MORRIS AGENCY INC., 1350 AVENUE OF THE AMERICAS, NEW YORK CITY, N. Y. 10019, U.S.A.

Jack Bruce itineraries. Courtesy of R. Forrester.

Larry McNeny and Eddie Choran during the 1979 Bee Gees tour.
Courtesy of the Bee Gees and the Bob Sherman estate.

Larry, Jack, and Hugh Burns on Mount Pilatus in Switzerland. Courtesy of L. McNeny.

Larry McNeny and Marcy Levy on a ferry crossing to Europe. Courtesy of Mary Oldaker and the Oldaker Estate.

Japanese fans taking a lot of photos at the train stationas Ozzy and band depart for the next city on tour. Courtesy of L. McNeny.

Larry McNeny, the band days, 1970. Courtesy of L. McNeny.

Larry McNeny on tour with Clapton.

The name tag Eric Clapton put on the Yamaha acoustic guitar I got him while in the Minnesota hospital for his ulcers. He called himself "Walter Albino." Courtesy of L. McNeny.

Larry McNeny, Chuck Vollman (pilot), and Ben Palmer on Eric Clapton's private Viscount plane on tour. Courtesy of Mary Oldaker and the Oldaker Estate.

Marcy Levy, one of Clapton's backup singers, backstage waiting. Courtesy of Mary Oldaker and the Oldaker Estate.

One of our two station wagons on the first Jack Bruce tour in the US. Courtesy of L. McNeny.

Rob Fraboni, producer and engineer at Shangri-La Ranch Studios, listening to a playback of the Clapton album Rob produced. Courtesy of Mary Oldaker and the Oldaker Estate.

Clapton road techs Jeff (Bombs), Bradley, and guitar tech (Clapton and Barry Gibb) Willie Spears. Courtesy of Mary Oldaker and the Oldaker Estate.

The outside of the private European train in which we toured with Clapton. Courtesy of Mary Oldaker and the Oldaker Estate.

Ronnie Lane of Slim Chance onstage opening for Clapton.
Courtesy of Mary Oldaker and the Oldaker Estate.

On Jack Bruce tour across Canada—taking a break. Courtesy of L. McNeny.

The Bee Gees promo photo at sunset. Courtesy of the Bee Gees and the Bob Sherman estate.

The Bee Gees, 1979. Courtesy of the Bee Gees and the Bob Sherman Estate.

Tony Hymas, amazing keyboardist for Jack Bruce, Jeff Beck, and many others. Courtesy of T. Hymas.

Promo photo of the Bee Gees. Courtesy of the Bee Gees and the Bob Sherman estate.

Young power drummer Simon Phillips, with Jack Bruce. Courtesy of T. Hymas.

CHAPTER 6

The Sun Does Rise Again!

Back in the Comfortable with Eric.

While I enjoyed working for Eric, his manager, Roger, used to like to play card games, mind games, and who knows what other kinds of games. Although I was his assistant during most of our time on the road, he would quite often not include me on some of the more unique dates. For reasons only he knows, I did not go on the 1977 trip to Barcelona, Spain, and the Plaza de Toros bullring show in Ibiza. He also never took me to any of Eric's concerts in Jerusalem or to Japan, which Eric played often. Though unbeknownst to me at the time, I'd eventually travel to beautiful Japan and Spain as well as Southeast Asia dozens of times before my active career slowed. In fact, I got to know Japan better than most of EC's contingent ever would.

Oddly enough, a few years later I was working with Ozzy Osbourne during the recording of his *Bark at the Moon* album at the Ridge Farm Studio in Surrey, which was near Eric's home. We needed a guitar tech, and since EC was not on the road or recording himself, I hired Lee Dixon, who took care of Eric's guitars for a number of years after Roger fired the whole Tulsa lot, including Willie Spears, Eric's former tech.

On a day off from recording, Lee suggested we go visit EC at home. I had been to his house a few times in the past and was comfortable going along. Besides, Lee did not drive then, so he needed me to take him. Plus, I had use of a nice BMW!

We went over to Eric's estate and sat around in his kitchen chatting for a while. I happened to mention how the first time Roger brought me to England to work with Jack Bruce, Eric and Roger put me in a gloomy one-room basement flat for about a month of rehearsals.

I expressed how depressing the apartment was, and Eric said to me, "That was Roger's plan." I asked what he meant by that, and Eric told me that Roger had thought I was almost too good to be true on my first American tour with EC, so he wanted to see if putting me in the gloomy basement flat would break me.

I wondered if he thought I'd quit and go home. Instead, I survived the experience, in part because I had always wanted to visit London, and here I was with someone paying my way and for my room. And I was getting a paycheck as well.

However, I'll admit hearing Roger had that side to him didn't make me very happy. He could be extremely gracious and kind or distant, one never knew. Like the way the Tulsa Band was fired! There is another story about Roger and a knife in my back, but I'll save that for later. That one I'd never forgive him for.

I want to add a side note here about touring. Being on the road during a concert tour wasn't always filled with mile-a-minute, exciting activity or drunken brawls or jewelry shopping in an elevator. Not by a long shot. Mostly it was work, a job for me and others. Many, no, most days were given to just trudging through the downtime, thus one of the reasons for pool tables—to keep minds occupied and people out of trouble. They helped make the tour dates go by faster.

Starting a five-month tour of forty-five to fifty shows seemed daunting at first, but once we hit the road, going from stage to stage, hotel to hotel, all of a sudden, we'd have completed over half the shows and be in the home stretch. It was the knockout punches coming out of the blue that caused a tour to slow down and become drudgery, despite the excess of luxuries. Checking off dates was a good thing, an accomplishment. A good example of the opposite, you might recall, would be Jack Bruce's USA tour. That seemed like it went on forever.

An example of a smooth, quick-moving, and enjoyable tour would be Eric's. There was never a lot of troublesome antics that could derail the schedule. Except for showtime and traveling, a few of his band members often just stayed in their hotel rooms, doing whatever they carried in their little medicine kit.

Not all the band members were so inclined, though. Marcy Levy, Yvonne Elliman, George Terry, and sometimes Jamie Oldaker would go out. Heck, even Eric left this room to play pool or eat. He was more social than the extremely talented rhythm section, who were busy "resting."

It was with all this in mind that I began a North American tour with Clapton's band in February 1978. As an opening act, we had an RSO-signed group (part British, part American) called Player, who had a fairly large hit with a song titled "Baby Come Back." They were friendly and sounded fairly good when I got to hear them, but for some reason they just didn't fit the show. Meaning, they weren't the right act to open for Eric. But I guess since they were on the same label, someone talked Roger into letting them have the opening slot, which was probably the last time that ever happened.

Having the right opening act was an important part of touring. A popular band could help sell more tickets, and while you didn't want their music to be the same as the headliners, at least being in the same genre was good.

Also on this tour was a gentleman—and I mean gentle in the kindest way possible—named Ben Palmer. He was Eric's old friend and bandmate in the Roosters. Ben, who lived in Wales, was married to Carl Radle's former girlfriend, and Carl told me he still carried feelings for her.

Ben was extremely thin and had a fairly long, pointy nose. He was always polite and seemed grateful EC and Roger had taken him on this tour because he needed some work and maybe some purpose. Ben was to serve as the tour accountant, at least for the band side of things.

We flew out on our own Toby Roberts Tours private DC-3 plane with Chuck Vollman at the controls, just as he had been for the last couple of US tours. We all had a great deal of trust in Chuck.

The first show was in Vancouver on February 1, 1978. Roger had, for some reason, decided that on this tour we'd primarily stay in less expensive hotels when possible, Holiday Inns, and everybody could take it or leave it. No one left it.

After playing two concerts in Canada, we traveled to Seattle to do a couple of shows and based there for a few days. Then it was off to Portland on February 9—yep, another Holiday Inn—before heading to Oakland for a concert and to check out their Holiday Inn situation.

Moving down the coast, we played back-to-back nights in Santa Monica, February 11–12, and since we were in Southern California, why not stay at the famed Chateau Marmont hotel (where many celebrities lived and died) just off Sunset Strip? Next, we slid into Las Vegas to play the Aladdin Theatre, which could host an impressive amount of people, especially considering most casino showrooms didn't hold too many. But the Aladdin's capacity was seven thousand, so we had a decent-sized audience, and we stayed there as well.

So far so good. No major flubs from Eric, the band, or me. The tour was going all to plan. There were shows in Denver and Minneapolis and their Holiday Inns. Ames, Iowa, the same. Kansas City, the same. They were all great concerts.

St Louis, Chicago, and Louisville brought more cool, calm sailing, so to speak. You see, the dates could tick off just as quickly as the days on a calendar if everybody did their job well. And we did.

On our private airplane, several of us would get into a card game they called Pontoon, although it was actually just a version of Twenty-One. Roger was good, Alphi was good, Eric was all right, and I was, well, not as good as Eric. I remember one game in particular where I knew I was going to win with Pontoon (twenty-one). These were real betting games, and so as the money was creeping higher and higher, I bet one hundred dollars, feeling quite confident.

Of course, I lost. I can't remember to whom, but it came back to haunt me as Ben, who'd been watching over our shoulders, put the negative on my account. After the whole tour was over, and I got a final check and statement, I saw there was a one-hundred-dollar deduction for a gambling debt. Thank you, Ben. Or perhaps thank you, Roger, for reminding Ben to make sure the loss was recorded and deducted. I never played Pontoon with them again.

As we often did with Eric's tours, we continued to work out of a base hotel located near several short-hop flights to shows in other cities. This gave us a chance to unpack, settle in, check laundry, and get a little rest. The system Roger was again using worked as well as before.

We flew into Nashville after a concert in Kentucky and took the ever-ready limos—thanks to my advance calls—to the Holiday Inn on West End Avenue. As always, I had arranged for a pre-check-in with the keys and room lists to be ready upon our arrival. It was already late, probably close to midnight, so I passed out the envelopes and told the band the luggage would follow as quickly as possible.

It wasn't five minutes before one, then another, and then another of our touring party came back to the parking lot where the luggage was being unloaded. Everyone said there were people using their rooms, and they were in bed, naked, and indignant that they were being interrupted. Seems we had stumbled onto the local hang-on-to-the-room-key brothel! Ladies of the night would take johns to these rooms since usually they were mostly empty. That is until Eric, or rather Roger, decided to come to town. More of the touring party came down, and all of us were stupefied. I went to the desk person in the hotel lobby but got no satisfaction.

I believe it was with the help of our promoter's representative, Jay Hagerman, who is a close friend of mine now, that we found a five-star hotel not too far away that had enough rooms for us and were pleased we were going to be there several nights. We reloaded the cars and made a speedy getaway, waving Holiday Inns and Roger's experiment to save money goodbye for the rest of the tour. I think he was insulted by what happened and a bit embarrassed, funny as it was.

Every room in the second hotel was a suite of sorts. There was no restaurant, so all our meals had to be ordered through room service, which was great. And the food was great as well. Since we would be headquartered here for this leg of the tour, I had time, or rather the travel agent had time, to rebook the second half of our journey with better hotels. Whew, what a relief.

We spent the days there and flew out for shows in Huntington, West Virginia, Nashville, Memphis, and Birmingham, Alabama. That wrapped up the tour's first half. Everyone went home for a two-week break and Player, well, they'd played their last date with EC.

Again, going home was a very odd thing, not only this time but every time, and it wasn't just me. Most everyone I have met who toured had the same experience, especially if they stayed out on the road for weeks on end. Even though I called home often, when I arrived it was as if I was a stranger in my own home. And it was not always the fault of the one who was left behind; they shared some blame as well. The person arriving home expects a celebratory steak dinner and champagne, basically a warm welcome.

I'd been away with an entirely separate group of people who were all doing the same thing on the road, making sure the show went on as planned.

We developed our own inside jokes and a sort of road language, although not out of any predestined plan. It just happened as a way of surviving while being away from everything normal in the world.

Life on the road was not normal at all. It cost many marriages and ruined many steak-and-champagne dinners. I would not advise it if you're seeking a loving, long-term relationship. I know many couples who have made it, but I know more who didn't.

The two-week break gave me the opportunity to make sure everything was still there at home, which included reaffirming that love, if it existed before, was still there as well and would continue to be there after this next leg of the tour was over. I'd also catch up with my few friends, where we'd talk about the shows and what had been going on in Tulsa.

Then, before you know it, the time comes to repack the suitcases and book a taxi to the airport. It was a sweet-and-sour affair. I loved being home, but I loved being on the road.

Figuring out how to travel light took me a short while to learn, and I'm still working on it. When I first went to Europe for Jack's tour, I carried two suitcases, a suit bag overpacked with sportscoats and the like, and my briefcase. I don't know how many pairs of shoes I took along, but it was way too many. While I still find minimizing my necessities for a trip hard, I am much better now and have traveled abroad for a month or more with just a carry-on suitcase. That's progress, but I still lugged so many of my own damned clothing around for way too long. I must have been a slow learner or just wanted to be, as ZZ Top sings, "a sharp-dressed man."

On March 18, 1978, we flew from Tulsa to Miami to begin leg two of the Clapton North American tour. Revving the traveling operation back up was always exciting. Unfortunately, we had to say at a Holiday Inn near the Miami airport as the location was convenient for our plane and us. The hotel was also the only one available that could accommodate so many rooms. It was a tower hotel and not at all like many of the other Holiday Inns where we'd stayed. After that, though, we'd be in Hiltons, Sheratons, and generally better accommodations everywhere we went.

On this portion of the tour, we had a new and more appropriate opening act. This was a friend of Eric's named John Martyn, and he could play guitar extremely well. In fact, his show consisted of just him, solo, playing and singing. He was magic on stage, a fireball of energy, his fingers flaming across those strings. And his voice was equally as good. John could also seduce an audience with his ballads and the lovely melodies he could produce on his guitar.

However, off stage John was often Eric's compadre in the alcohol realm. He could put down drinks with the best of them. Though I liked John, I remained cautious of him after recent experiences.

We did a couple of shows in Florida and then one in Savannah, Georgia, on March 21 before flying the next day to Macon, where we stayed at the Macon Hilton. After a sizable concert that evening, we were back at the bar for a couple of bevvies. Suddenly, having gone to the show himself, Greg Allman of the Allman Brothers Band came in. He and Eric had been friends since Greg's brother, Duane Allman, had collaborated on the Derek and the Dominos album *Layla and Other Assorted Love Songs* in 1970.

He and Eric visited and had a drink together, and at first, we thought it was nice of Greg to stop by and say hello. But then he stayed, and they kept drinking.

I had been sitting at a table nearby with Alphi, who'd just gone up to bed, when Eric came by and said, "Greg wants to take me out to see where Duane is buried." Duane had been killed in a motorcycle crash there in Macon in 1971. I understood. It was late, dark, and EC was a bit inebriated, and he really didn't like these types of things anyway. He said to me, "Get rid of him, I'm going to bed."

Great, now I had a chore on my hands. When Eric didn't come back from the bathroom, which he had used as an excuse to get up and depart, Greg came over to my table and asked where Eric was. I told him that Eric had gone to bed. Greg explained how he wanted to take Eric to show him where Duane was buried and that Eric wanted to go. I replied with something along the lines of Eric wasn't feeling well and had gone to bed. I then paid my bill and started heading to the elevators myself.

Being drunk, stood up by his friend, and now alone in a hotel bar with no one to talk with, Greg was none too happy with the situation. But I made it to my room and was getting ready for bed, thinking my work was done for the evening. My hope was Greg would just eventually go home and that would be that.

Oh no, Grasshopper. Down the hall I heard Greg banging on doors and calling out Eric's name. I stuck my head out of my room and told him that

Eric was already asleep and that he wasn't even on this floor. Greg called me a liar and kept banging. I stepped into the hallway, closing my door behind me, and caught up with him. I told him a bit more sternly this time that Eric was not on this floor and was not going anywhere. Greg may have had another drink or two at the bar, but that didn't cool him off any. By this time, he was angry Eric had skipped out.

Next thing I know, he pulled out a .22-caliber pistol and put it to the side of my head. He said, "Tell me where Eric is, or I'll fucking shoot you." I must say this was much more than I had bargained for.

Just then, behind Greg, I saw Alphi, wearing only his trousers, step out of his room and quietly creep up behind my potential executioner. Alphi grabbed the nerve on the neck and shoulder area of Greg's gun hand. The gun fell to the ground and so did Greg. He was out. How Alphi had learned these things, well, I never asked. But he incapacitated him completely.

I was so grateful that Alphi heard the commotion and came out to see what was going on. Then again, he had been with me during Jack's tour and, like me, was used to these out-of-the-blue emergencies.

Alphi said to grab Greg's feet, and he'd take the shoulders and gun. We carried him to the elevator, took his still limp body to the lobby, lugged him to the front of the hotel, and gently laid him in the gutter by the curb. Alphi then emptied the bullets from the gun, put them in the trash can, and slid the .22 into Greg's jacket pocket. With that, we returned to our rooms.

I obviously told Alphi how grateful I was and hugged this gentle giant of a man before we separated. When I got back to my room and realized how close I came to dying, I was a wreck. I believe I did something I never, well, hardly ever did—I raided my minibar for a gin and tonic to calm down.

Macon, the Allman brothers' hometown, was our base for shows in some other southern cities, but even though we were there a few more days, we never heard another word from Greg or any of his people in retribution. Thank goodness! I couldn't take those kinds of Eric's "friends."

We got a thank you from Eric and Roger, but neither Alphi nor I got a raise for fending off the marauding hoard that was a drunken Greg Allman. At least this was altogether easier than touring with Jack.

The shows continued to go well, and Eric's band was good every evening despite the alcohol he drank and the other illegals some members of the band were partaking in. Good thing we traveled on a private plane. And John was always great to catch if we got there in time. He was masterful on the guitar, and the crowds loved him.

We finished our southern stretch with three straight nights of concerts, March 24–26, before heading up north to Detroit and that area for a run of shows. And again, the band and EC did what they did while we filled our days waiting until it was time to leave for the next plane and show.

We were going to play Radio City Music Hall in Manhattan on April 3, but due to high ticket demand, the venue was changed to Nassau Coliseum on Long Island. We were staying in New York City and took three limousines out to Uniondale for the show. I was in the front seat, where I preferred to ride, when a voice came over the driver's walkie-talkie as we neared the Coliseum. The voice said they were limo number four from the same company and had a guest who wanted to take the arena's underground ramp with us as he was a celebrity coming to the show.

I explained what was happening to Roger, who was in my car while Eric rode in a different one and so was not aware of the situation. When asked who was in this mystery limo, the response came back, "Mick Jagger." *Interesting*, I thought, as I'd never met him. Surprisingly, Roger then piped up to the driver, "He's not to follow us down the ramp and into the arena." I was a bit perplexed, but Roger always had a reason—some good, some questionable. I knew this might alienate Mick or at least royally piss him off.

Sure enough, the three Clapton limousines entered through the arena's large roll-up door, but the fourth limo was locked outside the gate and did not make it down the ramp. I'm sure the drivers were wondering why Mick was not allowed in, but the deed was probably done because Roger tried to keep these kinds of distractions out of Eric's life. Plus, we had a show to do. The incident was mentioned backstage but nothing was reversed, except the limo carrying Mick on his way back to the city.

After a date in Springfield, Massachusetts, on April 5, we were off to Montreal, Canada. When we got to the hotel, I went to have dinner with drummer Jamie Oldaker in the restaurant. We got a drink and ordered some food, and I noticed, as did Jamie, that a number of people were staring at us. And it did not seem to be because they thought we were famous.

So I asked our waiter why everyone was staring, and he said it was because of the jacket I was wearing. While in Chicago, we were all given Chicago Blackhawks hockey jackets, which were nice, but apparently the Blackhawks were heated rivals of the Montreal Canadians. The waiter suggested I take the jacket off immediately so people would stop staring. I did so tout de suite, but who knew? I'm from Texas, and we didn't have professional hockey then, so the sport wasn't something I kept up with. Glad we didn't have our meals dumped on our heads. Another close call!

The final date on the docket was a bit reminiscent of a Jack Bruce tour. Eric's last show was in Toronto on April 8, and we stayed at the Windsor Arms, which was a large hotel that featured different antique furniture in every room. The decor made for a nice change from the fancy modern hotels we normally reserved, where the furniture was all similar.

We did the show at Maple Leaf Gardens, and the following day all the band and crew flew home, except for me, Alphi, Roger, Eric, and John. Their flight was not until the next day, so Roger asked me to stay over and, if needed, help Eric and John.

Now with time on their hands, those two hunkered down in Eric's suite and began drinking—all day long as it turned out. Eric did not need encouragement to drink and neither did John. Together they were pounding them down.

Roger asked me to go to Eric's room to see if I could help keep things calm and maybe slow down the imbibing. So off I went, knocking on EC's suite door. He opened it and said immediately, "Oh, Rog sent you down to keep an eye on us?" There was no getting one by on Eric, even in that condition. I said, "Well, of course, he did," going along with the game. He invited me in, but only if I would drink with them, which I did.

I had a few gin and tonics, and they watched TV while continuing to drink copious amounts. After a couple of hours, I was ready to leave, tired of the midafternoon socializing. I never liked drinking in the daytime, so I said goodbye to the two slurring, singing celebrities and went off to my room. I called Roger and said that it was time for Alphi to take over. He responded, "Fine," and I hung up.

Strangely, the quaint hotel that seemed so warm and enjoyable suddenly felt dark and dank. I think it was a combination of all the band members, my friends, being gone and the drinks. I don't really remember having any dinner that night, although I may have. That day was primarily a blur and best gotten over with.

The next morning we all headed to the airport, and the four of them went to their overseas airline while I took my plane to Tulsa and home—probably while nursing a good headache.

Eric Clapton 1978 *Slowhand* North American Tour Dates

February 1, 1978: Pacific Coliseum (Vancouver, British Columbia)

February 3, 1978: Northlands Coliseum (Edmonton, Alberta)

February 5, 1978: Paramount Theatre (Seattle, Washington)

February 6, 1978: Beasley Coliseum, Washington State University (Pullman, Washington)

February 8, 1978: Paramount Theatre (Portland, Oregon)

February 10, 1978: Oakland Coliseum (Oakland, California)

February 11, 1978: Santa Monica Civic Auditorium (Santa Monica, California)

February 12, 1978: Santa Monica Civic Auditorium (Santa Monica, California)

February 13, 1978: Aladdin Theatre (Las Vegas, Nevada)

February 15, 1978: McNichols Sports Arena (Denver, Colorado)

February 18, 1978: Metropolitan Sports Center (Bloomington, Minnesota)

February 19, 1978: Hilton Coliseum, Iowa State University (Ames, Iowa)

February 20, 1978: Municipal Auditorium (Kansas City, Missouri)

February 21, 1978: Kiel Auditorium (St. Louis, Missouri)

February 23, 1978: Chicago Stadium (Chicago, Illinois)

February 24, 1978: Louisville Gardens (Louisville, Kentucky)

February 26, 1978: Huntington Civic Center (Huntington, West Virginia)

February 28, 1978: Nashville Municipal Auditorium (Nashville, Tennessee)

March 1, 1978: Mid-South Coliseum (Memphis, Tennessee)

March 2, 1978: Boutwell Auditorium (Birmingham, Alabama)

March 19, 1978: Miami Jai-Alai Fronton (Miami, Florida)

March 20, 1978: Lakeland Civic Center (Lakeland, Florida)

March 21, 1978: Savannah Civic Center (Savannah, Georgia)

March 22, 1978: Macon Coliseum (Macon, Georgia)

March 24, 1978: Charlotte Coliseum (Charlotte, North Carolina)

March 25, 1978: Carolina Coliseum, University of South Carolina (Columbia, South Carolina)

March 26, 1978: Von Braun Center (Huntsville, Alabama)

March 28, 1978: Cobo Hall (Detroit, Michigan)

March 29, 1978: Civic Arena (Pittsburgh, Pennsylvania)

March 31, 1978: Baltimore Civic Center Arena (Baltimore, Maryland)

April 1, 1978: Spectrum (Philadelphia, Pennsylvania)

April 3, 1978: Nassau Veterans Memorial Coliseum (Uniondale, New York)

April 5, 1978: Springfield Civic Center (Springfield, Massachusetts)

April 7, 1978: Montreal Forum (Montreal, Quebec)

April 8, 1978: Maple Leaf Gardens (Toronto, Ontario)

CHAPTER 7

More Train Time

Back in Europe Happily Comfortable with Eric.

After a rather lengthy break at home in Tulsa, which I must say was needed, as burning the candle at both ends will take it out of you, we were notified that a European and UK tour had been planned. We were to meet up in London for some brush-up rehearsals before heading to Madrid, Spain, in early November.

Again, Roger had worked his magic. We would be traveling by private train, except this time we had our own engine so would not have to rely on other trains to pull us. We could leave and arrive on our own schedule. And we'd still have use of the German DSG sleeper, the dining car from the Orient Express (complete with French chefs), and Hermann Göring's lounge car. I was looking forward to this. The last train tour was so great, and this one would be even better with our own engine.

Another treat, albeit one EC was somewhat reluctant about at first, was Roger had arranged for the opening act on the tour to be Muddy Waters, an idol of Eric's and for most blues guitar players in general. The first few dates, when we arrived at the venue, Eric would hear Muddy and his band playing and stop to listen for just a bit away from the stage. Then one day he told Roger he didn't want to arrive until after Muddy had finished his set. It turns out that Eric felt having such a legend open his concerts was all wrong.

Luckily, after a while everything settled down, and Eric and Muddy spoke often. Eric would even visit their dressing room, and he became friends with Muddy's band. By the end of the tour, he would regularly stand at the side of the stage and listen to these great musicians. We all would.

In addition, Roger arranged to have a few dates of the train tour made into a documentary, which was directed by Rex Pyke. The film, titled *Eric*

Clapton's Rolling Hotel, was never officially released, although DVDs of the movie can be found, and there is concert footage on YouTube. I had a few scenes, including one with a press person that stands out, and there were other shots as well that ended up on the cutting room floor. Probably best.

We were in Europe for fifteen days, and for most of them I saw the sun start to rise before going to bed. I'm sure a few brain cells were lost along the tracks.

The rehearsals went well and were short because these musicians were such professionals that it only took one time playing through a song to get their groove back. Then we were off to Madrid by airplane to open the tour with a show on November 5. We had a lot of fun, the food was great, and the city was extremely interesting. As the train tracks in Spain were a different gauge than the other dates in Europe, we had to fly to Barcelona to perform a concert there the next night. Already I was really having a great time seeing all these beautiful places. How lucky could I be?

Following Barcelona, we flew to Lyon, France, where we picked up our train and settled into our cabins. Ah, fond memories. After a show there on November 8, our train chugged onward to Germany—with a nice French meal, I am sure. I had become familiar with Germany and liked the country very much. It seemed somewhat Americanized but still German.

We played five dates in Germany, where on days off we'd go to a nice hotel to take a break. For the concert in Munich on November 12, we stayed in a hotel so we could all shower, and so the film crew could get some shots away from the train.

After the show, I was in the bar and got a phone call from the production manager, my friend Keith Bradley, who told me that the promoter had put the crew in a different hotel, albeit not too far away. Their rooms either had a bath or shower, but the toilet was down the hall. That or the rooms had a toilet but no bath or shower. Either way, the situation didn't sound so nice.

To make matters worse for the crew on their day off was their hotel had no bar. No bar? What was the promoter thinking? Or not thinking?

Though I could not change their hotel, to remedy the situation I invited the whole crew, twelve or more members, to our hotel bar to drink with the band. They were there in a flash, and soon some of the pain of their inconvenient accommodations was alleviated with a few drinks and maybe a room service spread or two. In the end, I told the bartender that the bill was all going on the promoter's tab, as he was also staying in our hotel. Everyone was grateful and felt he deserved this retribution.

The following morning, as we got on our bus to head back to the train station to go to Düsseldorf, the promoter, whose name was also Eric, was the last to board as usual because he was making sure I had paid all the incidental room charges for the band and Roger. He came on the bus rubbing his head in amazement and said something to the effect of, "I must have been really drunk last night to have run up a nearly $3,000 bill."

I had already alerted Roger, who had not been in the bar when this happened but agreed it was the right thing to do. The promoter should not have treated our crew that way. Eric Clapton had been on the bus for a while also knew, and everyone else just sort of played dumb, as if we had no clue what he was referring to. But soon enough, the promoter knew, and he knew why because the crew let him know in a flourish of very blue expletives.

We did the show in Düsseldorf and again stayed in a hotel for a night off. I had one of the best and most expensive meals I'd ever enjoy on the second evening. The band, Eric, Roger, and I were not paid a per diem. We just ate and drank what we wanted, which was usually nothing very extravagant. That was one great thing about Roger. He was extremely generous in this way.

However, on this night, guitarist George Terry asked if I wanted to have a meal with him in the hotel's very fancy restaurant, to which I agreed. I let him order the wine since he seemed to know more about wine than me back then, and he requested a 1957 bottle of Château Lafite (or some famous year, supposedly). I saw the price and it was around $200 a bottle, but once I tasted it, I knew I was drinking something very special. It was extremely delicious.

The meal itself also was memorable as I had venison, a specialty of the restaurant, with some vegetables. It ranked right up there with the wine. By the end of the meal, after three bottles of the same wine and with a cigar in hand, I knew I wouldn't eat or drink like that often in my life, so I savored the experience for as long as I could. Thank you, George, for the darn good grub.

Somewhere along the way, Eric asked Muddy to travel a night with us on the train. We sat in our dining car having a chat and drinking as we rumbled down the tracks. At the table was Roger, Eric, Muddy, and me. One of Muddy's favorite things to do after playing a show was to go back to his hotel and have a good meal with a bottle of champagne. We did not disappoint.

As we were talking, somehow the question came up about where we thought the prettiest women in the world could be found. Muddy and I agreed on Texas, my home and one of his favorite places to play. I told him I was from Dallas and grew up with a musician named Jimmy Vaughn, who later moved to Austin. Muddy looked at me and said Jimmy was his favorite guitar player and that he loved the Fabulous Thunderbirds, Jimmy's band. Eric was kind of stammering, like who is this Jimmy Vaughn and the Thunderbirds, and how come I don't know about him? It didn't take long, though, for Eric to get familiar with Jimmy, the Thunderbirds, and eventually Stevie Ray Vaughn, Jimmy's little brother. That was a great evening.

We played Hamburg on November 16 and then went on to Paris for our day off, staying this time, I believe, at the Hotel Concorde La Fayette, which was very nice. Someone heard Rickie Lee Jones had a concert that evening, a call was made, and the next thing I knew we were in a theater watching her perform solo on stage. She was very good.

We played our show in Paris in a venue that used to formerly be an abattoir, or as we call it, a slaughterhouse. This was where animals were killed and cut up for sale to stores and restaurants. The place was now one of the largest concert venues in Paris, and no, it did not smell like rotting meat.

From Paris to Brussels to Amsterdam, we enjoyed the train to its fullest. We realized we may never get to do this again.

Roger had tagged on two dates at the end of the UK leg that we would have to fly to. It was behind the Iron Curtain in Czechoslovakia and Romania—at the time, and still, mysterious places. I thought the idea sounded great, but the Tulsa band members went to Roger and said they expected to be paid the equivalent of or more than their normal show rate. Well, Roger didn't like the way it was put to him, so he canceled the dates.

Instead, after Amsterdam we flew straight back to London for a few days off before starting the UK part of the tour. Great, guys!

Following three days off in London, where we had a great time at the historic Montcalm hotel, we headed out for a show in Glasgow, Scotland, a place I had been to before with both Jack and Eric. We played the Apollo with the balcony that bounced slightly when the crowd became excited about the music. Kind of a scary sight, but it never came crashing down.

Again, Muddy and his band opened all these shows, and as expected, his playing went over well with every audience. And now that Eric was friends with Muddy, things were comfortable. Even Muddy and his harmonica player were invited onstage occasionally to play along with Eric, which always brought the house down.

We did ten shows in the UK, including a pair of concerts on December 5–6 at the Hammersmith Odeon theater in West London. After a performance at Guildford Civic Hall that included guest appearances from George Harrison and Elton John, our wonderful European/UK jaunt then came to an end at a smaller venue, Dingwalls Dancehall, on December 11. What a great time we had.

Then, as always, it was time for an awkward return home just in time for Christmas. I admit having such a fantastic job was nice. I was listening to amazing music almost every night, eating and drinking like a king, and being paid well. And now I had a nice, comfortable bank account.

Eric Clapton with Muddy Waters 1978 Europe and UK Tour Dates

November 5, 1978: Pabellón de la Ciudad Deportiva Del Real Madrid (Madrid, Spain)

November 6, 1978: Club Juventus (Barcelona, Spain)

November 8, 1978: Palais des Sports de Gerland (Lyon, France)

November 10, 1978: Saarlandhalle (Saarbrüken, Germany)

November 11, 1978: Festhalle Frankfurt (Frankfurt, Germany)

November 12, 1978: Olympiahalle (Munich, Germany)

November 14, 1978: Philipshalle (Düsseldorf, Germany)

November 16, 1978: Congress Centrum Hamburg (Hamburg, Germany)

November 18, 1978: Pavillon de Paris (Paris, France)

November 19, 1978: Forest National (Brussels, Belgium)

November 20, 1978: Jaap Edenhal (Amsterdam, Netherlands)

November 24, 1978: The Apollo (Glasgow, Scotland)

November 25, 1978: Newcastle City Hall (Newcastle, England)

November 26, 1978: Manchester Apollo (Manchester, England)

November 28, 1978: Victoria Hall (Stoke-on-Trent, England)

November 29, 1978: Gala Ballroom (West Bromwich, England)

December 1, 1978: Gaumont Theatre (Southampton, England)

December 2, 1978: Brighton Centre (Brighton, England)

December 5, 1978: Hammersmith Odeon (London, England)

December 6, 1978: Hammersmith Odeon (London, England)

December 7, 1978: Guildford Civic Hall (Guildford, England)

December 11, 1978: Dingwalls Dancehall (London, England)

CHAPTER 8

Loyalty to EC

State Your Name, Please. Which Arm?

What did I think I was doing, sitting in that small hospital-examination room, which smelled of alcohol (rubbing, not drinking) and antiseptic? It reminded me of all the real emergencies that may have occurred in that room, people clinging to life while I was here for some other type of artificial "emergency."

I sat with my left shirtsleeve rolled up above my elbow, and I was squeezing a rubber ball. It wasn't me who was getting married to Pattie Boyd, who had enjoyed conjugal visits with one of the top models of the 1960s. I wasn't going to reap any of the wedding-night benefits, and I sure as hell wasn't Eric bloody Clapton!

Yet here I sat at 7 p.m. on March 25, 1979, in a Tucson, Arizona, hospital emergency room, having *my* blood drawn because Eric was afraid of needles. And he could not, by state law, get a marriage license without first having a blood test. The fact a renowned former heroin addict was afraid of needles did dawn on me, although I appeased myself by imagining he just snorted the drug.

Alphi O'Leary, Eric's personal assistant, and I had held off going until after normal hospital hours were over, hoping there would be fewer gawkers and less of a wait. To our surprise, it was pretty quiet. Or was it celebrity privilege?

I checked in successfully with the help of Alphi and the occasional "Yes" or "No" in my poor British accent. (Side note: hardly any American can do a passable British accent, and I have heard many. I am married to a Brit, and people try it out all the time just to sound clever.) Alphi had explained to the staff why we were there and who I was, or rather pretending to be. He also said that I couldn't talk much because I had a bit of laryngitis and needed to rest my voice for the sake of the tour.

The hospital staff was outwardly excited but bit their tongues and kindly withheld any questions they'd already formulated to ask this "rock star." The less I had to speak the easier it was for me to pull off this charade. I just kept my head down because everyone knows celebrities are usually introverts in public.

I had, for several years, been used occasionally as a decoy for Eric since we had the same-shaped face, beard, and a similar build. I was even convincingly filmed doing an interview on the train while pretending to be Eric. Mostly this likeness came in handy after concerts. I'd help draw the backdoor autograph seekers away prior to the real Eric casually making a quiet getaway out the door and into his awaiting limousine. Many people might think this would be a cool and exciting thing to do, being mistaken by so many for a celebrity, but I found it awkward and embarrassing. I really felt like such a fraud.

In the hospital, the nurses knew this was obviously a special case. I don't imagine many celebrities came through the ER doors there in Tucson, and they were making the most of it. We even offered them some tickets to the show, so I was led back to a room fairly quickly to have my blood drawn. Now a fellow was tapping on my vein, ready for a stab. Looking away, I saw Alphi snickering to himself in the corner and probably dying to have a Rothman.

Within a minute, it was all over. Blood taken, Band-Aid on my puncture, and we were cleared to depart. We paid cash for the blood test and were told the results would be ready to pick up in the morning. I signed a couple of autographs—Eric's signature was not difficult—and we were back in a cab, headed to the hotel to report our success.

Roger, Eric, and the band all had a good laugh that we'd actually pulled it off, and I imagine Roger even thanked me, although I'm not sure. He was never too demonstrative or complimentary because I think he believed it showed signs of weakness. Or maybe he felt doing so put him in a position of obligation? He was definitely a good boss, but unique.

Although public information, Eric marrying Pattie was not really a well-known fact. He loved her, but Roger also forced the issue one evening by betting Eric he could have his name on the front page of the London newspapers the following day. I think the bet, which Eric took, was one hundred pounds. Small-time gambling was a pastime within the Clapton organization, especially the card game Pontoon.

Eric had just finished an early March tour in Ireland and was at home in Surrey. However, he and Pattie had a tiff, and so she left for California. They had now been separated by the Atlantic Ocean and several time zones for a short while, as couples who have spats will do, especially if money is not an object. Pattie was spending some time in Los Angeles with friends while EC was back in London preparing to embark on a tour of the US.

As it happens, once the bet was down and Eric had left, Roger, never one to wager unless he was sure to win, picked up the phone and called a friend at a major London newspaper office and gave him a scoop: Eric and Pattie were finally getting married. He gave the reporter an exclusive, which at the moment was not at all true.

I wonder how many other times Roger used these methods. Funny enough, in most rock-and-roll band/manager relationships, it is the manager who has all the best contacts and a sizable amount of money when separations happen.

The next morning, Eric woke up to see his name on the front page. He knew he'd lost the bet and, by the headline, his bachelorhood. Once Pattie awakened in LA eight hours later, the news was in papers around the world: "Eric Marries His Layla!"

Soon after that, EC paid his one hundred pounds to Roger, and they boarded a plane to Tucson, Arizona, where the tour was scheduled to begin. I imagine it was a chilly ride in first class that day. Eric also phoned Pattie and apologized for whatever it was they were arguing about, and he did in fact ask her to marry him. No going back now. It was all over the globe.

We were all put on alert and had to work double-time to get this wedding together. No expense spared, remember. Assisted by the hotel staff, we found a nice church and a priest to perform the ceremony. We also arranged a reception at our hotel, a fancy but small two-story place in a Tucson suburb. Roger was being cool and trying to second-guess the press, so he had us stay away from a big hotel and it worked. He was clever that way most of the time, and while some of his methods in handling Eric seemed questionable, he always made EC's best interests and well-being a priority.

While we were discussing the arrangements with the priest, he explained that Eric needed a marriage license, which he could get from city hall, but it would require a blood test first. Back at the hotel, as we were telling Eric what needed to happen, he exclaimed, "Blood test? No one said blood test to me. That wasn't part of the bet!" He refused to take the blood test and left Roger's suite.

I remember this as clearly as if it were today. We were sitting in Roger's room with Alphi, Roger, and some others, discussing the problem, when Roger turned suddenly to me and said, "Ah! Larry, gosh, you look just like Eric. You can take his blood test."

And that is how I ended up with an extra hole in my arm. I was taken by surprise and a bit flattered, but I also felt somewhat used. *This was Eric's responsibility, not mine*, I thought. *Why should I take his blood test?* Job security was the answer.

Despite everything else going on around us—tour plans, notwithstanding—Eric and Pattie were married on March 27, with the attending crew and staff in rented tuxes and nice attire. All in all, the occasion was very nice. I think only one or two press photographers found out, but in the end, the affair was very low-key.

The reception after the wedding was held in a second-floor gathering room of the hotel and was catered with sandwiches, crudités, punch, champagne, beer (lots of beer), and Eric's ever-present brandy and lemonade. Naturally, this could not be a normal cheery reception, this was rock and roll, so of course it had to end in a cake fight. Everyone looked too good to stay that neat. I think Roger even paid for the cleaning of those rented tuxedos.

In all the years I'd know him, I think only twice did I ever see Alphi hit anyone. One of those times was that evening. We were outside the motel-style hotel, which had open corridors at the ends of the hallway. A fellow, who was most likely high or drunker than we were, had gotten word of the party and just wouldn't leave the area near one of the stairwells. After we reasoned, pleaded, and even apologized that he could not be invited in, he still insisted on seeing Eric and was being belligerent. Alphi finally had to coldcock him, spark out! I think Alphi felt worse than the guy he hit, and it took him a couple of days to return to his old happy-go-lucky self.

This was just another example of us being in our own world, on the road, where the rest of the world did not exist. Except, that is, when it related to putting on concerts in whatever city we were in. We had a show to get on stage on a given night at a given time, and no matter what, that was going to happen. And it always did happen.

Five days after the wedding, we were in Midland, Texas, for a concert. The crew had gone by buses and the equipment via trucks while we flew out on our private plane. On April 1, Roger bought Eric a present for his birthday, which had been March 30. I remember Eric badgering Roger for a decent birthday present this time.

Dodge had just come out with its newest dual-rear-wheel pickup truck, meaning four tires in the back, so Eric and Roger went to the dealership and picked one out. I believe the sales price was around $16,000, a whole lot less than a pickup in today's world. As usual, Roger paid with the cash he'd acquired from my friend Jay Hagerman, who worked for our promoter, Concerts West. Cash was always available and in large amounts, if given some notice.

The truck was delivered to the hotel later that day. Eric was all smiles while Pattie played the happy-for-her-husband wife. Not only did Eric have a new wife named Pattie, he now had a brand-new pickup he named Dooley. Life was great.

The only problem was he didn't have a US driver's license. Or insurance. No license, no driving. In addition, I don't think Concerts West, which had a sizeable investment in this lengthy tour, would be thrilled with the idea of Eric driving a truck to tour dates around the country, especially as close as he and his best friend Courvoisier were.

Promoting a fifty-city concert tour is both a major expense and production, logistically, and though Concerts West was insured, having Eric behind the wheel was not a good idea. Later, on another big tour, we'd find out just how expensive canceling shows could really be, but that's another chapter.

So who was next in line to drive Eric's truck? You guessed it, me. I drove Eric around Midland for the afternoon and to the show that night. However, the decision had been made—between Eric and Roger, I'm sure—

that I would leave after the Midland concert and drive this hefty vehicle to Dallas, 330 miles to the east. Eric, Roger, and the band would all take the private plane and fly. Heck, they didn't want to drive all that way in the dead of night.

We were staying at the Anatole Hotel, so I knew when I got there I would have a nice room to greet me. But leaving Midland at eleven o'clock after the show and driving to Dallas tired and alone was not my idea of fun. Though we were off the following day, I was in no mood to dillydally. I got a little white pill from a truck driver, a couple of cassette tapes, and I hit the road, although I must admit with a frown on my face and a few foul words passing my lips.

Between Midland and Fort Worth, there is really nothing much to see, except for a few one-horse towns and truck stops. What's worse is it was dark, very dark. But at least it wasn't raining. I decided to see how this truck could handle, and before long I was passing just about everything on the road doing one hundred miles per hour. I did have a CB radio and was tuned into channels to see if I could pick up on any highway patrol stakeouts.

With the truck being new and having new tires and all the bells and whistles, I assured myself with a false sense of security that it could handle what I was giving it. And with God as my copilot and a gas stop—just to be sure, even though it had dual gas tanks—I reached the hotel in three hours and ten minutes with no tickets or trouble. The band had only been there for just over an hour and a half. I was even fortunate enough to talk a barman cleaning up out of a large gin and tonic to help me wind down.

For the next eleven days, we based out of the Anatole, flying off to do shows in that part of the US when necessary and returning to the Anatole each night. Every day I would take Eric to Peaches Records and Tapes, where he'd buy a few cassettes, and then we'd go to the same Sonny Bryan's Smokehouse barbecue restaurant and have lunch. Eric loved the ribs; I preferred brisket. We'd go by a western-wear store where he bought clothes and several pairs of boots. Once done, we'd listen to the new cassettes on the way back to the hotel. Sometimes one of the band members would join us.

One day after Eric had bought boots in a variety of styles, some salesman mentioned having a custom pair made. Well, that caught Eric's attention. For the next hour, he picked out colors, leathers, and styles, and even spoke to a representative from the Tony Lama factory in El Paso. The boots had been decided on, and they featured several colors, including blue and even Kelly-green patent leather. Oh well, I didn't have to wear them. We paid for the custom pair in cash of course, despite them being much more than the normal off-the-shelf offerings.

As the time neared to move on to our next base city, I made arrangements, per Roger's instructions, with an international freight agent in Grand Prairie to ship Dooley from Dallas to England, where it would be delivered to Eric's house. *A mighty big truck for those narrow English roads,* I thought. I stupidly imagined they might leave it with me for Eric's use when he came back to the US.

I ran the pickup to nearly empty on gas, took everything off that could be stolen or broken, and then turned the truck and around $3,000 in cash to cover the shipping fee over to the company to make it happen. That was the last I ever saw of Dooley.

A couple of years later, Roger called and asked me to contact the Tony Lama factory where Eric had ordered his custom boots. Seems they had never arrived in England as instructed. So I made some calls and soon was talking with Tony Lama Jr., who then ran the operation his father had made famous. I explained the situation, and he said he'd investigate and call me back. It wasn't long until he phoned and told me that when they got the order from the store in Dallas, they couldn't imagine making a pair of boots that they thought would look terrible, so they simply didn't. They just assumed someone must have made a mistake.

I assured them that it was indeed a real order from Eric Clapton, and he really did want those boots. After a harrumph from Mr. Lama, he said they would make them and ship them to England as quickly as they could.

A few years later, after Stigwoods had closed its doors, I was visiting with Roger in his office at Regents Park and asked if Dooley the truck had ever made it to England, as I'd never heard about it again. Roger related a story that it had in fact been delivered to Eric's house in Surrey and that the first time he took it out for a spin—mind you, it still probably had under two thousand miles on it—he misjudged the distance between himself and a Jaguar coming the other direction, and his driver-side mirror, being extra-wide for the dual-wheel setup, ripped a hole in the top of the other car.

Roger said Eric never drove Dooley again and sold the truck immediately.

Well, not wanting to forget about the other special UK shipment, I asked if the cowboy boots ever made it. Roger laughed and said they did arrive, but Eric took one look at them and decided they were too ugly—he never wore them. I guess happiness really is hard to buy. Tony Lama was correct!

While we were at the Anatole, where Pattie and Eric were still celebrating their marriage, word came that once we left Dallas for shows in Louisiana, Mrs. Clapton would be heading back to their house in Surrey. There were some reasons offered, but most of us knew the drill. Quite often she preferred to be home, as touring for her was boring. Her leaving was also sometimes suggested by Eric when he got the urge, if you know what I mean.

After a show in Monroe, Louisiana, on April 14, we arrived late in New Orleans, where we would set up base at the Royal Orleans Hotel. Eric, Alphi, and I went out to Pat O'Brien's, which is famous for a drink called the Hurricane. Delicious! The following day, Jennifer, one of the twins of Jennifer and Susan fame, flew in from England. Eric, who had cavorted with her previously, made plans without anybody's knowledge, not even Roger's. This could well have been what Eric and Pattie's original spat had been about. Who knows?

No one on the touring team was too thrilled with this development, and a funny thing happened, at least as I remember it. I don't know who had the idea, but once we found out this girl had arrived only two days after Pattie had flown home, and only about two weeks after they were married, the crew rallied together and approached Roger, asking him to deliver Eric this message: either Eric honored his marriage vows to Pattie while in their presence or they (the crew) would leave the tour. The crew stood up for what was right. If I got some of the details wrong, guys, I'm sorry, but it was a terrific stand of might and right. I was proud of the crew for doing what needed to be done.

Needless to say, Roger told Eric in no uncertain terms that Montana, a code name, had to go now or the tour was off. She left immediately, and we toured.

Regarding the blood test, I never gave it much thought at the time, but when looking back, I've never felt good about it. When I heard years later that Eric and Pattie were divorcing, I wondered, *Was the marriage entirely legal anyway?*

That tour itself was a rather long one, which, as you can see from the list of dates at the end of this chapter, meant a fruitful year. Getting into stride on these tours was always a bit slow at first, but once we settled into a pace, the dates suddenly seemed to whiz by. Touring is a way of life that is difficult to explain and even more difficult to understand for those left behind at home.

It was always like that. We'd have a list of dates looming months into the future, and to think of being away that long from friends and loved ones seemed almost unbearably painful. Then the tour, or the rehearsals preceding the tour, would start, and everyone would do whatever they had to do to find their path and settle in. Those who made a lot of money could choose a number of paths. Those who made little had few choices but to grin and bear it.

Once the first couple of weeks were under our belts, the next month or two would seemingly pick up speed, and before you knew it, we'd been on the road for three months. We would normally get at least a two-week break to go home before heading out again for the second half of the tour. And usually falling back into stride was easier. Going home, while enjoyable and natural, was never easy, as most every touring professional will attest.

In fact, life on the road was in no way a normal or near normal way to live, no matter how hard you tried to make it happen. It is a unique, special, sometimes dangerous, yet always changing way of life.

We were somehow chosen to work, experience, and even suffer in a world unique unto itself that only a few got to enter, at least all the way. I would say nine out of ten people who lived on the road touring for a substantial number of years, if asked, "What was it like?" would answer, "It was the hardest thing I have ever done in my life," and then continue with, "but I'd do it all again in a heartbeat."

I had a banner year in 1979 because when Eric's tour wrapped up in Seattle, Washington, on June 24, the following day Jay and I flew to Dallas, where the Bee Gees' *Spirits Having Flown* tour was about to begin. After spending nearly a year and a half with Clapton, we were now both signed up for another nine months on the road. There was no stopping.

This was the Bee Gees' first tour since the popular movie *Saturday Night Fever* and the accompanying soundtrack that produced the Bee Gees' biggest hits came out in 1977. We wondered what to expect.

Eric Clapton 1979 US Tour Dates

March 28, 1979: Tucson Community Center (Tucson, Arizona)

March 29, 1979: Albuquerque Civic Auditorium
(Albuquerque, New Mexico)

March 31, 1979: Special Events Center, University of Texas-El Paso
(El Paso, Texas)

April 1, 1979: Langford Chaparral Center, Midland College
(Midland, Texas)

April 3, 1979: Lloyd Noble Center, University of Oklahoma
(Norman, Oklahoma)

April 4, 1979: Hammons Student Center, Missouri State University
(Springfield, Missouri)

April 6, 1979: Tulsa Assembly Center (Tulsa, Oklahoma)

April 7, 1979: Pine Bluff Convention Center (Pine Bluff, Arkansas)

April 9, 1979: The Summit (Houston, Texas)

April 10, 1979: Tarrant County Convention Center (Fort Worth, Texas)

April 11, 1979: Municipal Auditorium (Austin, Texas)

April 12, 1979: San Antonio Convention Center (San Antonio, Texas)

April 14, 1979: Monroe Civic Center (Monroe, Louisiana)

April 15, 1979: Municipal Auditorium (New Orleans, Louisiana)

April 17, 1979: Freedom Hall Civic Center (Johnson City, Tennessee)

April 18, 1979: Knoxville Civic Coliseum (Knoxville, Tennessee)

April 20, 1979: Memorial Coliseum, University of Alabama
(Tuscaloosa, Alabama)

April 21, 1979: Omni Coliseum (Atlanta, Georgia)

April 22, 1979: Mobile Municipal Auditorium (Mobile, Alabama)

April 24, 1979: William & Mary Hall, College of William & Mary (Williamsburg, Virginia)

April 25, 1979: Mosque Theater (Richmond, Virginia)

April 26, 1979: Capital Centre (Landover, Maryland)

April 28, 1979: Providence Civic Center (Providence, Rhode Island)

April 29, 1979: New Haven Veterans Memorial Coliseum (New Haven, Connecticut)

April 30, 1979: Spectrum (Philadelphia, Pennsylvania)

May 25, 1979: Augusta Civic Center (Augusta, Maine)

May 26, 1979: Cumberland County Civic Center (Portland, Maine)

May 28, 1979: Broome County Veterans Memorial Arena (Binghamton, New York)

May 29, 1979: Onondaga County War Memorial (Syracuse, New York)

May 30, 1979: Rochester Community War Memorial (Rochester, New York)

June 1, 1979: Buffalo Memorial Auditorium (Buffalo, New York)

June 2, 1979: Richfield Coliseum (Cleveland, Ohio)

June 4, 1979: Toledo Sports Arena (Toledo, Ohio)

June 5, 1979: Saginaw Civic Center (Saginaw, Michigan)

June 7, 1979: Riverfront Coliseum (Cincinnati, Ohio)

June 8, 1979: Market Square Arena (Indianapolis, Indiana)

June 9, 1979: Dane County Coliseum (Madison, Wisconsin)

June 10, 1979: St. Paul Civic Center (St. Paul, Minnesota)

June 12, 1979: Chicago Stadium (Chicago, Illinois)

June 13, 1979: Wings Stadium (Kalamazoo, Michigan)

June 15, 1979: Athletic & Convocation Center, Notre Dame University (South Bend, Indiana)

June 16, 1979: Brown County Veterans Memorial Arena (Ashwaubenon, Wisconsin)

June 17, 1979: Omaha Civic Auditorium (Omaha, Nebraska)

June 19, 1979: Kansas Coliseum (Wichita, Kansas)

June 21, 1979: Salt Palace (Salt Lake City, Utah)

June 22, 1979: Spokane Coliseum (Spokane, Washington)

June 24, 1979: Seattle Center Arena (Seattle, Washington)

CHAPTER 9

Staying Alive One Day at a Time

Never Seen or Heard Anything like It.

We pulled away from the curb at the back of the Beverly Hilton, where we had been staying during our time in Los Angeles. We must have taken up forty or more rooms. The bus was negotiating its way around the block and into early rush-hour traffic as we headed to Dodger Stadium for the sound check. I was standing at the front of the bus as usual, having counted everyone as they boarded, and had given the driver the go ahead to get us on our way.

About ten minutes into the journey, although we'd not gone very far, everyone was chatting and starting to get excited about playing at such a prestigious and large venue. That's when someone called out from behind me, "Where's George?"

"What? George?" I went through the bus quickly, and damnation if I hadn't forgotten—only this one time, mind you—to grab George Bitzer and escort him to the bus. George was our blind keyboard player, and while I did not have to constantly look after him, I normally picked him up from his room when it was time to head to the show. Unfortunately, I had in fact failed to stop by and get George. And his playing would have been missed, for sure.

I instructed the bus to return to the hotel amid all sorts of abuse (lightheartedly), such as "That's right, Larry, forget the blind guy!" or "Yeah, George doesn't want to see Dodger Stadium." There was a bus full of my tourmates making fun of my mistake, and I could do nothing about it since I had indeed screwed up. No excuse.

Of course, after I retrieved George and we were back on the bus, the verbal barbs all began again. Even George jokingly started to have a go at me. I deserved their digs, I know, and it was funny, but the situation could have been a more serious dilemma, say, if we'd made it all the way to the stadium. Whew!

Only two weeks before, I had successfully completed a lengthy tour of the US with Eric Clapton. Remember, I've said that Eric's tours were pretty much anything and everything, as money was not an issue, and this most recent one had been no exception. It, too, was full of fun and excess.

I flew to Dallas to join up with the band and crew of the Bee Gees' *Spirits Having Flown* tour, which was already in rehearsals at the Tarrant County Convention Center in Fort Worth. Imagine renting out a whole massive arena just to rehearse. I don't think Eric ever did that.

Jay Hagerman, the Concerts West representative who would be handling business affairs during this tour, had been out on the entire Clapton run with me. He and I checked into the Hilton Fort Worth hotel in downtown Cowtown and fell right back into the swing of things. Another circus, different name.

Not that there was any competition, but this new tour was going to be more money-no-object excessive than Eric's were. The exception was the band for the Bee Gees, being so large, were on per diems, where the expenses for EC's group were all paid for by Eric's manager. On those tours, there were no per diems for the band, Roger, or me. I liked that much better. However, I could immediately tell this was going to be fun.

This tour was actually supposed to hit the road earlier than 1979 in order to follow up on the popularity the brothers gained from the Stigwood-produced hit film *Saturday Night Fever.* The soundtrack from the movie had delivered numerous hit records for the Bee Gees and others. I had been discussing my participation with their manager, Dick Ashby, for well over a year (at least since early 1978) and was assured a spot, but for some reason things had been delayed. Maybe they were waiting on the *Spirits Having Flown* album to come out. In the end, everything worked out well as I was able to do both Clapton and the Bee Gees—a very fortunate stroke of luck and financial security for me.

I'd have to admit that initially I was not too sure how thrilled I'd be listening to disco music every night. Yes, I liked some of their songs, but I think back then I viewed Barry, Robin, and Maurice Gibb as more of a teenybopper group originally and then as a disco bunch. I knew, though, that they were extremely popular, and if nothing else, this would be a fun tour to be on since everything would be top-notch.

And boy was I mistaken in my skepticism of how the brothers would perform. They were fantastic each and every single night, and I was extremely sad when the tour ended.

The Bee Gees had an incredible band. The main guitarist, Alan Kendall, drummer Dennis Bryon, and one of the keyboard players, Blue Weaver, had been with the brothers for many years. But complementing them was the second keyboard player George, guitar player Joey Murcia (formerly of Andy Gibb's band), conga player Joe Lala, the six-piece Boneroo Horns, the Sweet Inspirations, who were Elvis's backup singers, and bass player Harold Cowart, who allowed Maurice, a bass player himself, a bit more freedom on stage. Not a bad batch of musicians to have behind you. They were loud, exciting, and admittedly none of the songs sounded disco. And if they did, they were so powerful they could have passed for hard rock music anywhere.

Throughout the entire tour, we traveled with the band and their families, including kids, parents, wives, and assorted in-laws. Also along for the ride was Dick, head of security and former special agent with the FBI Orin Bartlett, Joe Esposito, one of the so-called Memphis Mafia who worked with Elvis, and retired New York police officer who served as security personnel. In addition, there were personal assistants for each of the Gibb brothers, Jerry Schilling, another former Memphis Mafia member who managed the Sweet Inspirations, a PR man, a wardrobe mistress, and sometimes Robert Stigwood. And this did not include the dozens of crew members, drivers, and technicians.

Then there was me. I was in charge of the band, making sure they were all together and there on time for the show. The band and assorted staff, as well as any unexpected guests, went from the hotel to the private plane by Greyhound coach, which I arranged ahead of time using Dick's advance preparation. Usually, there were about thirty people or so. Throw in luggage, purses, and other various bags, and the bus was pretty full.

I usually stood in the exit well up front, so I had control over where we went. I was also there in case of any trouble or delays. Dick normally sat in the seat behind me, and through our chats, we became pretty good friends. I must say, he is one of the funniest men in the music business and probably the most organized person I've ever seen. Going to his hotel room for a meeting or just to talk was an experience. He didn't book a suite like Roger did, instead opting for a room with double king beds. The brothers had at least three suites, and their mother and father maybe had another, although I never went to their room. In Dick's room, he had one of the king-sized beds neatly organized with rows of files and miscellaneous papers. He was seemingly always on the phone coordinating something. I admired him, and he is still someone I very much enjoy speaking with.

I am fortunate in that I make friends quickly, and in addition to everyone in the band, I made a good friend in Mickey Spensley, who was Maurice's brother-in-law. Mickey was about my age, and the girls thought he was especially good looking. And he had a British accent, which made things even better for him. Mickey and I had a lot of fun and many late nights together, and he was a huge help to me in many ways. I was terribly saddened when I heard that many years after that tour, Mickey suffered several strokes at once one evening while out at a club in Miami.

I was told early on we would only be touring through the US and would not be traveling abroad. This was a disappointment because it was going to be such an incredible tour. So much work and effort, not to mention money, preparing for it, had already taken place. At the time, it was reportedly the biggest and most expensive tour since Paul McCartney's Wings Over the World tour in 1975–76, which Jay also helped with while working for Concerts West. I decided I'd enjoy every date we were able to share together and just hoped whoever made the decision would change his mind and take this tour out of the US.

As I pointed out, the start of the tour took a long while to get going, but once the time finally came and rehearsals began in Fort Worth, yes, it was magical. The stage had a huge underlit, multicolored, disco-style floor (in the days before LEDs). There were different levels for the drums, guitar players, horn section, back up singers, and the brothers, although Barry, Maurice, and Robin could wander the stage wherever they wished. Additionally, we carried a custom-made, ten-foot-diameter mirrored disco ball that hung from the center of the arenas and stadiums. When "You Should Be Dancing" was played, and the ball lowered with the spotlights hitting it, the scene was an amazing sight. Flashes of multicolored Vari-Lites bouncing off the mirrors created a wonderful effect each night, filling each venue with magical illusions. The audiences loved that portion of the concert as much as anything.

Not only were the optics of the show worth the price of admission, but the band is still the loudest I've ever worked for. Needless to say, the cutesy disco teenybopper myth was quickly forgotten. Every song they played was a certified hit, and the audience reacted as such.

The band rehearsed for a few days, and then the time came to hit the road and share this special show with the public (at least in the US). Being based in Fort Worth to begin with, our first date took place there on June 28. Vari-Lite and Showco, the company that provided the sound, were both located in Dallas, and most of the tech crew were all local personnel. That made it cheaper to rehearse in nearby Fort Worth because they could go home each evening, saving a bit on hotel rooms. And if there were special technical needs prior to the tour's start, getting something fixed, rebuilt, or replaced was easy.

The whole tour was already sold out, so we knew audiences were going to be in abundance everywhere we went. We played in Austin and then in Houston, where *Saturday Night Fever* star John Travolta came on stage, and flew home to the Fort Worth hotel each night. That was nice and sort of what I was used to with EC.

Oh, I forgot to mention that when we moved from city to city, we traveled by the chartered Caesars Palace Boeing 720 jet, the same airplane that was used by Led Zeppelin for their 1977 tour. The plane's interior was fitted with sofas, recliners, lounges, and bars with food and snack areas as well. It was very, very opulent. They also had the outside of the plane painted to match the tour's logo—black and red with outlines of the brothers' heads on the tail fin. Seeing that plane fly overhead must have been great for people on the ground.

The next date was in Denver on July 3, which was followed by a Fourth of July show in Salt Lake City. Denver was a piece of cake, but Salt Lake was not going to be easy. This was one of those famous dartboard dates that booking agents often came up with. It was a widely known fact that everyone on a tour felt booking agents did not really plan well. They didn't think of timing and miles and could the band, including multiple trucks, make it to the next city on time. So it was said that booking agents just randomly threw darts at a map to decide where the next show would be!

I remember a meeting where some of the primary staff, which I was fortunate to be a part of, and the truck drivers discussed how we were supposed to get all of that equipment over the Rocky Mountains from Denver to Salt Lake City and have it ready for a show the next night. Not only was it a long way, but the weather was questionable. One of the truck drivers mentioned they used double drivers before on such long treks like this, but this was a bit farther and more dangerous in the mountains. Someone said, "How about triple drivers? Two in the seats and one in the bunk?" The truck never stopped, except for fuel, and that was how it was done.

Thanks to ten trucks and thirty drivers, the Bee Gees hit the stage in Salt Lake City on time and sounded great. This was also the first show attended by younger brother Andy Gibb, who I'd later manage briefly for Stigwood, and he was brought onstage with his brothers for a song or two. The crowd went nuts seeing all four of them together.

We stayed in Salt Lake City at a hotel directly across from the Mormon Tabernacle. Both the hotel and its view were outstanding, especially when the church was lit at night.

The next date was in San Diego on July 6, then we played Los Angeles the following night, where the soon to be famous leaving-George-Bitzer-behind episode was to take place. While the brothers did press and promo, I was able to spend time with the band and some of my LA friends.

It was nice being back in Southern California and not having to live on an aspiring-rock-star's budget (meaning zero dollars) like when I was trying to become famous with my band Big Punks. I had left that life behind a number of years before and did not regret doing so one bit. Thank goodness.

I got to be friends with Joe Lala, who would later go on to become an actor as well. A funny guy, he shared some good stories and memorable experiences about the bands and celebrities he'd been around. I also got close with Alan Kendall, who'd been with the Bee Gees for a long time by this point. We were quite close . . . or so I thought. Twelve years down the road, he showed his true colors.

The show in LA was pretty spectacular as it was at Dodger Stadium, and for one of the only times ever, the ballpark took out the main light pole so the stage could be set up in center field. Shows at the famed stadium were rare back then, so this was a special deal. And all those fans! I must say I'd never seen anything like it in my career thus far.

On July 28, we played the Pontiac Silverdome outside of Detroit. Even with part of the gigantic stadium curtained off, I still think it held about thirty-five thousand people. However, I was unable to make the show as I was diagnosed with walking pneumonia and told to stay in bed a day or two and take the antibiotics I was given. Seems I had been on the road for so long—surely burning the candle at both ends—that the touring grind had finally caught up with me. I needed to rest. I felt terrible but allowed myself only twenty-four hours in bed. Two nights later, we were scheduled to play back-to-back concerts in Chicago. I made those shows.

After a few more dates, including a concert in Tulsa on August 3, we were ready for a two-week break. Everyone booked commercial flights back home except the Gibb brothers and their families and friends, who probably took the private jet to Miami, where they were living.

Breaks were an oddly welcomed part of a long tour. While being home was nice and you could really get some rest and catch up with "real" life, I think almost everyone wanted to just get back on the road—at least after two or three days.

Following the three-week respite, we were off again, starting in New Haven, Connecticut, on August 27. We then played a couple of dates in Canada before working our way down the East Coast, which included a five-night run at Madison Square Garden, September 7–12.

There was a show where one of the horn players thought it would be funny if he doused me with ladies' perfume right when we arrived at the concert venue. I smelled like a hooker the rest of the night, and yes, where the smell came from was very obvious. I don't think it was even a good, quality perfume. I don't know why he choose me because we'd never had a run-in before or actually much communication at all. However, it was me he chose to pick on.

I was obviously not very happy with this carrot of a horn player and was made fun of by a few of his fellow unfeeling Boneroos and others. But I decided I'd wait for my chance at revenge and held my temper. I came up with a plan, and when we played the second of two nights at the Omni in Atlanta, a major-sized arena, I was prepared to get him back.

Along the way, I stopped at a magic shop and purchased what used to be called Skunk Perfume, which smelled like the worst fart ever produced. The odor was sickening, like an old, well-used latrine. I suspect it was made from sulfur and other nasty-smelling chemicals.

When the band came off the stage in the dark at the end of the show and before the encore numbers, I casually sauntered over to where everyone was gathered. They were all celebrating a good concert and wiping sweat from their brows. It was then I emptied the whole tiny bottle of foul-smelling perfume on my intended victim. Suddenly, they were back on stage, and no one even noticed . . . yet! I was safely backstage observing.

The brothers launched into their first encore song, and as the horn section began to play, I noticed several of them looking around, wondering where that terrible smell was coming from. They had to perform anyway, but I could tell they were having trouble getting a good breath due to the stink. By the second encore song, several of the horn players realized who was the source of the smell and distanced themselves from the offender. In fact, most of the horn section told him to leave the stage as the stench was making them ill.

Feeling somewhat dejected and understanding the odor was coming from him, he came down the stairs, saw me, and realized what had happened. The favor had been returned. I don't believe he spoke to me for the rest of the tour. A well-deserved retribution, I felt. My only regret is that the other horn players had to suffer trying to breathe that putrid smell. All in all, it was pretty funny.

We played four more dates after that, with the last show of the tour sadly coming on October 6 in Miami. As quickly as it had started, following many months on the road with Clapton, it was over. The Gibb brothers returned to their homes and the band and crews to their respective hotels, and that was that. At least that's how it felt.

There may have been a party, but nothing stands out in my mind. I'm sure that a few of us staying at the famous Miami Fontainebleau had a few drinks before calling it a night. For something so very expensive and widely attended all across North America, you'd have thought a celebration would have been planned, even if it had been at someone's home. But I have wracked my brain and cannot remember any final send-off to end one of the most successful and profitable tours of that era.

To this day, that tour still stands out as one of the top-three highlights of my career on the road. The Gibb brothers were great to work for as was Dick. And to my surprise, this would not be the last time I'd tour with the Bee Gees.

Bee Gees 1979 *Spirits Having Flown* US Tour Dates

June 28, 1979: Tarrant County Convention Center (Fort Worth, Texas)

June 29, 1979: Frank Erwin Center, University of Texas (Austin, Texas)

June 30, 1979: The Summit (Houston, Texas)

July 3, 1979: McNichols Arena (Denver, Colorado)

July 4, 1979: Salt Palace (Salt Lake City, Utah)

July 6, 1979: San Diego Sports Arena (San Diego, California)

July 7, 1979: Dodger Stadium (Los Angeles, California)

July 9, 1979: Oakland Coliseum (Oakland, California)

July 10, 1979: Oakland Coliseum (Oakland, California)

July 11, 1979: Oakland Coliseum (Oakland, California)

July 13, 1979: Seattle Center Coliseum (Seattle, Washington)

July 14, 1979: Seattle Center Coliseum (Seattle, Washington)

July 15, 1979: Pacific Coliseum (Vancouver, British Columbia)

July 18, 1979: Memorial Coliseum (Portland, Oregon)

July 21, 1979: St. Paul Civic Center (St. Paul, Minnesota)

July 22, 1979: St. Paul Civic Center (St. Paul, Minnesota)

July 24, 1979: Hilton Coliseum, Iowa State University (Ames, Iowa)

July 25, 1979: Dane County Coliseum (Madison, Wisconsin)

July 26, 1979: Market Square Arena (Indianapolis, Indiana)

July 28, 1979: Pontiac Silverdome (Pontiac, Michigan)

July 30, 1979: Chicago Stadium (Chicago, Illinois)

July 31, 1979: Chicago Stadium (Chicago, Illinois)

August 1, 1979: Checkerdome (St. Louis, Missouri)

August 3, 1979: Mabee Center, Oral Roberts University (Tulsa, Oklahoma)

August 4, 1979: Myriad Convention Center (Oklahoma City, Oklahoma)

August 27, 1979: New Haven Coliseum (New Haven, Connecticut)

August 28, 1979: Providence Civic Center (Providence, Rhode Island)

August 29, 1979: Providence Civic Center (Providence, Rhode Island)

August 31, 1979: Maple Leaf Gardens (Toronto, Ontario)

September 1, 1979: Montreal Forum (Montreal, Quebec)

September 2, 1979: Montreal Forum (Montreal, Quebec)

September 4, 1979: Civic Arena (Pittsburgh, Pennsylvania)

September 7, 1979: Madison Square Garden (New York, New York)

September 8, 1979: Madison Square Garden (New York, New York)

September 9, 1979: Madison Square Garden (New York, New York)

September 11, 1979: Madison Square Garden (New York, New York)

September 12, 1979: Madison Square Garden (New York, New York)

September 14, 1979: Buffalo Memorial Auditorium (Buffalo, New York)

September 15, 1979: Riverfront Coliseum (Cincinnati, Ohio)

September 16, 1979: Riverfront Coliseum (Cincinnati, Ohio)

September 21, 1979: Spectrum (Philadelphia, Pennsylvania)

September 22, 1979: Spectrum (Philadelphia, Pennsylvania)

September 24, 1979: Capital Centre (Landover, Maryland)

September 25, 1979: Capital Centre (Landover, Maryland)

September 26, 1979: Scope Arena (Norfolk, Virginia)

September 28, 1979: BJCC Civic Center (Birmingham, Alabama)

September 29, 1979: Omni Coliseum (Atlanta, Georgia)

September 30, 1979: Omni Coliseum (Atlanta, Georgia)

October 2, 1979: Greensboro Coliseum (Greensboro, North Carolina)

October 3, 1979: Carolina Coliseum, University of South Carolina (Columbia, South Carolina)

October 4, 1979: Jacksonville Coliseum (Jacksonville, Florida)

October 6, 1979: Miami Stadium (Miami, Florida)

CHAPTER 10

Andy Gibb's Blank Check

Your Mom Sewed Money in the Laundry Room?

The manager from Robert Redford's Sundance Resort in Utah said he had some ideas and would phone me back. While drinking coffee and eating breakfast made from supplies the lodge had stocked in our cabin fridge, Andy, Scott, and I sat amazed at the amount of snow that had fallen overnight and wondered what solution they might find. This was more than a snowfall. From what I was seeing, in my mind, it had been a blizzard.

When the phone rang, the ski resort manager told me they had previously used a helicopter to land on the hill behind the cabin where we were staying to shuttle people out, but to do so would cost over $3,000. I spoke to Andy, and we agreed that despite the beautiful snow drifts, we had to get out of there in order to stay on schedule for a TV show appearance in Florida, which would be followed by a flight to New York and then another to London on the Concorde.

"Let's go for it," I said.

This all started after the Bee Gees' *Spirits Having Flown* tour when Andy's former manager, Alan LaMagna, resigned his position, and the Robert Stigwood Organization (RSO) was looking for someone to fill that role. In December 1979, I received a call from Dick Ashby, asking if I'd be interested in managing Andy. I immediately said yes, as I knew, or so I believed, this would be a long-term and financially lucrative job since he was a young star with such potential—not to mention he had three very famous brothers.

I flew to Los Angeles for an interview, which was conducted by a person who was a top executive in the Stigwood company but a new face to me. We met in his suite at the Beverly Hilton. Before I left for LA, I was led to believe the deal was pretty much already done, as long as this fellow liked me. If so, he'd fill me in on the salary and other financials.

I was hired by Freddie Gershon, who was the COO of Stigwood's. After leaving RSO, he went on to write a best-selling book, *Sweetie, Baby, Cookie, Honey,* and then served as chairman and CEO of Music Theatre International, a company that licenses stage rights for musical theater shows. In other words, he's one of the biggest there is.

Mr. Gershon gave me the report on Andy. He was basically bankrupt, and RSO was going to give him one last push using its own money to see if his popularity could be resurrected. Andy had produced a rather large hit with his second album, *Shadow Dancing,* which featured four singles that charted highly in 1978. Unfortunately, not a lot had happened since then. He was racking up more expenses than the income he was generating. Having said that, the salary I received was satisfying.

Andy's lifestyle was very expensive. After I was hired to act as his manager on behalf of RSO, I made my way over to where Andy and Scott Sands, his personal assistant, were sharing a two-bedroom suite at the same hotel for a cost of more than $900 a night. I'm not sure how long they had been there by that time, but we ended up staying another month before we headed to Sundance. If you do the math even poorly, the total comes out to a very expensive month, given the cost of the rooms, room service, which I seldom ever used, bar tabs, and phone calls. Oh, I forgot to mention the cost of "smoke" as well.

In that month, I saw money virtually flying out the window as Andy fought to keep up a lifestyle only his brothers could really afford. This was no cheap hotel. I had a separate room on another floor that helped give me some peace and space. There was also a Mercedes 450SL convertible in the valet garage available for Andy's use, another sizable cost. I ended up driving the car quite a bit instead of the rental sedan I was given. It was a blast.

One of the first things Andy asked me to do was get him $600 cash so he could buy some smoke, his term for pot. *Well, that was straight to the point and rather confident of him,* I thought. After a few phone calls, I found out that Janis Lundy, who worked for Al Coury, president of RSO, could arrange to get me a cash advance as requested, plus some additional working capital. She didn't seem phased at Andy's request and what the money was for. Apparently, this was commonplace with him.

I gave Andy his $600, and he bought two bags of marijuana, which must have been pretty good stuff as a normal bag of pot in 1980 averaged from forty to sixty dollars. These were $300 each.

I popped by his room once, as I did daily for a briefing, and was greeted by several trays of leftover food and drinks from the pricy room service. Seems he and possibly Scott had huge appetites, especially after smoking two bags of expensive pot in three days. First off, I was flabbergasted that anyone could smoke so much in such a short amount of time, and secondly, that they could have eaten so much food. In only one round of room service that I witnessed, they devoured hamburgers, french fries, steak and potatoes, cake and ice cream, milkshakes, and another few trays of no telling what else. Scott confided in me that he had only partaken in a few hits of pot and that Andy had consumed almost all of it on his own.

While Andy did not usually drink alcohol, he succumbed to his other vices. He also was a really nice guy, good looking, and could have had his way with any number of women whenever he so chose. However, during the entire time I was managing him, I didn't see him go off with any females. He wasn't gay, just uninterested or too high to be bothered. I am sure, though, he broke hundreds, no, thousands of hearts.

Now here we were in Sundance on the morning of January 27, 1980. Outside, the area was covered in a thick blanket of snow, which is why we came. Andy had wanted to ski one more time before we headed to Europe for a promotional tour arranged by our employer, RSO.

I had slept extremely well the previous night, having enjoyed a few drinks after we'd left the Osmonds concert and a backstage reception at the arena in Provo, Utah. Andy and his mom, Barbara, had been friends with the Osmond family for some time, and he and Marie Osmond would later date for a while. The show was good and, as expected, there was no alcohol in the reception room, only punch and a pitcher of milk, if my memory serves me correctly. Maybe that was there for fun.

Andy, Scott, and I steered our little four-wheel-drive Subaru rental car back to the resort and went inside the gathering hall to see what was happening and to get a stronger drink. And darned if Robert Redford himself wasn't there in the flesh. Mr. Redford said hello to Andy and us, but the greeting wasn't long—well, not as long as I would have liked it. *Nothing like a meaningful chat with such a great actor,* I thought.

Regardless, the drinks were top notch, and we ended up speaking with an older fellow who was a regular photographer for *Playboy,* which promised to be an interesting conversation but ultimately wasn't. He mainly talked about what kind of cameras he was now using. Andy had been to Sundance before, and being a casual celebrity, some wanted to meet him and some not so much.

Before long we made our exit and returned to our cabin up on the hill. It was a very nice cabin at that, featuring large, sumptuous beds and duvets. The furniture and kitchen in this rental were as good as those in any house I'd ever seen. The snow was now coming down in large flakes, making the night peaceful and relaxing, albeit with the help of the gin, I am sure.

The next day we were scheduled to head off to Miami to meet up with Andy's fifty-eight-foot Hatteras yacht. We would take that up the coastline to Jupiter, Florida, where Andy would then tape an appearance with Dinah Shore on her daytime show, *Dinah and Friends.* From there we were to cruise the boat back to Miami, fly first class to John F. Kennedy Airport in New York, and then board the Concorde to London to begin the promo tour. Oh, yawn, what a life! If you ever get a chance to fly first class, do it. The experience, though, is better and more fun if you don't have to pay for the pleasure.

However, during our last night in Utah, we may have slept, but the snow did not. By morning, it was several feet high, and we were obviously housebound. There was snow drifting nearly to the cabin's roof, and the car was completely covered. The scene was beautiful, and if we'd not been on such a tight schedule, I would have enjoyed it. No, I enjoyed it anyway, but a problem was looming.

The phone rang with the lodge manager confirming we were snowed in and that we should just stay where we were. I explained the situation and said we had a noon flight to Miami we *had* to be on. He laughed before responding that getting out might be impossible. I put on my nicest voice and pleaded for some solution, noting that they must have run into this situation before with some other celebrity who had to make such a critical escape.

With my approval, the manager made the arrangements for a helicopter from Salt Lake City to land on the hill directly behind our cabin. We packed quickly, and within half an hour, we heard the whirling blades overhead. Outside, we saw it touch down not one hundred yards away, up a snow-covered drive. I helped Scott and Andy carry their bags up the hill and helped them into the helicopter since it would only hold two passengers with the pilot. I backed away while they lifted off and got a great blast of fresh snow blown all over me. Needless to say, I was now definitely awake and feeling like I was in a scene from some film.

About forty-five minutes later, the pilot returned for me, and I was off. As we flew over the snow-covered mountains, I could see skiers high up, skiing down threatening, steep mountainsides. The lodge had assured me they'd return the car for us and also send the bills to Stigwood's accountants, including the cost of the helicopter. Again, money was not a real consideration. Whose idea was that?

I had flown in helicopters while working with Eric, and this was seemingly no different, except we were flying over mountains, not Chicago. About fifteen minutes later, I saw a vast space ahead, which was the Salt Lake City airport. I figured we'd land somewhere nearby, and then Andy, Scott, and I would take a taxi around to the terminal. No, the helicopter landed within thirty yards of the already-boarded airplane to Miami.

I got out of the copter with my bag, thanked the pilot, and climbed the stairs into the plane. Everyone on that side of the aisle was looking out their windows to see who was boarding. I suspect they did the same for Andy, which must have been a bigger thrill than my entrance.

From Salt Lake City, we flew to Miami and took a taxi to a boatyard where his beautiful Hatteras was floating in the water next to a dock. I'd never been on a yacht such as this before and was excited, as you might expect. Andy spoke to the attendant, who he knew well, and then to his mom and his niece (his sister Lesley's daughter). They, too, were coming to Jupiter. All in the family.

While I had done some cool traveling and had my share of fun on the road, my head was spinning at what had taken place that day. We'd been snowed in at Sundance just a few hours earlier, and now we were cruising at sea in shorts and T-shirts.

Andy was the captain of the *Shadow Dancer*, his yacht. I was told when his career as a singer began, he was given a rather large advance from RSO Records, and Andy had used a sizable portion of that advance to eventually buy this boat. He loved it, and he knew how it all worked and how to handle her, as a good captain should.

We took the channel out to the open water of the Atlantic Ocean before heading north toward Jupiter. This was the first time I saw flying fish in their natural habitat, flying from wave crest to wave crest right beside the boat. We traveled just a couple of miles offshore, so land was always in sight, but still the ride was fantastic. I had my own cabin, which was very nice. Not a great suite like the captain had but a single bunkroom, well-appointed. While on the bridge cruising and checking the various gauges, Andy became hungry and asked his mom for a couple of sandwiches. Boy, this skinny fellow could eat.

Barbara was a wonderful mom to Andy and her other talented sons. Obviously familiar with the galley of the boat, she cooked Andy two bacon and egg sandwiches that consisted of several strips of bacon, a fried egg, and bacon grease spooned on the bread, instead of the traditional mayonnaise or mustard. Andy was in heaven having his mom cooking for him again. The journey wasn't too long since the distance from Miami to Jupiter is not far, but it was enough to give me a feel for his favorite method of travel.

As late afternoon approached, we pulled into a prearranged marina, with Andy on the radio communicating with the dock master. The marina was small. There were no individual boat slips but rather one long wraparound dock, which was full with the exception of one slot that appeared to be fifty-nine feet in length. Andy's boat was fifth-eight feet. But by golly, he parallel parked that boat as smooth as could be, right in the slot without ever bumping another vessel. It was like watching an artist paint. He knew exactly what to do and did it meticulously. If he was nervous, he didn't let it show.

That first evening we attended a performance of the Broadway hit *Same Time, Next Year* with Carol Burnett and Burt Reynolds in the starring roles. Fittingly, the play was being held at the Burt Reynolds Dinner Theater, and we got to meet Burt and a few other people who took great care of us. We then were driven by limo to our floating hotel for the night.

The next day, January 28, we were picked up and taken back to the theater, where the stage had been transformed into the set for the then popular *Dinah and Friends* afternoon talk show. Andy was a guest and would sing two songs. Every time he appeared on TV to perform, I had to call Dick and make arrangements to get the necessary backing track created in the right format and then have it shipped to the show's producer. Usually, this happened at the last minute, but for some reason it always worked. I attribute that to Dick's organization. I'll say it again, he's the most organized person in the music business.

The show was good, fairly uneventful, and Andy was a hit with the audience as he always was. But after the show, we discovered actor Martin Sheen outside in the parking lot shooting baskets. He turned out to be a nice man and invited us to shoot some with him. Duh! I'm not a big sports fan, but I had played Horse and Clock as a kid and quickly agreed. It was a fun hour or so. Martin was at the theater rehearsing for *Mister Roberts*, which would be the next play to take the stage there.

Later that afternoon, we departed Jupiter on the boat and took the inland waterway back as the sea was a bit rough and no one wanted to get seasick. Because of this, the ride was longer, although somewhere along the inland waterway we saw Robert Stigwood's yacht, a one-hundred-foot former navy vessel. It was vacant and in the facility for some fittings.

We couldn't make it all the way to Miami, so we stopped for the night after I made arrangements with a local dock master (really he was the barman as everyone else had gone home). Using our generators for light, we were then able to get some takeout food from a nearby café. Not the lobster dinner I was hoping for, but the grub filled the hole.

The following morning, we finally made it back to Miami where a very large mansion on Biscayne Bay had been rented for us, fully furnished. We tied the boat up in back and spent the evening quietly repacking for Europe the next day.

A storm developed close by during the night though, and the waves in the bay were somewhat large and, well, wavy. Andy's yacht was bashing up against the wooden pilings fairly ferociously, and he did not want it to get damaged, so Scott, Andy, and I went out and did our best to retie the buoys that kept the boat from slamming into the dock. The whole affair was silly. Here we were, the three of us, trying to manhandle this massive boat away from the dock against heavy waves and wind while trying to put the buoys where they'd be most effective. I remember quite clearly pulling my thumb out of the way just milliseconds before the bow of the boat slammed into the wooden piling. I'd have lost my thumb had I been any slower. Despite our efforts, there was some minor exterior damage to the Hatteras, but heck, have the yacht fixed and put it on the bill.

While we were there at the rented mansion, Andy received a birthday gift from Stigwood, a handheld underwater-propelling device for snorkeling or scuba diving, which I thought looked pretty sleek. But Andy said, "This is the second one of these he's given me." *Hmm, I'll take it,* I thought.

We were up with the sunrise, and within a short time were on the way to the airport, as always in a limo. The boat would be collected and put in dry dock, so we didn't have to worry about it. I enjoyed this don't-worry-about-it mentality, although I personally couldn't afford it. However, I found it irresponsible that we were traveling all over in expensive vehicles when supposedly Andy was bankrupt and owed back plenty of advance money to RSO or someone else. *Who,* I wondered, *had let him get in such a predicament?* I was to find out later.

We flew first class to John F. Kennedy Airport and upon arrival were greeted by a couple of RSO New York staff members who escorted us to the British Airways Concorde terminal. I was excited to be traveling on the fastest commercial plane in the world.

Once aboard, we found ourselves in a fairly vacant plane. The seats were only two wide on each side of the aisle, so Andy and Scott sat together while I sat in a row by myself. Surprisingly, the cabin was not large on the inside. On the contrary, it seemed small compared to most commercial flights, and compared to a jumbo airliner, it was tiny.

After taking off around two o'clock in the afternoon, the pilot came over the loudspeaker and explained we would not increase to supersonic speed until we were a number of miles off the coast of New York. Doing so would cause a sonic boom, something the neighbors below weren't too fond of.

As we snacked on champagne and nuts, we felt the throttle being pushed forward and the speed increase until we were flying at just over Mach 2. I touched the inside of the window, and it was very warm from the friction outside. As we flew, we saw the sun going down and shortly thereafter coming up again as we approached the UK. That was fast.

While in the air, we were served a very nice restaurant-quality meal with dessert, and afterward we enjoyed brandy and cigars. They served cigars on an airplane? Sure, smoking was still allowed on planes but cigars? I even had one, at lease a bit of one.

We arrived in the UK and were quickly ushered through customs and to our hotel, the Hilton near Heathrow Airport. Since we were off the next day for the European promo tour, there wasn't enough time to get into the heart of the city and back, but, oh well, as much as I loved London, the Hilton would have to suffice. Was I getting spoiled?

We met with the record company executive, Mike Hutson, who would accompany us on the promotional tour. He gave us the lowdown on where we were headed and what was expected. "Do not travel with any drugs!" was a mandate. Andy knew that was a no-no anyway.

The tour to promote his *After Dark* album was about three weeks long, although doing a promo tour was much simpler than a concert tour and went at a much easier pace. There was more time to have fun.

Our first stop was Amsterdam, where we stayed at the Hotel Pulitzer, sparing no expense. Andy couldn't wait to get there because he knew he could acquire some hashish from a club. It seemed to be expected. Since we had a day off, of course Andy, Scott, the record people, and I had to go to this place of procurement ASAP.

We went to a hippie-looking building, and inside, were several floors of head-type shops as well as a few clubs with music emanating from them. We went in a bar and ordered a drink while wondering how this worked. We figured why not ask the waiter, so we did. The next thing we know, a small Saran-wrapped packet arrived at the table with hash in it. Mike, I think, paid the fellow the required Dutch guilder, and we left posthaste, noticing that the building was directly across the street from an Amsterdam police station. Supposedly, the location was planned that way so the police could help keep an eye on any trouble that might arise. How convenient.

We did several days of print press (music magazines) as well as radio and TV interviews. Or rather Andy did, although we were always there to help him out of embarrassing situations, especially when someone wanted him to dress up in an Amsterdam idea of a cowboy outfit. Why? He wasn't a cowboy or even an American, much less as Texan as I was.

We were in Amsterdam for four days, and the evening before we were to depart for Munich, Scott and I were sitting in Andy's suite. He said he had about half the cube of hash left and needed to get rid of it before we left so as to avoid traveling with it. Smart boy. Looking back on it now, I should have been surprised there was any left, knowing how he imbibed.

He had smoked as much as he could, but the hash needed to be mixed with tobacco in order to smoke it with rolling papers, and the tobacco burned his throat and lungs. Scott and I agreed to split it with him and eat a small chunk, so there would be no waste or evidence. I was not an enthusiastic pot smoker at all, but I swallowed the hash whole to avoid tasting it. I then went to my room to pack and get ready to leave the next day. Instead, for some reason, I decided to go to bed and get up early to pack. After all, this wasn't a band tour and therefore wasn't as rigorous from a time standpoint.

I slept well, but when I arose the next morning, the hash had taken its desired effect on me during the night. I was moving slowly. Packing my one suitcase took me over an hour (I told you I'd learned how to travel lighter). I kept forgetting what I was doing and would just sit down and relax. It was almost like an out-of-body experience that I did not enjoy at all.

Finally, we made it to Munich, where we checked into the Munich Hilton, a hotel I had stayed in several times before and knew to be nice. As we were checking in, I spied a member of the band Queen heading to the elevator. They, too, were staying at the hotel while they recorded their album *The Game* at Musicland Studios.

In Munich for six days, we did our promotional obligations as Mike directed, but Andy and I ran into Queen's Freddie Mercury in the lobby one afternoon, and he invited us to the recording studio. Later that evening, Andy, Scott, and I did indeed go down there and were given a warm welcome. We even got to listen to some tracks that had been recorded.

Before long, someone suggested Andy sing backup harmony on the song "Play the Game," which he tried. Although the effects of the hash had long since worn off, the overall experience of being there was surreal as all of us were fans of Queen. They wound up not using his vocal track on the record, but we still left having had a very cool evening.

The next day was a Sunday, and Andy said Freddie had invited him up to his suite to watch a film. Because we were all aware of Freddie's lifestyle by then, Andy did not want to go alone, so Scott and I were happy to tag along. We all sat around chatting and watching some movie while outside the rain came down.

As the afternoon wore on, the fact that Freddie was attracted to Andy became obvious, which made Andy uncomfortable. He was giving Scott and me eye movements like, *Let's get out here!* that Scott and I just pretended not to understand while holding back our laughter. Watching Andy squirm was hilarious. Finally, I said we had an appointment, dinner with some local promotional people, and we made a hasty exit. Andy was not amused, but in the elevator, Scott and I laughed all the way down at the uncomfortable situation Andy had gotten himself into. At least we enjoyed the movie, and Freddie was great and always polite.

Then we were on to Paris, the last stop on the promotional tour. We stayed at the Hotel George V, at the time the most prestigious hotel in the world. The place was extremely nice, though nice in an old classic European way. Remember, money was no object, or at least not spoken of.

Andy did his required interviews, TV appearances, and photo shoots while Scott and I watched and kept an eye on things. Back at the hotel one night, Andy was wishing he had some pot or hash to smoke, but instead I took him and Scott downstairs to the basement level where the hotel's fancy restaurant, with its well-stocked and wonderful wine cellar, was located. Having been around Europe several times by now, I was becoming familiar with the better foods and wines of life.

There was a gate on the cellar, but all the wines were visible in the deep, dark vault. I pointed to the wine and said to Andy, "Here, my friend, are the best, most expensive wines in the world. Right there in front of you is the best wine selection you'll ever see, and the record company is paying for it. We need to take advantage of this tonight, and you can worry about getting high another day." Andy saw the smile on my face and agreed.

For the next couple of nights, the three of us ordered some very nice cabernets, merlots, and a variety of high-priced wines to taste (or gulp down) before ordering a wonderful room-service meal featuring very fine French cuisine. It was a time I'll never forget. The wine, food, and company, not to mention the laughs, all made for a wonderful last night in Europe. Hangover? Never! Not at those prices.

As we checked out of the George V, we were about to head to the waiting limo when we were stopped by hotel security. One of them asked in a broken English accent, "Bathrobe?" and held out his hands. We were seemingly being accused, or at least one of us was being accused, of taking an expensive bathrobe from this fine hotel. This was a major no-no, we were told. I knew I had not taken it, though I'll admit I had thought about it, so it was either Andy or Scott. I pulled them aside and said, "These guys are serious."

No matter what kind of money we offered them to get out of this mess, they only wanted the bathrobe back. Both Andy and Scott denied it—that is until the conversation went on for way too long, and it looked as if the French police might be called in. At that point, Scott piped up that he in fact had the bathrobe in his suitcase. He was embarrassed and ashamed at being caught, but he coyly retrieved the stolen article from his bag, handed it to the security men, and we were escorted out to our waiting cars. I don't think Scott forgot that incident for a long time. He was a convincing liar, and we had one on him now. Likewise, Mike was not impressed with this shenanigan either.

We flew back to England with Mike, where we again checked into the Heathrow Hilton for a night, as our flight to the US, also on the Concorde, was not for a couple of days. Andy had a few interviews in London the following day, which all went well.

On Tuesday, February 26, 1980, we were picked up from our hotel and transported to the Café Royal in London, where a very posh ballroom was set up for the British Rock and Pop Awards that would broadcast the next night on BBC TV and Radio 1. This was similar to the American Grammy Awards that aired the same evening from Los Angeles.

We were shown to a large round table near the front, close to the stage. Suddenly, our table guests arrived, and my mouth dropped open. Joining us would be Paul and Linda McCartney as well as Bob Geldof and his future wife, Paula Yates. Well, if lunch turned out to be cardboard chicken and cheap wine, at least the company would be interesting.

Conversations ensued, and food was served before the show took place. Trying to eat while not spilling anything down the front of my jacket or accidently spitting something across the table at Paul kept me on my toes. And while I chatted a bit, I remember I ate slowly and listened mostly as this moment wouldn't happen very often in my life. The afternoon was great, and we had fun chatting with our tablemates. Andy served as a celebrity guest presenter and handed out the honor for the Best Band or Group, which was the Police.

The following day, Mike and an assistant picked us up and took us to Heathrow's Concorde terminal and walked us to the boarding gates. This was 1980, and security wasn't what it is today. We said our thanks and goodbyes, and within a short time we were speeding at over Mach 2 back to New York. With a layover that night since our flight to LA was not until the next morning, RSO put us up at the Waldorf Astoria, another very expensive and fancy hotel. Our room? The three-bedroom Cole Porter suite with Mr. Porter's own white grand piano in the lounge. Why not? Money was no object.

Scott and Andy wanted to hit the streets of NYC, but I decided to stay in the room and enjoy the atmosphere, as this, too, might never happen again. So they went out, and I turned on the TV to relax and enjoy being in such a plush environment. I promptly fell asleep on a very comfy sofa and didn't awake until the next morning when it was time to pack—well, I hadn't unpacked—and head to the airport. I'd fallen asleep due to jet lag and missed a whole evening of lounging in a suite at the Waldorf. What a lame brain.

My time with Andy didn't last very long as I had a home in Tulsa where I wanted to be, and Andy really had no home at all. He either stayed in hotels or rental houses for short spurts. I ended up convincing RSO to let me hire an assistant to stay with Andy sometimes so I could go home, and I was able to persuade a trusted friend, Marc Hulett, to help. I knew Marc from the Bee Gees tour. He was the nephew of Tom Hulett, the cofounder of Concerts West. Marc was a great and capable guy, and he was single and diplomatic—a perfect fit. I spoke with him daily when I was not there.

One day I got word that Andy's taxes were coming due, and the amount was about a quarter of a million dollars. Surprise! I'd asked several times since the job began if someone, an accountant, had put money aside to pay the taxes on his very sizeable advance from RSO. No one ever gave me an answer, just a shoulder shrug.

Well, now Andy was in the Bahamas relaxing on his boat with Marc and Scott, and I'm sure having a great time. I had to give him the bad news about the taxes and that Robert Stigwood would cover the tax bill with the IRS. But to do so, he would require the *Shadow Dancer*, Andy's yacht and true love, as colleterial. Andy went bananas, saying it would never happen.

Fortunately, I was sixteen hundred miles away and did not have to face his ire in person.

I am sure Andy phoned his brothers and then Dick, who calmed him down somewhat and told Andy he had no choice. Dick phoned me and suggested I get myself to Nassau for the signing of the agreement with Stigwood, so I was on the first plane to the Bahamas. I stayed at a hotel by the marina where the yacht was docked—it and hundreds of other very expensive vessels, many much bigger than Andy's fifty-eight-footer, which was pretty large itself.

I visited Andy at the marina to discuss the situation. He was still angry but somewhat resigned to the fact that the decision had already been made. I explained that someone should have put aside a sizeable amount of the advance to pay the eventual tax demands. The position Andy found himself in caused him, I feel certain, a great amount of depression. He told me he hated the situation and asked, "Why could someone not have been better at expecting this?" He was not blaming me, as he knew I was not around at the time, but instead was infuriated with his bookkeepers in New York.

Regardless of how he or anyone of us felt, the next day an accountant from RSO made his appearance at my hotel with Andy and crew in tow. Andy then signed the papers, agreeing to mortgage his beloved *Shadow Dancer* to Stigwood in exchange for paying his taxes. It was very bittersweet. I think he spent the rest of the day on his boat reminiscing.

We all flew back to LA to "get on with Andy's life" a day or two later, and upon landing, we were met by a limousine that was to take us to a Holiday Inn in Westwood, not the Beverly Hilton. I had reserved us rooms and Andy a suite there in an effort to save money since we didn't know how long we'd be in LA.

I was sitting in the front of the limo while Scott, Marc, and Andy were in the back. Unexpectedly, Andy asked the driver to head up to Sunset Boulevard because he needed to stop by somewhere on his way to the hotel. I stayed calm, waiting to see what he was up to. As we were traveling just past Tower Records headed east, I slid the dividing window down and motioned for Scott to lean forward so I could speak to him. I asked, "Where is Andy wanting to go?"

Scott looked coyly down and said, "He wants to go to his dealer's house to get some weed." We had not even been back in town an hour. For some reason, the only thing I could think was, *This is how he got himself into so much financial trouble.* He had no money to pay taxes, no songs for a new album, and he was waiting on a brother or two to write him some new hit songs when I knew perfectly well he could write darned good songs himself.

I said to the driver of the limo to pull over to the curb and stop the car, which he immediately did. I asked him to open the trunk. I got out of the car, grabbed my suitcase, walked around to the passenger side of the limo and opened the back door. I stuck my head in, looked directly into Andy's eyes, and said to him. "Give me a call when you grow up!" I then shut the door, and the limo drove off.

I'd just quit an impressive and great-paying job that I was mostly enjoying. I just did not want to watch this handsome, talented young man take a trip down a road I had by now seen a number of times. It was too painful to watch.

I doubt Andy ever gave me a second thought. After I made my way back to the hotel, I phoned Dick and told him I'd quit, but that Andy was safe with Scott and Marc.

Marc Hulett worked a few more years for Andy, which included Andy's period dating Victoria Principal and his time hosting the *Solid Gold* TV show. Marc then went on to serve as a personal assistant for Barry Manilow and still does to this day. He remains a good friend of mine. I never heard from Scott again.

I have to say I think Andy, growing up in such a privileged life, wasn't set up to be a strong enough man to handle what fame would throw at him. He once told me that when he was a young boy in Australia, with his brothers already becoming famous and money beginning to flow into the household, he thought his mother, Barbara, went into the laundry room and sewed money. That she basically made the money he saw keeping the Gibb-family machinery working and thriving. Like many of today's youth, I think he felt entitled and that life should be easy, that he should have whatever he wanted.

I wish he were still alive to share time with his brother Barry, who I know misses him as desperately as he must miss Maurice and Robin.

Andy Gibb 1980 European Promotional Tour Dates

February 8, 1980: Fly from New York, New York, to London, England

February 9, 1980: London, England

February 10, 1980: Fly from London, England, to Amsterdam, Netherlands

February 11–12, 1980: Amsterdam, Netherlands

February 13, 1980: Fly from Amsterdam, Netherlands, to Munich, Germany

February 14–18, 1980: Munich, Germany

February 19, 1980: Fly from Munich, Germany, to Paris, France

February 20–22, 1980: Paris, France

February 23, 1980: Fly from Paris, France, to London, England

February 24–25, 1980: London, England

February 26, 1980: London, England, British Rock and Pop Awards

February 27, 1980: London, England

February 28, 1980: Fly from London, England to New York, New York

A replica of the 58-ft. Hatteras owned and captained by Andy Gibb. Courtesy of A. Gibb Estate.

Brad Gills and friend on Ozzy's bus. Courtesy of L. McNeny.

Bee Gees 1989 tour laminated pass.
Courtesy of L. McNeny.

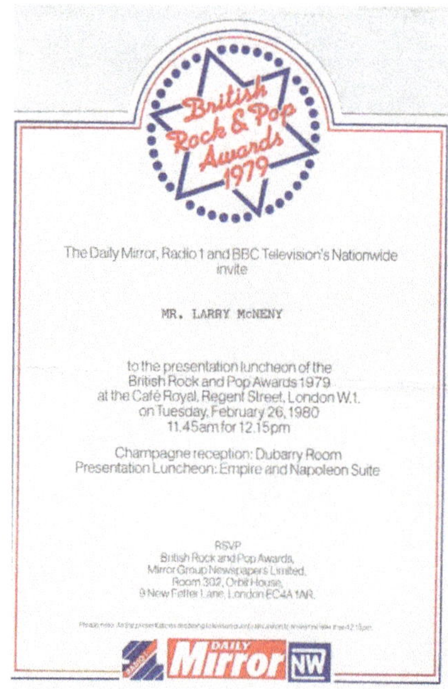

British Rock & Pop Awards 1979

The Daily Mirror, Radio 1 and BBC Television's Nationwide
invite

MR. LARRY McNENY

to the presentation luncheon of the
British Rock and Pop Awards 1979
at the Café Royal, Regent Street, London W.1.
on Tuesday, February 26, 1980
11.45am for 12.15pm

Champagne reception: Dubarry Room
Presentation Luncheon: Empire and Napoleon Suite

RSVP
British Rock and Pop Awards,
Mirror Group Newspapers Limited,
Room 302, Orbit House,
9 New Fetter Lane, London EC4A 1AR.

Daily Mirror NW

Invitation to British Rock and Pop Awards,
1979 (Andy Gibb and I attended in London).
Courtesy of L. McNeny.

Andy Gibb, Kim Chamberlin, and Larry McNeny, 1980. Courtesy of A. Gibb Estate.

The Bee Gees and producers in studio. Courtesy of the Bee Gees and the Bob Sherman estate.

Ticket stub to board the Concorde flight (my name misspelled). Courtesy of L. McNeny.

Three Dog Night promo photo. Courtesy of Three Dog Night.

Larry McNeny, Omar Abderrahman (production manager supreme), and promoter with some friends in Singapore. Courtesy of L. McNeny.

An original "Night Fever" 45 RPM single in sleeve in great shape. Courtesy of the Bee Gees and the Bob Sherman Estate.

Ozzy Osbourne laminated backstage pass. Courtesy of Sharon Osbourne.

Ozzy Osbourne onstage with screaming fans. Courtesy of Sharon Osbourne.

Ozzy Osbourne mug shot.
Courtesy of Sharon Osbourne.

Sharon always taking care of business.
Courtesy of L. McNeny.

Ozzy Osbourne with band and crew, last show photo, 1982. Courtesy of L. McNeny.

In Japan with Sharon, Ozzy (seated behind), Tak (promoter), and Brad Gillis. Courtesy of L. McNeny.

Larry McNeny relaxing in a hotel room on Ozzy tour. Courtesy of L. McNeny.

Limo pass for the premier of *Fame*, 1980. Andy and I sat behind Christopher Reeve and his wife. Courtesy of L. McNeny.

Pig roasting on the spit before Ozzy and Sharon's wedding, which I helped plan! Courtesy of L. McNeny.

Crew and me after Ozzy's bachelor party. Courtesy of L. McNeny.

Protester outside one of Ozzy's concerts. Courtesy of L. McNeny.

Laminated backstage pass for Steve Wozniak's US Festival where Ozzy performed. Courtesy of L. McNeny.

Rudy Sarzo and Don Airey of Ozzy's band on a train in Japan. Courtesy of L. McNeny.

Rob Cowlyn, Ozzy's production manager, arriving in Hawaii for R&R and wedding on the way to Japan. Courtesy of L. McNeny.

One of the few photos of Sharon and Ozzy's wedding in Maui, with her father on the right. Courtesy of L. McNeny.

Three Dog Night. Courtesy of Three Dog Night.

Sharon and Ozzy getting married, finally! Courtesy of L. McNeny.

CHAPTER 11

Clapton Is Back with Lee, Brooker, Stainton, Spinetti, and Markee

New Blood, but This Time Not Mine!

Back home in Tulsa, still reeling from the Andy Gibb debacle, I was doing my normal household chores and going to clubs periodically to listen to local music. In a surprise move, following the conclusion of Clapton's US tour in June 1979, the band had all been fired, not by Eric himself, but by his manager, Roger Forrester. Whether Eric even knew this was happening is questionable, although I believe his name was signed at the bottom of the telegram. There wasn't even a courtesy phone call, just a piece of paper that read something like, *No gigs imminent. Suggest you seek other employment. Eric.*

As I was working on the Bee Gees tour at the time, I did not receive one of these callous pink slips that notified my friends that the leader of the band they had played with for five years was firing all of them. Pretty harsh, I'd say.

To my knowledge, all the telegrams were identical, and though I do not know for sure, I suspect everyone got one: Carl Radle, Dick Sims, Jamie Oldaker, and Marcy Levy. By that time, George Terry and Sergio Pastora were no longer touring with Eric and his band. I had received the news from Willie Spears, who was EC's guitar tech and was out on the road with me doing Barry Gibb's guitars during the *Spirits Having Flown* tour. The news came as a shock to all of us.

Mind you, while I adamantly agree the way the firing was handled was in very poor taste, the band themselves had been pushing a good, no, great situation to the brink. There was that particular instance during one of our tours through Europe when Roger wanted to tack on a pair of show dates in Czechoslovakia and Romania at the end. Things there had calmed down somewhat politically since the Cold War, so we had a chance to play behind the Iron Curtain.

However, the band, sans Eric, told Roger they wanted to make sure they were getting paid their normal rate to play the additional dates. Since they had already taken home more money from previous concerts on the tour than many average people earned in a month toiling away at nine-to-five, blue-collar jobs, Roger assumed they'd just do these last two for free and enjoy the experience. There wasn't that much money being guaranteed for the shows anyway.

But when the band members made their demand, Roger told them to forget it and simply canceled the gigs. I, for one, was disappointed, as I really wanted to go to Romania where Dracula's Castle was supposed to be.

I think the band was shocked Roger stood his ground and canceled, and I know Eric was none too pleased when he heard why they weren't going. This was one of the numerous reasons I am sure the telegrams were eventually sent. Contentment and comfort seemed to breed greed.

I must admit that after Eric, or rather Roger, fired the Tulsa band, things had changed and attitudes were different in town. Who could blame them? I saw Dick, Marcy, Jamie, and Willie socially, and they had no animosity toward me, or so I felt. But now everything seemed a bit different. Not necessarily personally, but we no longer had that life-on-the-road bond we'd once had.

Tragically, Carl took the news the hardest. On May 30, 1980, eight days after I had returned home, he was discovered dead in his house in Claremore, Oklahoma. His death was ruled an accidental overdose, but who knows? It was a very sad affair.

As was told to me, not too long after Eric heard about Carl's death, he phoned Carl's home telephone number and left a message on his answering machine, saying something to the effect of, "There are more things coming up, so stay well. I'll get back to you." And with that, he hung up.

This odd and poorly timed call was discussed around a select group of Carl's friends in Tulsa, and the conclusion was that EC was feeling a great deal of guilt, possibly because of the way the firing was handled. Or perhaps he lacked knowledge of the telegrams. Or maybe he was visiting heavily with his friend Mr. Courvoisier and, under the influence, tried to shake off some of the guilt he may have felt.

No matter, I believe the impersonal feeling of the telegram arriving at his doorstep contributed to Carl's depression, considering he had been a friend and bandmate of Eric's for so long. Sadly, I doubt Roger even considered handling Carl's release in a different way.

Carl was buried, a memorial show was held at a club in Tulsa, and Bonnie Raitt came in town especially for the evening and played. Then a month or two later, Carl's mother organized an estate sale of his belongings. She asked me to assist in gathering all his musical gear and pricing it. I felt good about being able to help, though was heartbroken for the reason.

So much changed when Carl died. After his death, everybody in the band and most of the community were not as thrilled with the name Eric Clapton as they had previously been. For a long while, Tulsans had seemingly thought of EC as a local boy, but no longer. In certain circles, he was looked on as being partially responsible for Carl's eventual drug overdose, although that was never really the case. If someone gives up hope and sane reasoning, the choice is theirs if they decide to take such dangerous risks with their own lives.

But as always with death, even one such as this, there comes a time when you have to put it behind you and move on with positive memories and thoughts. I still miss you, Carl.

Despite the circumstances, I'll admit I wondered if I'd get the chance to go on the road with Roger and EC again due to my close association with Clapton's now defunct Tulsa band. Fortunately, I would eventually receive a call from Roger. Eric had recorded a new album titled *Another Ticket,* and he wanted me to join them on their upcoming tour. I said yes, of course.

I was pleasantly surprised and overjoyed to have been asked. I suspect Roger wanted to take along someone who was very familiar with Eric's touring routine. But after the call, I did my best to avoid seeing the former band members, and I didn't mention the new tour if I did happen to run into them. Tulsa was not a big city and avoiding them was somewhat difficult.

Regardless, I was soon packed and headed off to Seattle for rehearsals, oddly the same city where I last saw Eric and his Tulsa band together. Rehearsals with EC's new band were being done in a large club Roger had rented. Everything was scaled down, but there were still more amps and PA equipment than that club had ever seen.

For his new band, Eric had hired some old friends from the UK who were exceptional musicians. They were preparing to do a fifty-seven-city US tour, and opening the shows would be the Fabulous Thunderbirds—led by Muddy Waters's friend and mine from my band days in Dallas, Jimmy Vaughn. I felt good that my enthusiasm on the train that night traveling through Europe with Eric, Roger, and Muddy could have played some small part in getting them on a major tour. They deserved it.

Eric's new group was impressive, and I was enjoying being around them. The drummer was Henry Spinetti, who'd played with Gerry Rafferty on his huge 1978 hit "Baker Street" and would later take part in the memorial concert for George Harrison that Eric helped organize a year after the death of the famous Beatles guitarist. He likewise played sessions and shows with Roger Daltrey, Paul McCartney, and Pete Townshend. Henry was a nice guy and funny as well. He was short, but his drumming was large.

Chris Stainton played piano and had a long list of impressive credentials as well. He seemed to always be jamming with someone somewhere. He played and recorded with Joe Cocker, the Who, Bryan Ferry, Bill Wyman, B. B. King, and David Gilmour, to name a few. Chris was a very polite and quiet person. I think he listened a lot. He did have a good sense of humor, but you had to be quick and on the ball to catch it. I believe he often still plays with Eric.

Albert Lee was a highly respected guitarist. A Brit, he was married to an American and lived in Malibu. Albert, like Chris, played and recorded with many celebrated musicians, such as Ricky Skaggs, Emmylou Harris, and Bill Wyman's Rhythm Kings as well as the Everly Brothers for more than twenty years.

Dave Markee handled bass. Another Brit, he seemed older than the other players but was a great musician. He was another kind but also quiet fellow. Some of Dave's previous credits included shows and sessions with Bing Crosby, Henry Mancini, Frank Zappa, Waylon Jennings, and Leo Sayer.

And to round out the impressive band, Eric hired friend and organist Gary Brooker of Procol Harum fame. He helped pen the celebrated hit songs "A Whiter Shade of Pale" and "A Salty Dog." Gary also played with Ringo Starr and his All-Starr Band and the Alan Parsons Project, and he owned a pub in the UK. I think he fancied himself as a bit of a James Bond. He was a character, and we got along well.

Together with Eric, this made for a very good band to follow on the heels of the Tulsa bunch. In addition, the road crew, most of whom were Brits, had worked with Eric when the Tulsa band was still with him and were also on this tour, so I already knew them, which made things more comfortable.

Eric's band rehearsed daily from just after lunch until whenever the band or EC felt they'd done enough for the day. We'd then head back to the hotel, which had a good restaurant and a nice dark bar. It was an extremely pleasant place to stay while rehearsals were going on.

We also used this hotel for the first several dates of the tour before we moved on to the next base city, and as usual, we had a pool table in Roger's room to occupy our time if needed. We became known not only in the hotel but around the local community as well. Having the staff know us better always made staying somewhere more enjoyable and personal.

During our lengthy time in Seattle, we ran across a few interesting people. Eric met a young man whose father owned a company called Lamiglas that made highly regarded fishing rods. Eric and his new friend talked fishing and fishing equipment for hours. I never knew EC had such an interest in fishing, but he'd eventually go on to be a respected fisherman and has since caught record-setting salmon in Iceland.

Also staying at our same hotel was English tennis star Sue Barker, who I did not know, but the entire British contingent was well aware of as she was their country's pride and joy on the court. The band members were a bit shy to speak to her (imagine that!), so I struck up a conversation, and we all got to be friends. My tour associates gave me a lot of grief for making friends with one of their celebrated countrymen, er, women.

Sue was playing in a World Tennis Association tournament there in Seattle and got us all tickets to the event. Most of us went and watched the match—back and forth, back and forth. I don't remember who won, but I do remember our decorum was not that of normal tennis enthusiasts. We applauded and whistled when we should have been silent, but after a while we caught on and decided we were better off just staying quiet. Later, Sue said she could hear her new friends in the stands, although she assured us we did not disrupt her game. After Sue's playing career ended, she became a respected TV tennis broadcaster in the UK.

Mostly we kept (or were kept) to ourselves at hotels since we were always on the move and often at odd hours. As mentioned, we'd occasionally meet friends or other celebrities who were staying at the same hotel, but normally we were our own best and only friends.

After a week or so of rehearsals, the shows were ready to start. The first one was a thrill, I must admit. There was always electricity in the air for opening night. The band was raring to finally perform in front of an audience, and there was the excitement of fans ready to see EC perform. So, as always, the energy was high. It was going to be a good night.

What caught me by surprise was seeing the show start with Albert, Henry, Chris, and Dave on stage without Eric. The lights went down, and Albert launched into "Country Boy." The crowd, although maybe not familiar with Albert, knew the song. He played his butt off, and the audience loved it.

Then Albert introduced Gary, and he came out, sat at his Hammond B3 organ, and played the oh so identifiable opening chords of "A Whiter Shade of Pale." The crowd went wild when they realized who he was. Hearing him play his biggest hit gave me chills, and the audience was content. He once played "A Salty Dog" instead and that got great applause as well.

I must say, I was surprised Eric let Gary play those songs before he came on stage. To me, following that performance would have been hard for any superstar. The concert could have ended then and there, and it would have been enough. But to top it all off, EC then came on, and the night really took off.

At some point, after a few dates in and out of Seattle, the time came to bid adieu to the hotel that had been our home for nearly a month and move on to the next city and hotel, which was the Radisson in downtown St. Paul, Minnesota. We had done seven shows around the Seattle region, which included stops in Montana and Oregon. Already this was shaping up to be a good tour.

Before we checked into the St. Paul hotel, we flew on our private Vickers Viscount plane to a date in Madison, Wisconsin. We did the show as expected, show number eight, and it went well. Afterward, we said we'd see everyone, even the Fabulous Thunderbirds and our crew, in the next city, and we took off to hunker down in St. Paul for a few days. But during the flight, Eric began feeling very ill. He sat in the back compartment of the plane on his own.

Unbeknownst to most of us, EC had been downing a British painkiller called Veganin that contained paracetamol and codeine, and in numbers that would have killed a small animal. The huge dosages had ulcerated Eric's stomach internally, and with all the Courvoisier, well, that wasn't good.

Roger realized on the plane how serious the situation seemed, and he wanted to take no chances with Eric's health. So after our plane landed and taxied to a terminal for private charters at the Minneapolis–St. Paul airport, Eric, Roger, and Alphi O'Leary took one of the limousines to the nearest hospital. The rest of us went back to the hotel to await the results.

Though very late at night, they went to the emergency room, and the surgeon on duty saw EC. He gave Eric some stomach medicine, and before sending him to the hotel, made him an appointment with a specialist the next morning. The surgeon believed Eric's stomach pains, while not appendicitis, needed attention.

Back at the hotel, we had checked in and taken Roger's, Eric's, and Alphi's suitcases to their respective rooms. Again, there was a pool table in Roger's suite, and we spent some time there discussing Eric's condition. Eric had gone to his own suite, but Roger told us the surgeon suspected EC might have an ulcer. At the time, his condition did not seem very serious.

Alphi came nervously into Roger's suite after having been to Eric's room to check on him. He'd obviously received a shock. It seems Alphi had walked into EC's room (we always kept a spare key for when he didn't answer) and spied Eric's shoes and jeans lying on the floor, protruding from behind the sofa area. Alphi's mind raced, fearing Eric had fainted or worse. Alphi ran to the sofa, only to discover that was where Eric had disrobed before going to bed. He had just left his shoes and jeans where they fell. Still, the scene gave Alphi quite a jolt, and he came to Roger's room a bit pale. It made for a good laugh, at least that evening.

At that point, unbeknownst to us, the crew, and the Fabulous Thunderbirds, Eric Clapton's fifty-seven-city US tour had done its last show. Everything was soon going to screech to a very bell-ringing halt.

On the morning of March 14, Roger, Alphi, and Eric went to the doctor's office as instructed, where a renowned specialist examined Eric before immediately admitting him to the hospital. With as little fanfare as possible, EC was checked into a private room on a floor several stories above the ground. The nurses knew he was there, but everyone was trying to keep it hush-hush.

Eric was diagnosed with three ulcers—one small, one large, and another that was near perforation. If that last ulcer had opened into his body cavity, he would have had about an hour to live before peritonitis sealed his fate. Once the doctor heard what EC had been doing, taking the large quantity of Veganin, twenty or more tablets, drinking a fifth of Courvoisier a day, and eating sparingly, he felt confident he knew the cause of Eric's ulcers.

Fortunately for Eric, the specialist, the esteemed Dr. Votel, was one of the doctors who researched and developed the newest ulcer medication at the time, Tagamet, I remember being told. He had plans to return him to full health, which included putting a halt to Eric's current tour.

Roger notified us back at the hotel what was happening and that the tour was being canceled. At first, we believed he was only kidding, but then we realized he was serious. We were canceling forty-nine of the fifty-seven dates on the tour. When Roger notified the tour agent and various people in LA and London who were involved in the logistics that the tour was being canceled for unforeseen medical reasons, everybody was flabbergasted. Nothing like this had ever happened before, at least to us.

We had to inform the truck, bus, and plane companies that it was all over. I was also told by Roger that when word reached Lloyd's of London, who had insured the tour in the UK, the news caused the company's Lutine Bell to ring, a feat not often done. I suspect their policy covered any costs for all such changes and cancellations for everyone involved, thereby buffering any significant damages to Eric or Roger personally, although I don't know for sure.

There was certainly concern in Duluth, Minnesota, where our crew had traveled to for the next scheduled show. They were now out of a job and had to look for new work immediately instead of counting on employment for the next six months.

Then there was notifying the Fabulous Thunderbirds that the tour was over for them as well. Doing so was terribly difficult since this was their biggest tour to date, and they'd purchased and refitted an old Flxible bus for the journey. Now they, too, had to reschedule new dates. That and they'd miss performing for all those potential new fans . . . and have to still make bus payments.

We expressed how sorry we were, and everyone took the news well—sadly but well. We all were pretty upset by the turn of events, including Roger. Eric was very apologetic, but I never really knew how he felt about letting so many people down. True, he didn't purposely do this to disrupt everyone's next six months. Initially, he was too ill to be very concerned as he was taking medication for pain as well as to relax and keep calm. I'm sure he had some feelings of responsibility and disappointment, but I never heard him voice any regret verbally. Maybe not his style, but I feel certain he thought about it.

Roger asked me, Alphi, and Eric's personal assistant and friend Nigel Carroll to stay in St. Paul with him and keep watch at the hospital around the clock to make sure fans and the press left Eric alone. This was great for me as it meant I'd be paid for at least as long as EC was laid up.

Updates about Eric being admitted to the hospital were all over the news globally within just a few hours, so Alphi, Nigel, and I immediately began our daily shifts, which meant sitting in a chair down the hall where we had a direct view of Eric's hospital room and the elevator. If anyone suspicious came off the elevator looking like they weren't supposed to be there, we'd intervene and divert them back to the elevator. In a few instances, we had to call security.

Eric spent his first days in the hospital relaxing, not doing much of anything except sleeping and watching TV. I'd work eight hours or so, Alphi would do eight, and then Nigel eight. We'd switch shifts every few days. The doctor said Eric's confinement might be as long as six weeks, so we needed to decide on a routine.

I would normally sit in the hallway between two rooms of ill and elderly people, and once I had to listen to someone dying in the room to my left. It was pretty upsetting for me, not to mention the family there with him.

We pretty much left Eric on his own unless he needed us for something or just wanted a visitor. Reading a lot of magazines helped the time pass, but as this was before computers and cell phones, we were basically isolated in a hospital hallway. Occasionally, I'd pop into Eric's room if I could tell he was awake, and we'd chat or watch some TV, and then I'd head back to my chair.

As time progressed and Eric's hospitalization became less and less newsworthy, our shifts would usually end when visiting hours were over. Alphi, Nigel, Roger, and I would then gather in Roger's suite or the hotel's restaurant for a meal and a drink. Well, Nigel and I would have a drink. Alphi didn't drink too much, and Roger didn't drink at all. Not because he didn't like the taste, that wasn't the reason. He liked the taste too much, so he gave up alcohol completely.

Alphi and Roger smoked like chimneys, and Roger drank coffee like water. Later, I learned that at the time, and possibly for a long time, he was addicted to Valium, which helped explain the need for the vast quantities of coffee he drank and his often extremely casual composition.

While at dinner and before wandering off to bed, we'd usually discuss EC's condition and the medical updates Roger had received. Eric's diet was unfortunately extremely bland, as ordered by the doctor, but he'd put himself in this situation and took the prescribed medicine.

Pattie, Eric's wife, flew in after about a week and moved into Eric's suite directly across the hall from my room. Having another friendly face to visit with was nice. Plus, Pattie drank, so she was at least someone I could get tipsy with at the bar after a long and boring day at the hospital.

She'd visit Eric every day, and they would chat or watch TV. But Pattie quickly became extremely bored as well of this solemn existence that was pretty much void of any activity, especially with her husband. The hospital was depressing.

A week into Eric's treatment, I was sent out to buy him a good classical guitar, so he could have something with which to occupy his time instead of just watching TV. I got him a nice Yamaha, one that I still have to this day since he did not take it with him back to the UK once this long ordeal was finally over. I started with two suitcases for the entire tour but returned with nearly twenty checked items, eighteen of which were luggage filled with items Eric bought or gifts he'd been given and didn't take home.

One morning, Roger informed us that Pete Townshend was coming all the way from London to visit and offer moral support. How nice was that? Pete was an old friend of Eric's and likewise an old friend of mine since I was sixteen years old when we first met. Having someone like Pete come for a visit would be a nice change to the boring routine, and I was exceptionally happy to have the chance to catch up since we only saw each other every few years. The last time I'd seen Pete was at the Rainbow Theatre in London when he'd convinced Eric to get his ass back on stage and finish the show, even joining EC for those final few songs in an effort to help him.

Pete and his lady checked into a suite at our hotel, and then we were off to visit Eric, who was pleased that his trusted friend had come so far just to see him. Later that evening, Pete, his date, Pattie, and I then ended up in a suite with some drinks and evidently some other extracurricular chemicals. However, it seemed to only be Pete and his girl who'd disappear for minutes on end into the adjoining bedroom to imbibe. There may have been some coke that was shared, but I preferred to stick with my gin and tonic.

The evening was special in many ways. Pete was not in very good shape then, having recently separated from his wife of many years and taken up with this new lady as well as obviously doing some serious non-prescribed self-medicating. Still, being alone with him in a hotel room and just chatting was nice.

I remember Pete turning to me at one point in the evening and saying, "You've held up pretty well," which was meant as a compliment. I said, "Thank you," although I desperately wanted to respond, "You, my old friend, don't look so well at the moment." But I bit my tongue and remained quiet.

There was a point that night—I suspect late as we were all several sheets to the wind—when Pete bemoaned that he was exhausted and wasn't sure why. For some reason, I decided to speak up and say something I'd thought for a long time. I had read several of Pete's magazine interviews, all of which were somber throughout. He is a highly intelligent person, and I am sure his mind is constantly thinking, but I said, "You know, Pete, maybe you take everything too seriously." And I meant it.

I don't remember what his reaction was, but I suspect since we were all pretty wasted, my words probably had little impact. And why should they?

Pete stayed another day or so and then was off to other places, but his visit with Eric did wonders as far as encouraging him to get healed as quickly as possible. Shortly thereafter, Eric's condition improved to a point that his doctor allowed him to be released from the hospital several times a week for a few hours during the day, as long as he was back for meals and did not eat outside of the hospital.

Eric had decided he wanted to be an outdoorsman, so each time he was released, I'd take him to the Eddie Bauer store, where he'd shop for flannel shirts, heavy khaki pants, and camping boots. Then we'd be off to a local fishing store. Eric took to buying a new fishing rod and reel every day we'd go. He'd have them wound with different line weight and chat with the staff about what reel would be best for catching what type of fish. And remember that Eric had made a friend in the young fellow whose father owned a company that made a top-quality fishing rod. Before long, Eric had fifteen to twenty complete fishing rods in his hospital room. I guess money was no object, and it was his to do with as he pleased. And he did!

A fun or at least time-consuming by-product of having all those fishing rods at the hospital was when I was on my security shift, I used to tape a five-dollar bill to the end of the line. I'd then leave the "bait" thirty to forty feet down the hallway near the nurses' station and elevator, just to fish for innocent passersby.

As expected, most people who saw the money on the floor would reach down to pick it up. They couldn't see the fishing line attached to the back of the bill, so I'd reel it in a bit. Quite often, people would follow along a few times, thinking the wind caused by their footsteps was making the bill scoot away. Others, though, knew immediately it was a trick. Anyway, the game occupied my time. Believe me, sitting there keeping guard on EC's room for an eight-hour shift seven days a week was very boring.

One interesting event that remains clear in my mind was the day I took Eric to the dentist office to have his receding gumline examined. This issue was the initial reason why he took the Veganin that got us all into this situation. As he and I drove along to the appointment, we listened to the radio and Eric's biggest hit, "Layla," came on. I remember initially thinking Eric might not want to listen to himself playing his most popular song because he had to perform it so frequently live on stage. I went to change the channel, but he stopped me. He said he wanted to hear it.

I remember thinking, *Here I am driving in a car with the guy who wrote and made hugely famous this rock-and-roll anthem, and no one else around us knows*. We listened to the entire song, and when it finished, Eric told me about recording "Layla" and how he stacked six guitar tracks to get that special dreamy guitar sound. I had no clue and filed it away as some interesting piece of information someone might like to know one day. It was an out-of-body experience for few minutes.

On April 16, after being in the hospital for a month with visits from friends, Pattie coming and going back to the UK, and trips to various stores for shopping, the time came for Eric to be released, at least temporarily. The doctors said he could take a few weeks off and go on a camping trip, maybe fish and relax, but they wanted him to return for a final examination before being cleared to fly home to London.

Prior to his release, Eric, Nigel, and I spent a few days planning a trip while Roger carried on with his business from the hotel room. We rented a Winnebago and bought all the necessary gear, including bedrolls, cooking pans, and utensils—everything we'd need for a camping trip. And, of course, Eric brought all his fishing rods. Heck, we even rented a canoe and strapped it to the top of the RV. I had been a Boy Scout and was an experienced camper.

Then one day we set off, heading out to camp and fish. I can't say the experience was a great deal of fun, as I am not a fan of long road trips after having traversed the US so many times, but we drove along and listened to music. Once we reached a destination, we camped, cooked, and went to bed early.

A couple of days into the trip, Nigel discovered EC had been sneaking into his prescribed medicine supply and was overmedicating on the pain pills. We started our expedition with maybe thirty tablets and within three days were down to less than ten. Nigel had to lock them away and hide them from Eric.

We made it all the way to Oregon, and on a chilly, rainy day we fished on a river with the Lamiglas fellow, although no one caught anything except maybe a cold. We also went up to Seattle to see some recently made friends and used a good-sized boat to fish for salmon around Puget Sound. Eric caught a large one that we took back and cooked, making for a great meal.

On April 22, while riding back to our campsite outside the city, the car Eric was riding in was hit by another car that ran a red light. The police came, and he and the driver were taken to a hospital just to make sure they were all right. Eric suffered cracked ribs but was otherwise fine.

Unfortunately, the next morning in the Seattle newspaper and on the Associate Press wire across the US and world, including the UK, it was reported that Eric had been in a car wreck. The media had already reported that he was no longer in the St. Paul hospital, but no one, not even Roger, knew where we had gone, which made front-page news. Typical.

Well, we called Roger to assure him everything was all right, but he said to get Nigel and Eric on a plane back to Minnesota. I was tasked to drive the Winnebago back. He wasn't mad or anything like that. He just didn't want to further complicate an otherwise busy and unpleasant few weeks.

After a couple of days driving alone, I made it to the hotel in St. Paul, only to find that Eric had been given the all clear on his ulcer problem, and he, Nigel, and Alphi had already flown back to the UK. Roger stayed behind to meet me and help clear out the numerous possessions Eric had collected. Basically, the only things EC wanted to take home were his fishing rods and reels.

As I said, I started the tour with a couple of suitcases and returned to Tulsa with a lot of extra luggage, including all the camping gear and the nice Yamaha classical guitar I bought for Eric. Not only was it sad to have a great tour come to a screeching halt, it was terrible to have our camping trip ended abruptly too.

Roger and I parted ways at the airport between the two cities and unfortunately never worked together again. That wasn't the last time we spoke or visited, but it was the last time I ever toured with Eric.

I kept in touch with Roger and saw him periodically, including one time that ended in a rather tasteless incident. A few years later, I was doing some work with Yamaha for an international battle-of-the-bands-type competition that would be held in Tokyo. Knowing my connection to Eric, they asked me to see if EC would come to Japan and be a judge.

I flew to London to meet with Roger, and when I proposed the idea to him, he said maybe Eric and Beatles great George Harrison, who were then hanging around together, would both attend if I could get Japanese promotor Seijiro Udo to confirm this was a good deal. Udo not only endorsed the idea, he also offered to pay all their expenses plus give the two legendary guitarists a sizable stipend just to come and judge for one night. Roger then asked that he receive a payment as well and a new grand piano, which Yamaha agreed to do.

But after not hearing anything for a month or two, I finally spoke to Roger again, and he told me that Eric and George wouldn't be available. Even worse, soon thereafter I found out the two were instead planning to do a tour of Japan together around the same time of the Yamaha event. It seems Udo and Roger decided that if Eric and George were going to go to Japan, why not do an actual tour and make a lot more money.

And that was that. I had been stabbed in the back by Roger and Udo. I found two other artists to do the judging.

When I was in Japan for the competition, I saw Udo in the lobby of my hotel as I checked in, and he looked down, knowing that I was aware of what he'd done. He then came up to me and bowed low in apology for his deception. Nothing was ever admitted, but we both knew the whole idea of a tour came up because of my original inquiry.

Roger never said a word about it, and neither did I.

I have seen Eric perform on a few occasions since then, even in Japan, but the shows I caught never had the magic and excitement of those I experienced when I worked with him. During that show in Japan, Peter Jackson, EC's tour manager at the time, invited me to come backstage afterward, but when my good friend Alphi asked Roger and Eric if they'd like to see me, he was told an emphatic no. The two of them then slid out the back door, careful not to be seen.

In 2002, I went to visit Alphi for the last time. He had stomach cancer and was dying. While there, he told me the reason Eric didn't want to talk to me that night was because he did not like seeing the people who knew him closely in his past life, when he was drinking so much and was in such a poor state.

Roger, on the other hand, had another reason for not wishing to see me, a low blow he possibly felt some guilt about . . . or should have!

Eric Clapton 1981 *Another Ticket* US Tour Dates

March 2, 1981: Veterans Memorial Coliseum (Portland, Oregon)

March 3, 1981: Spokane Coliseum (Spokane, Washington)

March 5, 1981: Paramount Theatre (Seatle, Washington)

March 6, 1981: Paramount Theatre (Seatle, Washington)

March 7, 1981: Paramount Theatre (Seatle, Washington)

March 9, 1981: MetraPark Arena (Billings, Montana)

March 10, 1981: Four Seasons Arena (Great Falls, Montana)

March 13, 1981: Dane County Coliseum (Madison, Wisconsin)

All the following dates were canceled:

March 14, 1981: Duluth Arena Auditorium (Duluth, Minnesota)

March 15, 1981: St. Paul Civic Center (St. Paul, Minnesota)

March 17, 1981: Hilton Coliseum, Iowa State University (Ames, Iowa)

March 18, 1981: Kansas Coliseum (Wichita, Kansas)

March 20, 1981: Hammons Student Center, Missouri State University (Springfield, Missouri)

March 21, 1981: Kemper Arena (Kansas City, Missouri)

March 22, 1981: Devaney Center, University of Nebraska (Lincoln, Nebraska)

March 24, 1981: LSU Assembly Center, Louisiana State University (Baton Rouge, Louisiana)

March 25, 1981: Municipal Auditorium (New Orleans, Louisiana)

March 27, 1981: Mid-South Coliseum (Memphis, Tennessee)

March 28, 1981: SIU Arena, Southern Illinois University (Carbondale, Illinois)

March 29, 1981: Kiel Auditorium (St. Louis, Missouri)

March 31, 1981: Barton Coliseum (Little Rock, Arkansas)

April 1, 1981: Hirsch Memorial Coliseum (Shreveport, Louisiana)

April 3, 1981: Frank Erwin Center, University of Texas (Austin, Texas)

April 4, 1981: The Summit (Houston, Texas)

April 5, 1981: Reunion Arena (Dallas, Texas)

April 7, 1981: ASU Activity Center, Arizona State University (Tempe, Arizona)

April 8, 1981: San Diego Sports Arena (San Diego California)

April 9, 1981: Long Beach Arena (Long Beach, California)

April 11, 1981: Oakland Coliseum (Oakland, California)

May 1, 1981: Market Square Arena (Indianapolis, Indiana)

May 2, 1981: Riverfront Coliseum (Cincinnati, Ohio)

May 3, 1981: Joe Louis Arena (Detroit, Michigan)

May 5, 1981: Allen County War Memorial Coliseum (Fort Wayne, Indiana)

May 7, 1981: Michigan State University Arena (East Lansing, Michigan)

May 8, 1981: Chicago Stadium (Chicago, Illinois)

May 9, 1981: Richfield Coliseum (Cleveland, Ohio)

May 10, 1981: Civic Center (Pittsburgh, Pennsylvania)

May 12, 1981: New HavenVeterans Memorial Coliseum (New Haven, Connecticut)

May 13, 1981: Broome County Veterans Memorial Arena (Binghamton, New York)

May 15, 1981: Nassau Coliseum (Uniondale, New York)

May 16, 1981: Providence Civic Center (Providence, Rhode Island)

May 17, 1981: Cumberland County Civic Center (Portland, Maine)

May 19, 1981: War Memorial Coliseum (Rochester, New York)

May 20, 1981: Spectrum (Philadelphia, Pennsylvania)

May 22, 1981: Capital Centre (Landover, Maryland)

May 23, 1981: Norfolk Scope Arena (Norfolk, Virginia)

May 24, 1981: Greensboro Coliseum (Greensboro, North Carolina)

May 26, 1981: Charlotte Coliseum (Charlotte, North Carolina)

May 27, 1981: Carolina Coliseum, University of South Carolina (Columbia, South Carolina)

May 29, 1981: Hollywood Sportatorium (Pembroke Pines, Florida)

May 30, 1981: Jacksonville Coliseum (Jacksonville, Florida)

May 31, 1981: Sun Dome, University of South Florida (Tampa, Florida)

June 2, 1981: Grand Ole Opry (Nashville, Tennessee)

June 4, 1981: Mississippi Coliseum (Jackson, Mississippi)

June 5, 1981: Mobile Municipal Auditorium (Mobile, Alabama)

June 6, 1981: BJCC Civic Center (Birmingham, Alabama)

June 7, 1981: Omni Coliseum (Atlanta, Georgia)

CHAPTER 12

Three Dog Night

The 1981 Comeback Tour.

After the abrupt halt of Eric's tour and our shortened camping expedition, I was back home in Tulsa. Of course, what was I going to do now? Touring with Eric seemed over as he was taking time off and learning how to become a renowned trout fisherman.

But out of the blue, I got a call from my good friend who I really owe a great debt of gratitude to, Jay Hagerman of Concerts West. Three Dog Night was planning a comeback tour, and Jay asked if I'd be interested in acting as tour manager on the company's behalf. I was most definitely interested.

In the late 1960s and early 1970s, Three Dog Night had been one of the world's most popular rock bands. They had numerous hits, such as "One" and "Joy to the World," and this newest version would include most of the original band members. They didn't even have a new album coming out. They were just going to see if their audience was still desirous of seeing and hearing them. After all, the band had registered twenty-one consecutive top-forty hits and sold almost fifty million records between 1969 and 1975. It was worth a try.

Concerts West would pay for and book their tour, and with income from the shows, not big arenas but large clubs, they wouldn't lose too much. Of course, they probably wouldn't make any money either.

I flew to Los Angeles and met with Tom Hulett, cofounder of Concerts West, which was also owned by Jerry Weintraub, who went on to produce some fine films, and Terry Bassett. Tom explained that this was Three Dog Night's last and only chance with them to see if they could still survive in this new marketplace. I'd be traveling with the band, taking them and a good crew on tour across the US, along with a representative from

Concerts West, John Meglan. He would act as my assistant and an accountant in settling the shows, although they were a flat fee anyway.

I agreed, and a few days later I was on a plane with the band headed to Portland, Oregon, for a show on June 11, 1981. Once again, I was with a bunch of strangers who I'd read about over the years and admired but did not know at all. Oddly, most tours I did started that way, with me not knowing a soul, except maybe a crew person.

Forming in 1967, there was Cory Wells, Danny Hutton, and Chuck Negron—the three Dogs. The rest of the band was made up of keyboardist Jimmy Greenspoon, Mike Seifrit on bass, guitarist Michael Allsup, and drummer Floyd Sneed. Getting to know everyone didn't take long, especially since I was thrust upon them by management. A couple were a bit leery, but thankfully Jimmy made things bearable. He was one of the funniest guys in the music business.

We would be traveling by an older-model bus due to budget restrictions. I remember a bit of moaning and groaning about the mode of transportation and how they used to be able to get better rooms. Fortunately, Danny and Cory always intervened, telling the others this was how things were now and to quit complaining or leave. Knowing they had already enjoyed their heyday, they now had to sacrifice if they wanted to make a comeback or at least make a living at this and not go work at a burger joint, which none of them wanted to do. That's a fact.

We'd stay at Holiday Inns, Ramadas, and similar-priced hotels, which back then were better but still a far cry from the top-of-the-line Hiltons or Sheratons. At least we all had our own rooms, except for the crew, who traveled separately.

Early in the afternoon before, I believe, the second show, I got a call from Chuck, asking me to come to his room. Happy to oblige, I did so, but after he let me in, he then climbed back under the covers, fully dressed. I wondered what was up, though I had a suspicion, having dealt with similar quirks with a member or two of EC's band.

Chuck confided in me that he'd come off a methadone rehab program too early in order to do the tour. It seems overcoming his heroin addiction was a prerequisite of the management company as well as Cory and Danny. Chuck had to get straight. He had been an addict for a while and supposedly was trying to get clean, but he had no more methadone with which to mask his desire for the heroine.

He asked me to find him something, anything to help him get on stage. Otherwise, "There would be no show." I was supposed to keep this between the two of us. I admit I was at a loss. Despite having been around drugs and a massive amount of alcohol with touring musicians, I didn't know what to try or where to get what he was looking for. This was a new area for me.

I'm sure Chuck and I had a good question-and-answer session, and after a call or six, we were soon on our way to a clinic, emergency room, doctor's office, halfway house, or something. I can't recall which as we visited all of them a few times over the next several weeks, hoping to acquire what he needed.

The hunt sort of went like this. Look up a likely facility in the Yellow Pages, make an initial phone call, introduce myself and my purpose for being in their city, and explain that one of the main singers was coming off a methadone program too early and needed some help. The nurse would frequently let me speak with a doctor, although on occasion they'd give me the cold shoulder and I'd get nowhere, meaning I'd have to humiliate myself with the same sob story yet again. People were always interested to find out who the band was, regardless of if they were going to help or not. No matter, in every city I attempted this, I was ultimately met with success.

The doctor would want to meet Chuck in person (always a mandatory requirement), and after their discussion, he would give him a medication sample or shot that lasted long enough to see him through the night and get him on to the next town. Chuck convinced me to go with him on these visits, which I did because I had the money. He was allowed very little cash due to the fact that his mates and management did not trust that he could avoid spending it on drugs. So the next best option was to apparently have the tour manager pay the cab fare, office-visit fees, and medicine costs.

These doctors always had a quiet word in my ear that this was not the norm with them, giving out such strong medicine to a non-regular client, and that they felt he needed to be back in a program immediately. I happened to agree.

I'll give it to Chuck, though. He was on stage every time and sang his heart out. Honestly, in my opinion, Chuck Negron may have not been the most popular member of the band, but he was the most talented singer of the three. I found that to be true in other instances as well.

For example, Jack Bruce was a total mess and a terrible handful to deal with off stage. Whether from drinks or drugs, he became a very disagreeable monster when he got drunk or high, but I believe without a doubt he was the most talented musician in the supergroup Cream, and I know many others who felt the same. There are other instances of troubled musicians being the most talented but very seldom did their addictions do their careers any good. In many cases, those demons cost them dearly.

The band sounded great every evening they performed, and we were getting to know each other well, crew and all. Listening off stage was a thrill for most of us, getting to hear this legendary band perform hit after hit, night after night. But no one actually knew the lengths Chuck and I had to go through. Or rather what I had to go through. All he had to do was take the medication. I had to grovel while trying not to be embarrassed by what I did to get him, and in turn the whole band, on stage each night.

I got to be fairly good friends with Jimmy and Mike, and we hung around together somewhat. Floyd, while extremely nice, was a bit quieter and laid low. Seldom did Cory and Danny surface from their rooms, except when the time came to leave for a sound check and to join in on the crew and band meal before a show. This was the first time I had done backstage crew meals with any band. Normally, the crew had been fed by caterers prior to the band showing up to perform, but since our budget was extremely slim, the promoter slipped an additional number of dinner meals in for the crew, John, and me. The food was good, and it saved on per diems, which was nice though not up to the level of most profitable tours. Again, we were on a strict budget.

Chuck wasn't often hungry and rarely grabbed dinner. But the scene was casual, come if you wish. No one asked any questions about his absence, especially if he was on stage every night singing like a lark. Every once in a while, a conversation with Cory and Danny or some band member would drift to Chuck and drugs. I believe they all knew he was struggling and were possibly aware of what I was doing to help the show go on. Doing so did not cause any outward tension between me and them, but I am sure the other two Dogs felt hugely let down by Dog number three.

However, they only confided among themselves and not with me at all.

I did not purposely try to deceive anyone on the tour or cover up what was happening with Chuck. I liked the guy, and I had promised him I'd do my best to keep it quiet so as to avoid any trouble or him possibly losing his job. I kept my word.

We carried on like this, bussing from one town to the next, down to Arizona and into Texas. We'd check into a hotel in the wee hours of the morning, I'd sleep for a little while, usually waking up no later than 8:30, and after a quick shower, breakfast at the hotel or in a coffee shop—I did not like room service, too isolated—I'd head back to my room and start working the phone. My first and most important chore each day was always to advance the next several dates. Remember, we had no cell phones back then, so the hotel landline was my best and oftentimes most expensive friend.

I'd have already advanced most dates a few days or weeks out, but I was pedantic and made second and third calls to the promoter, the club, any local transportation or rental companies, and the hotel. I'd explain our ETA and how I wanted the rooms prebooked with keys in envelopes, ready for me to wander in bleary-eyed at some unholy hour, pick up, and pay for. I'd then go back to the bus, where the driver would be taking off the suitcases, and wake those in the band who were asleep. They'd take their key, grab their bag, and head (also bleary-eyed) to their awaiting rooms and beds for a more comfortable sleep.

As a rule, buses were not too pleasant, especially the older ones like this budget-conscious ride we traveled on during this tour. It wasn't a wreck, by any means. The old girl just had hundreds of thousands of miles on the clock and a bit of wear and tear showing in most places. The bus, though, was only part of the problem.

With the exception of Jimmy, John, and maybe a couple of others, this particular tour was a grueling affair most of the time. I remember a long evening staying up very late with John, chatting about the band, Chuck, and the tours we'd done. It was a fun, albeit long, night. John was a great guy and is unfortunately someone I have lost touch with.

The issue now, though, wasn't so much staying in cheaper hotels and the lack of frivolous trappings, but rather the attitude of the three singers, which trickled down to the rest of the band. Cory, Danny, and even

Chuck had an attitude of defeatism about the tour. They were going out as a group in hopes of saving their music careers, and they had a promoter who fronted the money, knowing they'd collect it back from show payments. But that did not quash the overall feeling of *I can't believe we are here playing clubs and staying in budget hotels instead of playing arenas and staying in expensive hotels,* as they had done several years earlier. Staying on top is not as easy as some artists and bands make it look.

I'm not sure why Three Dog Night stopped touring initially or fell out of favor in terms of popularity and ticket sales, but I have a sneaking suspicion the decline may have had to do with drug or alcohol abuse and generally keeping it all together. I know how tough that must have been, having experienced it with other bands of that stature, but we had to make the best of it.

We had a concert in Dallas on June 21, and as usual I had to find someone in my old hometown to help Chuck out. After making calls to a few local musicians who I knew might have an answer, I was given a name or two. I contacted them and once again went through the whole routine for a quick shot and a "way to go Larry" from Chuck. The show went on.

We had a couple of days off before the next show, which would be on June 24 in Houston. During that small break, I took it upon myself to phone Tom Hulett. I explained that even though we were only a month into the tour, I was constantly being humiliated due to Chuck's situation, begging daily for medication. I said the rest was not difficult, and the music was always great, but getting to the stage was exhausting—at least for me and I suspect Chuck as well.

Tom was a very kind man, and he told me what a great job I was doing, which felt nice, especially on this downer of a tour. He said not to worry. For my hard work and effort, they'd increase my salary an additional $250 a week out of their management commission. He asked me personally to stay on and keep the tour going. Deciding to continue didn't take a lot of thought as I did not want to let him down. I'd also never backed out of a situation or tour yet, despite the hardships or complexities. I agreed to stay.

With that done, I could relax knowing Tom and the Concerts West office were now aware of how hard it was getting Chuck on stage night after night. At least my efforts were appreciated.

The following morning, after what I am sure was a normal R&R night off, I got a call from Danny, the more logical businessman of the two-Dog duo. He asked me to come to his room for a minute. There is a first time for everything, so I went.

I got to his room, and Cory was there. To make a long story short, Tom had informed them about Chuck—why not as it was their band too—and that to keep me on, he was going to up my salary out of Concerts West's commission. Cory and Danny then said that was not going to happen, and if I didn't like it, I could go home. Luckily, I had a return plane ticket in my briefcase (always).

I tried to explain the money was Tom's idea because I was having to go beyond the call of normal duty to get Chuck to the show every night. The two Dogs responded that if Chuck could not get on stage, then so be it, they'd perform without him, but no way were they going to allow Concerts West to pay me anything additional.

I don't think their problem was with the money itself because they understood the humiliation and extra effort I had to expend to accomplish this task. Rather, I think there was a principal they were trying to uphold, an edict they had handed down to Chuck prior to beginning the tour. No drugs! Either he's clean or no tour. At least that was the feeling I got.

So I had been given an ultimatum: accept the same deal and keep dealing with doctors and embarrassing situations for another five months on Chuck's behalf (as well as Danny and Cory's) or pack my bags and head home.

I did one last concert with them that night in Houston, and by show time everyone in the band and crew knew I was heading home. Not by me telling them, but let's just say rumors spread fast on the road.

After the show, I was back at a Holiday Inn, sitting alone in the bar and having a drink by myself while the bus with the band and my pal John were headed to the next city. I did speak to Tom in LA and explained what I'd been told by Cory and Danny, although he already knew. While he didn't agree with them, he deferred to their decision in an effort to keep the peace and show he would back his artists. Tom apologized and assured me he was grateful for all I'd done to keep the tour on track. He also said he would be happy to employ me on other tours as the need arose.

The following day I made my way to the airport and boarded my plane for the short flight back to Tulsa, where I was still living at the time. Other than talking with Jimmy Greenspoon every few years, I never spoke to any of the others again. Jimmy and Chuck have since sadly moved on to the big concert in the sky.

John Meglan, my old friend, brought Concerts West back in 1998, several years after they had first closed their doors. Concerts West was eventually bought out and became a division of AEG Presents and is now one of the two biggest promoters in the world. I am sure most of you recognize the name.

Though I never gave Three Dog Night another thought, I'm sorry the live entertainment industry has boiled down to just a few mega-promoters and not several dozen like the old days. Everything worked differently then. You'd get good promoters and bad promoters, which made every deal a crapshoot.

If the promoter was good, you made money and had a great backstage and full house. If the show was backed by a lame promoter, then the money was lame, the backstage was lame, and the ticket sales were lame. It was always different.

I am sure most of the big touring bands love the new system, as they know from the outset exactly how much money they will have when the tour is all over. Today's promoters will guarantee them very large amounts to do a set number of dates. They have done their homework and know exactly what they'll be banking. If you ever wonder why ticket prices have skyrocketed, you only need to look at the entities who organize these tours and sell the tickets—not necessarily the bands.

But then that is another book someone else is already writing, I am sure.

Three Dog Night 1981 US Tour Dates

June 11, 1981: Paramount Theatre (Portland, Oregon)

June 12, 1981: Paramount Theatre (Seattle, Washington)

June 13, 1981: Spokane Opera House (Spokane, Washington)

June 16, 1981: Rainbow Music Hall (Denver, Colorado)

June 19, 1981: Gammage Memorial Auditorium,
Arizona State University (Tempe, Arizona)

June 20, 1981: Plaza Theatre (El Paso, Texas)

June 21, 1981: Agora Ballroom (Dallas, Texas)

June 24, 1981: Agora Ballroom (Houston, Texas)

I left the tour after the Houston date, which was not my choice!

CHAPTER 13

Ozzy, Sharon, and Pookie Hit the Road

Better than Reality TV.

Somebody inside the bus yelled, "Get the gun!" and automatically several other members of the band yelled the same thing, "Yeah, get the gun!" But all of us knew we had no gun on board our bus. This was just a pathetic attempt to scare off the marauding hordes.

The bus was being banged, kicked, and rocked from one side to the other. Sharon Arden, Ozzy Osbourne's soon-to-be wife, and the wardrobe girl were screaming, and Pookie, the miniature yorkie that Sharon traveled with, had disappeared under someone's feet. Of course, the band, including Ozzy, would have been screaming as well except we'd look like sissies, and if we survived, none of us would ever live it down. Nevertheless, we, too, were frightened by the way the crowd had turned violent so quickly. We could hear glass being broken and metal being bent and smashed.

Looking back, the scene was very scary. We were trapped in that bus. What would have happened if they'd breached the door or windows and gained entrance? Stripped naked and beaten to a pulp? Nice image.

This had gotten quickly out of hand. The bus was stuck and could not move for fear of running over someone. Ed Skillman, the driver and owner of the Entertainment Transportation bus company out of Pennsylvania, had done his best to maneuver away from what had started as a peaceful request for an autograph. This was outside the University of Michigan's Crisler Arena in Ann Arbor after Ozzy's show on May 31, 1982.

As always, we had waited at least thirty minutes or so after the encore for the cars in the parking lot to disperse enough for our bus to make a hasty departure and get us on the road to the next town. But as we drove up the long ramp from under the venue, we discovered the parking lot was still chock-full of cars also trying to make a hasty exit. No one was moving anywhere very fast.

Before the angry crowd gathered, a couple of girls came up to the door of the stopped bus and loudly asked if they could get an autograph from Ozzy. Someone opened the door slightly, was given a piece of paper by one of the fans, Ozzy signed it, the prized possession was handed back out to her, and the door was closed.

But suddenly there were several more knocks, and we quickly knew we should not have opened the door the first time. Realizing this was Ozzy's bus, dozens of other fans exiting the arena began gathering and demanding autographs. We crept along a few feet at a time, closely following the slow-moving parking lot traffic, but we were not going at a fast enough rate to stop the one hundred or so people who were now surrounding the beautiful virgin-white bus.

We closed the lounge curtain, so they could not see back into the bus. However, poor Ed had a ringside seat as he couldn't hide behind a curtain. When the calls for autographs were not answered, the requests instead became shouts of "Assholes!" and other foul names. The crowd had turned—the same crowd who only minutes before were screaming how much they loved Ozzy.

The shouts became louder with fists slamming into the outside of the bus. Then the crowd started pushing the bus, rocking it back and forth. Ed declared from the front that some fans had opened the engine compartment at the rear of the bus and were trying to bend off the engine cover, no easy feat. The sideview mirrors were broken.

Ed continued inching forward, hoping those in front would get out of the way, but the traffic kept us from making much progress. In the twenty minutes since we reached the top of the arena ramp, we had only gone maybe one hundred to two hundred feet. And the scene seemed to be escalating.

A member of our loyal road crew, who was beginning to load the equipment truck parked down at the base of the ramp, spied our bus still in the lot. Having thought we were already long gone, he was now seeing the bus surrounded by a screaming, violent mob. He quickly rounded up the rest of Ozzy's crew, several dozen, as well as the local workers and made straight for the bus. Together, they started busting heads.

While none of us wished to see anyone, especially our crew or ourselves injured, their arrival was like the cavalry had come to rescue us. Soon enough, the front of the bus was cleared of people. Ed then circumvented the stopped cars by driving over a curb and through a grassy area, honking the horn in hopes people would get out of our way. They did, and we were on the move and not stopping (we hoped).

Within a minute or two, we turned and went down the wrong side of a major street for a couple of blocks with cars pulling over or onto the median to avoid us. Finally, we passed all the slow-moving traffic and were away from the riot—alive and still clothed.

Now on our way to Ottawa, Canada, for the next show, we didn't stop to survey the bus for damage until we were quite a few miles down the freeway. The bus had taken a harsh beating, but everything could be repaired. We even spotted blood on the engine cover, which meant whoever did the deed hurt himself as well.

The following day, we got in touch with the crew and found out they were all right. They'd suffered a punch here and there, but no one was hurt. For the most part, they actually enjoyed the break from the routine. What a great crew they were to come to our rescue.

I joined Ozzy's team on April 5, 1982. I was at home in Tulsa a few months after leaving Three Dog Night's employment when the phone rang. In fact, the name of this book should be titled, *And the Phone Rang!* It was my good friend Jay Hagerman (again, thanks Jay) from Concerts West, which was promoting most of Ozzy's US dates.

I was sitting outside my house on the corner of Fifty-First Street and the freeway when he asked, "What are your doing right now?" I told him I was watering the lawn, and he said, No, I mean workwise?"

"Not a lot just now," I replied.

He asked if I'd heard of Ozzy Osbourne, and because of his mostly negative press from the last year, I told him I had. He said, "Would you be interested in managing the remainder of his tour?" Jay knew me well. He knew I was adaptable and could be flexible in any situation. He'd seen me in action with Eric Clapton on two different tours across the US.

Jay told me about the plane crash that had killed guitarist Randy Rhoads and what happened in the aftermath. In Sharon and Ozzy's opinion, tour manager Jake Duncan was to blame for allowing the bus driver to take anyone, much less any members of the band, up in a plane after being awake all night driving to their Florida location. Jay said they could not go on with Jake any longer. Besides the tragic accident, Sharon later offered that they felt he was not doing his advance job properly or efficiently.

Well, I had heard of Ozzy, knowing him from Black Sabbath and mostly from the recent press he'd generated after biting the head off a bat during a show in Des Moines in January 1982 and then urinating on the Alamo a month later. Ozzy was selling more tickets after every unintentional stunt he did because the media made a big deal out of them. Those antics just made more kids want to go see this crazy guy from England.

I agreed to take over the tour manager's role and flew to New York the next day, where the band was playing Madison Square Garden with a new guitarist. I attended the show and was amazed at the reception. After meeting Sharon, a preliminary deal on my employment was made, although I was told that the current tour manager did not know he was being replaced. What? I had to be low-key.

Brad Gillis was also there. A guitarist from San Francisco, he would eventually go on to find major success with Night Ranger. Brad was going to take over for the current guitarist, Bernie Tormé, who had done a few gigs filling in for Randy but wasn't seen as a good fit for the band. Unaware he was also being replaced, Bernie's last show would come five days later with Brad then taking over on April 13 in Binghamton, New York.

I would later learn, after a bus ride to the next hotel in Providence, Rhode Island, that Sharon wanted *me* to tell Jake he was being fired, and I had to also make sure to get his accounting books, receipts, and the advance work he'd already completed. The task was not a fun one, but to be honest, he was very nice about it. He said he understood and gave me all that was requested before saying goodbye to everyone and making a quiet exit back to Scotland. Jake has gone on to enjoy a long career in the music business, working with artists such as George Michael, the Cult, and Oasis. I slotted right in, and within a few weeks, once it became evident I was going to get along with everyone and knew my job well, I was given a sizable raise.

Not long after I started—maybe even the first date, for all I know—I was called to the arena early by one of the production managers. We had two at the time, John "Bugzee" Hougdahl and Rob Cowlyn, both top-notch in the industry. I was told there were some people who wanted to speak with me. I made my way to the arena and was directed to some gentlemen wearing suits and ties. Seems they were from the Society for the Prevention of Cruelty to Animals (SPCA) and wanted my assurances that there would be no animals used in the show or harmed in any way. Seems Ozzy had a reputation, though mostly unfounded, for biting the heads off critters.

To be honest, while Ozzy thought the bat was a toy prop, he did once purposely bite the head off a dove, and there is a composite of four photos showing him in the act. I was told that in 1981, the CBS record company was hosting Ozzy at its annual sales convention. Evidently, he got annoyed with a PR woman on hand, so he grabbed one of the doves that was to be used during a speech he was scheduled to give. The woman's expression turned from amused to aghast when she realized Ozzy had put the dove's head in his mouth and pulled apart the body. One photo shows a drop of blood falling from his lip as he spits the head out. But to my knowledge, that is the only thing he ever decapitated intentionally.

I assured the SPCA that there were no animals in the arena and showed them around to boost their confidence. I also told them all that talk was rubbish and was only a story that got out of hand, sadly becoming a legend. This was a tour-manager duty I'd not imagined.

I must admit I met with what seemed like one hundred SPCA people across America as well as several RSPCA (Royal Society for the Prevention of Cruelty to Animals) workers in the UK when we performed there. These encounters happened at least once or twice a week.

Regardless, the band was great, and the shows always sold out. This was a massive production and took a sizable crew to set it all up. There was even a little person named John Edward Allen, who toured with the crew and took Ozzy his drinks on stage. Known as "Ronnie the Dwarf," he'd be hung (with a harness under his robe) high in the Gothic arch above the drummer, usually during the song "Goodbye to Romance." Showbiz? Probably couldn't get away with that today.

Ozzy and Sharon had come up with a lot of interesting ideas for these tours and another, which I'm glad I missed, was the flinging of animal entrails into the audience. Not surprisingly, this activity was not taken to kindly by fans as often the previously frozen guts were not always thawed properly, and some people got whacked with hard pieces, not to mention the blood from said flying liver, kidneys, etc. I was told what really stopped the continuation of this stunt was when the crowd started throwing the gross entrails back onstage at Ozzy and the band. The meat was slimy and, well, not as funny as intended once they got a taste of their own theatrical medicine.

Except for the scary exit from Ann Arbor as cited at the beginning of this chapter, riding the bus was usually a lot of fun. There was always a drink or two and videos to watch. I think Ozzy sat through *The Thin Red Line* two dozen times. But usually after a show, when everyone was still riled up from the event and we were headed down the road, the bus would often start to get very funny. Setting Sharon off normally didn't take much. She would start to snicker or giggle at something someone said or maybe something she remembered, and then we were off and laughing. Her laughter was contagious. Quite literally, this could go on for half an hour or more until we were aching or she said, "I peed myself." It was fun—always.

Bus life was okay. Yes, I had been spoiled by private planes and trains, but I discovered that once I was on the bus after a show, for the ensuing hours it took to drive to the next city, I could relax and not worry about where anyone was or what trouble they might be getting into. They were all on the bus with me until we reached our destination. We'd normally arrive in the early morning hours or at daybreak and go to a previously arranged hotel, much like I did with Eric and the Bee Gees. There would be keys in envelopes, and everyone would take their day bag with them and off they'd go.

I was usually able to grab a few extra hours of sleep at the hotel, having already had a couple in my bunk on the bus. I'd wake up and take a shower, send out laundry sometimes, iron the day's clothes, and then get a bit of a meal, all before heading to the venue for the sound check. We usually ate dinner there with the crew, which was nice as it saved spending per diem money, another difference from the Clapton tours.

With the Bee Gees, Ozzy, and really most big tours, the staff, crew, and band got per diems. In 1982, I think we got thirty-five dollars a day or thereabout, so the less you spent of your allowance, the larger the paycheck felt at the end of the week.

I was able to save enough per diem on one tour to buy my wife a high quality one-carat diamond through a dealer I knew in Austria. During another, I got my wife a heart-shaped sapphire in Thailand, which I had made into a beautiful cross that she wears to this day.

In general, the money situation with Ozzy was quite like other tours. If it had to get done, it had to get done, no matter the price or effort. We had concerts to put on, and we did everything possible to make sure that happened. A few Ozzy shows were canceled, and often the reason had to do with too much alcohol too early in the evening for the main man. That would cause a cancellation when a death threat would not—odd that!

Sharon was great to travel with and work for if you were on her team. She grew up as the daughter of a rather infamous British music manager, Don Arden. He worked with Electric Light Orchestra, Black Sabbath, and Air Supply, among others, many of whom discovered they were broke or in debt when their time in the spotlight was over. Meanwhile, Don was still standing rather well off. And it seems Sharon learned how to wheel and deal with the best of them. *Just don't cross her,* was what I kept in mind.

There were several times when I received a call from the sound or lighting company claiming they had not been paid for several weeks, and that if she did not pay immediately, they'd pull their gear off the tour. We're talking about a sound system or a lighting rig, neither of which would be easy to quickly replace. I'd let her know about these calls, and she'd tell me she'd take care of the problem. I then had to try to convince the company that she was getting them the money right away, knowing full well the payment would happen in her own time.

Once she had a disagreement of some kind with the trucking company we had transporting our equipment. I think we had six or seven semis. Sharon called to tell me that after the trucks had unloaded the gear for that evening's show and the drivers had left to go to their hotel and sleep, another trucking company she'd hired was going to show up and move the trailers. When the drivers then came back later that night for load out, this new company's trucks would be in their place, and the old group would be told to hit the road. You did not cross her.

On our way to Japan for some shows, Ozzy and Sharon decided to get married in Hawaii. We were to do a concert in Honolulu and then move to a Maui resort for a week's break before heading to Asia. This was a great perk for the band and crew who got to go along. The wedding, which was to take place on July 4 at the resort, would be held on the beach at sunset with a luau prepared for the reception.

Together with Sharon, I helped make the arrangements. We wanted a band of sorts for entertainment, so the hotel catering manager gave me some names of local bands to contact. Although most of them had gigs already booked for the Fourth or were taking the holiday off, I finally found a Hawaiian-style group that played some cover material as well as a lot of island music—Don Ho and the like. They had a show earlier in the day at another hotel, but for five hundred dollars, they would come play our reception for two hours or so. They didn't care who it was for, I realized.

Sharon and her dad didn't speak for a long period of time, due in part to Sharon taking over as Ozzy's manger after Don had fired him from Black Sabbath. But she invited her mother and father, who surprisingly agreed to fly from Los Angeles to Maui for the event. The day before the wedding, I was summoned up to Don's suite. I'd never met the man, and for all I knew, he and Sharon were still not on good terms. Don asked me to go over the wedding and reception arrangements as well as the costs involved.

Everything seemed all right until I reported on the band and what their price tag would be. Don told me he wanted the band to drop their fee. Didn't they know whose wedding this was? The press they'd receive? The additional gigs they could get? I told him how many others I'd reached out to and that no one else was interested or could make it. This was the only band on Maui. I was told to try anyway.

I went to my room and, bolstered by the wrath of Don Arden, called and asked the band to lower their price for the event, citing the reasons Don offered. Their answer was, "No, we'd rather go home." Don didn't like to lose a money challenge, but in this case (and maybe with Sharon's intervention), we paid the five hundred dollars.

On July 3, we had a bachelor party, and there is a blurry drunken photo of a passed-out Ozzy to prove it hanging on the wall in my office. The wives and girlfriends who came to Hawaii with the band and crew also had a hen party with Sharon, but of that I know nothing.

If you are wondering why there are no videos of the special nuptials, only a photo or two, the reason is that video recorders were still relatively new to the general consumer. And though we purchased one for the occasion, Sharon assumed the best person to video the event was the tour's lighting designer, Paul Dexter. She gave him the camera and a tape to practice with. For a whole day, Paul went around videoing everything, checking the clarity and focus because he wanted to make the best possible video for her and Ozzy. Paul is a great lighting designer and had been on the tour for a couple of years at this point.

The day after the wedding, Sharon invited Paul and a few other people up to the newlyweds' suite to view the previous evening's vows and festivities. But when they put the video in the VCR and pushed play, nothing but snow appeared across the television screen. Paul checked connections and jiggled wires but still nothing. Then came the most tragic and funny revelation: Paul had filmed the entire event, or so he thought, with no videotape in the camera.

Though obviously shocked, Ozzy and Sharon saw the hilarity in it, and like me on the Bee Gees tour forgetting the blind keyboard player George Bitzer, it took a while for Paul to live this down. But he got to keep his job and ended up working with Ozzy for several more years. I'm sure whenever they meet, they have a good laugh about it.

I had an embarrassing experience during the wedding as well. I had made and oversaw many of the day's arrangements, including periodically watching the pig roasting on the open fire. When the guys who were cooking took it off the rotisserie and began slicing the meat, I brazenly asked if I might have a small taste. One of the fellows took a piece of the roasted pig off the table, handed it to me, and I popped it in my mouth. The bite was delicious, and I swallowed with satisfaction.

The Hawaiians cooking the pig all burst into laughter. Then I realized they were laughing at me. After some coaxing, I discovered they had evidently fed me the sphincter of the pig that had just come off the spit. Nice one guys . . . although it was tasty!

With the wedding behind us, we all were looking forward to two weeks in Japan. We were greeted at the airport by Tack Takahashi, a member of Seijiro Udo's staff, and were treated like royalty. They always made the visiting bands and crew feel so welcome and special. Udo Artists was Japan's largest rock-and-roll promoter, and they had touring in that country down to a fine art.

Their attention to detail made the experience much more enjoyable for everyone. Even our crew had their own Japanese version of themselves as none of our guys spoke the language. Plus, working with the local unions and venue people was mandatory.

In Japan, the shows started at 6:30 p.m., so many in the audience came directly from their work. This was a bit odd as most often there was no opening act, meaning the show would be over by 8:00, and we'd sometimes be back at the hotel and usually in the bar by 8:30. This led to more than the normal amount of alcohol being consumed. Timing is everything.

The logistical coordination was exact. We traveled between cities on the bullet train, and when a Japanese tour manager said to stand in a certain place on the platform, you stood there. And darned if the train door didn't stop right in front of you. One thing we never figured out was how the fans, mostly girls, we waved goodbye to on the platform in Tokyo, for example, were waiting for us on the next platform in Osaka, 246 miles away. We were traveling on the fastest mode of transportation in the country. It may seem impossible, but it's true.

There was a particularly interesting event that happened one special evening. Mr. Udo invited all the band members, Sharon, and me to dinner at a Kobe beef restaurant he owned. We were all flattered, having secretly hoped he'd ask us out. This kind of meal in Japan was extremely expensive, a meal none of us would have considered paying for ourselves.

Everyone dressed up a bit more than normal, and we were shuttled by waiting cars from the Capitol Hotel Tokyu, one Udo frequently used for his artists when in Tokyo, to a colorful part of the city where his restaurant was located. The establishment was upstairs, but down on the street were neon signs and people everywhere. Japan is a unique place to visit that I'd recommend to anyone.

We were seated, Japanese style, in a large private room—shoes off, legs crossed, and all facing each other in a big square. We ordered sake and beers but let Mr. Udo order the food for us. Again, this was Kobe beef, where the cows are supposedly fed beer and are massaged during their lives, which is supposed to make the meat especially tender, which it was.

The first course of miso soup and a small cucumber-and-seaweed salad was nice. Then the beef, which was cut into long thin strips and marbleized perfectly, was brought out and cooked there in front of us. Slices were placed on everyone's plates, and a nod was given for us to begin. It was magical. The beef was wonderful, the sake was great, and everyone seemed to be having the meal of a lifetime. That is until Mr. Udo asked a brooding Ozzy, "What is the matter? Is it not to your liking?" To which Ozzy replied, "No, I am sure it's fine, but I'm a vegetarian."

Everyone around the table dropped their forks, er, chopsticks and stared dumbfounded at Ozzy for having made such a bizarre comment to such an elegant host. Of course, he was not a vegetarian, but for some reason Ozzy didn't want to participate in the dinner and chose this way to make his feelings known. Only Sharon matched Mr. Udo's face in embarrassed redness. She glared at Ozzy as if she would poke his eyes out with her chopsticks if he said another word.

After looking around the table in amazement at what had just happened, the rest of us finished our meals, probably had an extra sake, and thanked Mr. Udo for a most wonderful and gracious supper. Ozzy, well, I'm not sure what happened when they got back to the hotel, but it wouldn't surprise me if there was a quick uppercut from his wife, putting Ozzy to sleep, Japanese style, on the floor.

Ozzy Osbourne 1982 *Diary of a Madman* Tour Dates

April 5, 1982: Madison Square Garden (New York, New York)

April 6, 1982: Providence Civic Center (Providence, Rhode Island)

April 9, 1982: Buffalo Memorial Auditorium (Buffalo, New York)

April 10, 1982: Rochester Community War Memorial (Rochester, New York)

April 13, 1982: Broome County Veterans Memorial Arena (Binghamton, New York)

April 15, 1982: Allen County War Memorial Coliseum (Fort Wayne, Indiana)

April 16, 1982: Roberts Municipal Stadium (Evansville, Indiana)

April 17, 1982: Freedom Hall (Louisville, Kentucky)

April 19, 1982: Roanoke Civic Center (Roanoke, Virginia)

April 20, 1982: Baltimore Civic Center (Baltimore, Maryland)

April 21, 1982: Richmond Coliseum (Richmond, Virginia)

April 23, 1982: Freedom Hall Civic Center (Johnson City, Tennessee)

April 24, 1982: Capital Centre (Landover, Maryland)

April 25, 1982: Baltimore Civic Center (Baltimore, Maryland)

April 26, 1982: The Spectrum (Philadelphia, Pennsylvania)

April 28, 1982: Mid-South Coliseum (Memphis, Tennessee)

April 29, 1982: Nashville Municipal Auditorium (Nashville, Tennessee)

April 30, 1982: Greensboro Coliseum (Greensboro, North Carolina)

May 1, 1982: Cumberland County Crown Arena (Fayetteville, North Carolina)

May 3, 1982: Nassau Coliseum (Uniondale, New York)

May 5, 1982: Fairgrounds Coliseum (Columbus, Ohio)

May 10, 1982: Glens Falls Civic Center (Glens Falls, New York)

May 20, 1982: Hartford Civic Center (Hartford, Connecticut)

May 21, 1982: Hartford Civic Center (Hartford, Connecticut)

May 22, 1982: Cumberland County Civic Center (Portland, Maine)

May 23, 1982: Brendan Byrne Arena (East Rutherford, New Jersey)

May 25, 1982: Fairgrounds Coliseum (Columbus, Ohio)

May 26, 1982: Hara Arena (Dayton, Ohio)

May 27, 1982: Prairie Capital Convention Center (Springfield, Illinois)

May 28, 1982: Poplar Creek Music Theater (Hoffman Estates, Illinois)

May 29, 1982: Alpine Valley Music Theatre (East Troy, Wisconsin)

May 30, 1982: Castle Farms Music Theater (Charlevoix, Michigan)

May 31, 1982: Crisler Arena, University of Michigan (Ann Arbor, Michigan)

June 2, 1982: Ottawa Civic Centre (Ottawa, Ontario)

June 3, 1982: Montreal Forum (Montreal, Quebec)

June 4, 1982: Maple Leaf Gardens (Toronto, Ontario)

June 6, 1982: Winnipeg Arena (Winnipeg, Manitoba)

June 8, 1982: Northlands Coliseum (Edmonton, Alberta)

June 9, 1982: Stampede Corral (Calgary, Alberta)

June 10, 1982: Pacific Coliseum (Vancouver, British Columbia)

June 13, 1982: West Anchorage High School Auditorium (Anchorage, Alaska)

June 14, 1982: West Anchorage High School Auditorium (Anchorage, Alaska)

June 15, 1982: Seattle Center Coliseum (Seattle, Washington)

June 16, 1982: Spokane Coliseum (Spokane, Washington)

June 17, 1982: Portland Memorial Coliseum (Portland, Oregon)

June 19, 1982: Oakland Coliseum (Oakland, California)

June 22, 1982: Centennial Coliseum (Reno, Nevada)

June 23, 1982: Irvine Meadows Amphitheatre (Irvine, California)

June 24, 1982: San Diego Sports Arena (San Diego, California)

June 28, 1982: Honolulu International Center (Honolulu, Hawaii)

July 9, 1982: Festival Hall (Osaka, Japan)

July 11, 1982: Nagoya-shi Kokaido (Nagoya, Japan)

July 13, 1982: Kyoto Kaikan (Kyoto, Japan)

July 14, 1982: Nakano Sunplaza (Tokyo, Japan)

July 15, 1982: Nakano Sunplaza (Tokyo, Japan)

August 7, 1982: Cotton Bowl (Dallas, Texas)

August 8, 1982: Tad Gormley Stadium (New Orleans, Louisiana)

CHAPTER 14

Bark at the Moon

Without a Dog.

After returning in mid-July from Japan, which I'd discovered was always fun because the culture is so very different from the American and British ways of life, we had some well-deserved time off. I know I did, but darn, the band and crew had been on the road much longer than I had prior to the plane crash.

It was a bittersweet pill I had to digest, taking over for the person who bore much of the blame for the crash and ultimate deaths of the great guitar player Randy Rhoads, whom I never got to meet, as well as Sharon's good friend, traveling companion, and band seamstress Rachael Youngblood. Being there as it happened must have been a tragedy.

We were off for about six weeks, and being home was nice, albeit sad because Eric Clapton's Tulsa group was no longer his band, and Carl was gone. However, I made the best of being home and enjoyed not having to meet with police or SPCA agents all the time.

On August 5, 1982, I traveled to Dallas a bit early to see my family and check out the setup for the Super Bowl of Rock N Roll concert at the Cotton Bowl that would be held two nights later. After I checked into my room at the Anatole Hotel, I got a call from Sharon, who was in the UK. It seems she and Ozzy had gone through a "bloody great row," and he had left the house. The following day, before boarding the Concorde for their flight to the US, she called me back and said that Ozzy had come home, but he had shaved off all his hair!

I wanted to burst out laughing, just picturing a pudgy Ozzy with a bald head jumping around on stage. Sharon, I could tell, was about to get a good set of the giggles as well, but she had to stay calm and did her best.

Maybe Ozzy was close by? She then proceeded to ask if I could find a place to buy a wig, sort of dirty-blonde in appearance to match Ozzy's hair. Another odd request of a tour manager but all in a day's work with Ozzy. Never a dull moment.

I really did not know where to go, but I was always up for a challenge, and this would be a good one. It was a Saturday, and back then no place was open that I was aware of, except maybe one of the many odd shops in downtown Dallas. So off I went in search of a wig. It still is rather funny.

After a couple of disillusioning stops, I stumbled across a store on Elm Street, which back them was still a rather questionable area, especially on weekends. It was before noon, and there lining one long wall were Styrofoam heads with wigs on them. And they weren't too expensive. I looked around, and sure enough, on a smiling plastic head was a dirty-blonde wig, which I felt looked as if it were Ozzy's color. I bought two of them in case of any mistakes. I had no idea how long he was going to wear a wig.

The next morning, the day of the show, Ozzy, Sharon, and guitar tech Pete Mertons arrived at the Dallas Fort Worth Airport via New York City. I was there to meet them in a van, as they never traveled with less than eight to ten suitcases. Pete rode up front with me while Ozzy and Sharon sat in the farthest rear seat. I could see Ozzy in the rearview mirror, and he had on a wooly beanie cap, covering his bald head, and sunglasses.

It was extremely hard not to burst out laughing, and we couldn't make it back to the hotel without a few "verbal snickers," which did not make Mr. O too jovial. He didn't see the humor, although I'm sure he was sorry he'd done something so spontaneous and irreversible. Once he disappeared after another row with Sharon and returned sporting the very sizable demon tattoo on the right side of his shoulder and chest.

We made it back to the hotel and up to their suite, having only a few hours before we had to be at the Cotton Bowl, as we were opening for Loverboy and Foreigner. We started chopping at the wigs trying to get them to resemble Ozzy's hair as the shave had been less than forty-eight hours earlier. Finally, we got one that looked very good. It was difficult to tell if it was a wig from a distance, though up close, wigs never look the least bit real.

Nevertheless, we headed to the Cotton Bowl with the entire band and went straight to our dressing room. The band was snickering as well.

Despite Ozzy having the wig on, when the crew would stop in, they, too, had to try their best to keep from bursting out.

The band before us finished, and our crew got Ozzy's gear and stage set for the performance. We were all curious if the wig would slip during the show, or if it would go without a hitch and no one would notice. Well, the time had come for Ozzy to perform, and the band gathered around him. He kept his head down on his way to the stage and up the stairs. At the side of the stage, he stood gazing at the eighty thousand people or so, and I am sure he was nervous—probably more than he'd been in a long time.

The band launched into the opening song, "Crazy Train," and Ozzy ran out on stage to cheers and screaming as usual. Then just as suddenly as he'd decided to shave his head, I'm sure, he grabbed his wig, ripped it from his bald head, and threw it into the crowd. All eighty thousand went bananas. We were stunned. Not that he did it, I don't think, but that the wig only lasted for less than a minute. All in all, it was funny.

Needless to say, camera flashes were extremely abundant, providing photos for publishing in upcoming trade papers. And like biting the bat or urinating on the Alamo, his bald head probably got him huge publicity and sold more tickets. Ozzy always had a way of coming out smelling like roses, and I'm sure Sharon's name was included somewhere.

We did four more US dates through the end of September, including a pair of performances at the Ritz in New York City that were recorded for the live album *Speak of the Devil,* and then took a few weeks off. Another well-deserved rest after only a few shows, but we had a long run coming up. Sharon was always one to make the most of a good thing while it was still good.

It was during this break that bassist Rudy Sarzo left to rejoin Quiet Riot, his former band. Their *Mental Health* album, which came out in March 1983, was a huge success. We had a bit of time, so ever-clever Sharon and Ozzy got on the phone and convinced Pete Way, former bassist of the band UFO, to join us for several shows.

In early December, we set out for some UK dates before Christmas in support of the *Speak of the Devil* album, except this time Sharon would not be accompanying us on the tour as she was pregnant with their first child. Mind you, it did not slow her down. We were in touch daily, and she never missed a beat. She even joined us here and there, as I recall.

All went as usual, including meeting with the RSPCA. Never mess with an animal as these people take their jobs very seriously! I ran into the animal protection people throughout my time with Ozzy and very often dealt with the police when people would send in messages threatening to harm or kill Ozzy on stage because of his outrageous actions. Some of these threats were very concerning, but Ozzy was a trooper and never canceled a show for this reason. His comment to me was always, "Well, I hope they take me down with the first shot as I'd hate to lie there wounded, writhing around on the stage in pain." Wow! Some of these threats scared even me, and I was not the target.

A show at the Royal Court Theatre in Liverpool on December 20 marked our final date of the year, and the concert went well. While Ozzy and Sharon then headed off to their home in a chauffeured car, I rode on the crew bus back to London. Prior to leaving Liverpool, someone decided they'd had enough of John, the little person who had been on the whole US tour and the UK leg as well. He was nice, but he drank way too much, especially for someone his size, and too often became a pain.

So one of the crew told the driver of our private tour bus to stop at a roundabout in Liverpool, and a couple of people carried John off the bus, set him and his luggage in the grassy middle of the roundabout, and off we drove with him cursing and screaming. That was the last time I ever saw John. I don't think anyone laughed at the time or ever mentioned his name again.

We returned for a night at a nice hotel in London before the Americans headed back to the US for Christmas. Surprisingly, that evening while producer Rob Cowlyn and I were sitting in my room having a drink, the concierge delivered two packages, one for me and one for Rob. They were gifts from Sharon and Ozzy. She gave me a very nice designer winter jacket, and Rob got a bottle of thirty-year-old (or so) brandy, which he told me he collected. I didn't know, but Sharon did. What a nice gift I received, though. I must admit I was thrilled. And I still have the jacket.

Our return after the holidays, still without Sharon, found us in Helsinki on January 12, opening a European tour for Whitesnake because over there they were bigger than Ozzy. Still, I think most of the audience came to see the Ozzman anyway. I had already been through many of those cities before, and while not new to visit, culturewise, I always had a good time and always saw something different and noteworthy. The tour was a success, no doubt.

We did thirteen shows in Europe, although not all with Whitesnake since we had pockets where we could fill a decent-sized venue alone. They had a stage manager, Steve Payne, who was a tough nut back then, but he became a great friend to me years later and, I am happy to say, is still after all these eons later.

(As a side note, Rudy Sarzo, who'd already left to go with Quiet Riot, and Ozzy's drummer Tommy Aldridge would eventually join a new incarnation of Whitesnake with David Coverdale in 1987.)

Following the show in Helsinki and some time spent back at the hotel bar, I had turned in for the night. Suddenly, my phone rang. It was a call from Rob, who was no longer on the tour and was still in the States. He was now the production manager for Diana Ross, having toured with her previously.

He asked me if I'd like to be their tour manager or some job similar, but I had heard enough stories about how her tours were and the strict rules involved, so I decided to stick it out with Ozzy. The money was very good, and there seemed to be an endless supply of dates ahead for him while Ms. Ross was only doing three months or so. I still believe I made the right decision, though some people might argue otherwise.

Anyhow, while I was bleary-eyed and a bit tipsy—all right, very tipsy—Rob proceeded to tell me that Sharon had contacted him and asked him to speak with me. She wanted him to tell me I was blowing my gig, as I was imbibing too much too often. That sobered me right up. We talked for a while, and I explained, trying to justify my drinking too much, that I was going through a rough spell in my personal life at home. Regardless, I was grateful to Rob for his honesty and concern, and I took note to make obvious changes. I did not quit drinking, but I sure as heck cut way back and made sure I left the bar earlier than ever before. Thanks, Rob!

During the break, Brad Gillis left to rejoin his band in the Bay Area, Night Ranger, who had an album (*Midnight Madness*) come out later in 1983 that made them a success as well. And we had to now find a new bassist because Pete did not really fit Ozzy's style, and they wanted new blood, so to speak. That left the band with Ozzy at the lead, Tommy on drums, and Don Airey on keyboards. We needed two new members.

A friend of Ozzy and Sharon's, bass player Dana Strum, had a few recommendations, and we all met up in Los Angeles at SIR Rehearsal Studios on Sunset Boulevard, set for an evening of auditions. There were several guitar players, maybe six, and all were pretty darn good. But when it came down to it, the one who seemed the most natural and fluid and had a good look to go with the rest of the band, was Jakey Lou Williams. We had a brief confab—Sharon, Ozzy, Tommy, Don, and me—and all agreed. The other potential guitarists were in the green room and were told they could go home while Sharon made Jake an offer.

Not only was it a heck of a great deal for Ozzy, but Sharon also suggested Jakey needed a better stage name, and they came up with Jake E. Lee. Fine with the financial offer and name change, wham, bam, he was our new lead guitar player.

Then it was time for bass. There were fewer bass players, maybe three. I'm not sure if they played solo while we sat and watched, or if they played along to some of Ozzy's tracks, but one fellow stood out as being Ozzy material. His name was Don Costa. He had the look, and, come to find out, Don had a lot more than just the look. He often had a cheese grater taped to his bass and would nick his fingers to cause them to bleed, so he would look a bit, well, more out there for a rock and roller. Sharon said that would not be necessary, like the rest of us, finding it a bit odd. Later in his stint with Ozzy, we'd find out more idiosyncrasies of Don's, but I'll save that for later.

Don was offered the same deal as Jake and took the job. To this day, I am still surprised that Sharon got away with the meager amount she offered these new band members. I'd venture to say their pay was no more than half what the least crew member was being paid weekly. But Sharon is a magician in many ways.

Regardless, we now had a new band, and rehearsals began in order to get these two newbies up to speed. And by newbies, I do mean youngsters compared to Ozzy, Tommy, Me, Don, and even Sharon, though she was still young.

After rehearsals and a short break, we were set to begin a US tour, which was scheduled to last about two months. It was February, and we started in Syracuse, where the weather was cold and snowy. We had a few all-night drives, and it was a bit concerning; however, our bus driver and owner of the company, Ed Skillman, was a very safe driver. We had no problems, thank God.

At one point, we were down south somewhere and had two days off, so Ozzy and I traveled to the Bahamas to check out Compass Point Studios for Ozzy's next album. Beautiful, right on the water, great view, and Iron Maiden, whose members were friends of Ozzy's, was currently recording an album there. He told Sharon the place would be ideal, so she booked it.

We continued with the tour, SPCA, police, and visits from the FBI to share less-than-welcome news also thrown in. Thankfully, all went well, and no one was hurt . . . yet.

Along the way, Jay Hagerman, the Concerts West representative, and I flew to Louisiana for a night to check out an upcoming outdoor date at the Baton Rouge State Fairgrounds. The next day, we met the event promoter at the proposed site and found it to be satisfactory, no problems. With that, Jay and I were off to the airport to meet back up with the band.

I remember the bus had driven from Tulsa about nine hours to the next stop in Biloxi, Mississippi, so not a real short drive. When Jay and I arrived at the hotel, though, we were met by someone from the band who told us there had been an altercation on the bus that previous night. As the story was told to me, Don Costa, the new bass player, and Ozzy were watching something on TV in the back lounge of the bus, which also served as Ozzy's bedroom when necessary. While chatting, Don tried to wrap his arms around Ozzy and kiss him, which, of course, no bat-biting, Alamo-urinating man would put up with. Ozzy whacked him a time or two across the face, putting a halt to any further advances, and then left the lounge.

I made my way to Don's room, and he had a black eye and very swollen lip. Sure enough, Ozzy had hit him. He tried to say the quarrel didn't happen, and since no one else was there, we only had Don's and Ozzy's stories to go on. Unfortunately, from then on it was a terrible feeling whenever the band was together backstage. We did manage to finish the remainder of the dates with Don keeping to himself and staying out of the dressing room, but when the final show was done, he was as well.

We traveled all the way to Austin, Texas, back up to Michigan, through parts of Canada, and then to New York, where we wrapped up the tour in

Glens Falls on April 5. We did thirty-six dates before taking nearly two months off.

On May 29, we were then set to play the US Festival in San Bernardino, California. For that concert, without Don on bass, Sharon and Ozzy brought in old friend, songwriter, and former Uriah Heep member Bob Daisley, who turned out to be a very nice guy.

We all met up in Los Angeles and stayed at the Beverly Hills Hotel, one of Sharon's favorites (and mine, I'll admit). That evening, a day or so before our date at the US Festival, Sharon said she was expecting a very large crate and a big box to arrive via air freight from the UK. She said they had a costume for Ozzy to wear on stage that was sure to get him a lot of press coverage.

I made several phone calls, finally tracked down the shipment, and arranged for the crate and box to be delivered to the hotel. At last, they arrived and were sitting in the Osbournes' suite. The crate was about five-and-a-half feet tall, the same widthwise, and around a foot thick. *Odd shaped,* I thought. I pried it apart with the help of Bobby Thompson, a beloved crew member and eventually Ozzy's tour manager after I left the organization.

Once opened, we discovered a gigantic headdress with a partial mask that covered the top of Ozzy's face, leaving his mouth free to sing. Ozzy put it on, and the feathers, about thirty-six inches long, nearly reached the high ceiling. The headdress was a mixture between a Native American look and something a witch doctor from the Amazon would wear, as it had a rubber bone through its nose. It was interesting but very outlandish.

In the accompanying box was an outfit with cloth fringe that looked straight out of an American Wild West image. The mask and costume didn't really go together, but then it wasn't my $10,000 that had been paid to make the press-grabbing pieces.

On the day of our show, we headed off to San Bernardino, checked into our hotel with all the other bands who were staying for the night, and then gathered in the lobby for the ride to the festival. We were scheduled to go on in the late afternoon, not after dark, which would have been better.

We arrived through a crowd of about two hundred thousand people and went to our dressing rooms. Sharon and I mingled with promoters and other bands, and we had a nice visit until it was time to prepare for Ozzy's time slot on stage.

Ozzy, Sharon, and an assistant went to the dressing room to help him get his outfit ready. The headdress was waiting at the side of the stage in its crate for a quick put-on before he went out to face the crowd. I remember it being a bit top-heavy.

So up the stairs the band went, taking the stage to huge applause and launching into the beginning song of the hour set. Out of sight at the side of the stage, Bobby and the crew helped Ozzy on with his headdress. Next thing you know, he ran on stage as he always did, back and forth, goading the roaring audience. The mask was getting a lot of attention, except suddenly he yanked the headpiece off and tossed it, not into the crowd this time (as it was damn expensive), but to the wings of the stage. He then carried on with the song and set.

Of course, everything went smoothly, but I don't believe Sharon was too thrilled at having spent so much for a minute or two of the headdress visualization. If you go to YouTube and watch the video of Ozzy at the last US Festival in 1983, you'll see the headdress for a few moments but don't blink or you'll miss it!

We drove back to Los Angeles the next day and were waiting in the airport lobby for everyone to gather when Ozzy came up wearing a beautiful red-leather jacket he bought from Fred Segal or somewhere posh. It was nice. Then, not five minutes later, Bob, the new bass player and Ozzy's friend for years, arrived wearing the exact same leather jacket.

It was too coincidental, but it *was* a coincidence. Ozzy immediately took off his jacket and handed it to me, saying, "You want this? I decided I don't want it anymore." You bet I took it, and, yes, it's still in my closet to this day. I've worn it a few times but not much. Funny what money will cause you to do. Bob had no idea Ozzy had that jacket but bought it himself because he liked it.

We boarded the plane in LA and flew to New York City, where the band rehearsed and prepared for recording its new album in the Bahamas. I was packed for a summer in the Caribbean, and so was everyone else.

In the same hotel was the band AC/DC, who was in New York as well, rehearsing for a tour or album. They were friends with our band and Ozzy, which made for some great bar visits and stories. They seemed very likeable and genuine.

About three or four days into rehearsals at the SIR Studios there, Sharon called me and said Ozzy had changed his mind and wanted to return to Ridge Farm Studio in Surrey, England, to work on the album—the place where he had last recorded with Randy Rhodes. He and I had flown to Nassau to check out Compass Point Studios. *What a great place to spend the summer,* I remember thinking. Ozzy loved it as well.

Now that was all off. Suddenly, we were no longer going to be recording in paradise but instead in the UK. And there was nothing I could do about it. I was given the task of rearranging everything, which Sharon and her UK office had not yet started on, so I spoke with the travel agent and got the flights changed. After about three weeks of rehearsing, once the band felt they had enough new songs and were ready to start recording, we then hopped on a plane and flew to London.

Tommy, Bobby, and I stayed in a flat on Gloucester Road, which was all right, while the band did some last-minute polishing of the songs to be recorded. One morning, Sharon phoned me and said to go pick up a car at the Godfrey Davis car rental that she had reserved for us, and she sent me Ozzy's, or rather John Osbourne's, credit card to pay for it.

So Bobby and I went to the London Victoria railway station. I needed him to drive since I'd never driven in London before, sadly or gratefully. We entered the car rental office and were greeted by a beautiful lady in a bright orange uniform. "How can I help you?" she asked. I had on a Hawaiian shirt and sunglasses, and she immediately clocked me as another loud American tourist. I explained we had a car reserved, a Ford Granada, for the entire summer.

She was gone for a few minutes, and when she came back, she was in an even worse mood, I felt. They were out of the Granada-rate cars, and the manager said they'd have to give me a BMW 7 Series, a nice, bright burgundy luxury sedan with leather seats and a sunroof. And even better, we'd have it all summer at the same rate as the Granada. Wow! We scored big time!

There was something else that had caught my eye there at the car rental, but I wasn't sure what it was. However, we were out of there once the car came up. On the way back to our flat, though, I realized the lady who waited on us was damned attractive, and I wanted to ask her out. Yes, she was my type.

After having broken up with my girlfriend of a number of years before going on tour again, I'd decided I would not fall in love with anyone unless they were royalty or an heiress or a famous actress who made lots of money and could take care of me in the manner I desired. Yes, I know that was very self-centered of me, but considering my job and the people I often met in that position, it was not something impossible to achieve.

So over the next two weeks, we rehearsed every day (except weekends) at Nomis Studios. We drove the Beamer daily and had a great time. One Sunday, we decided the car was dirty and needed a wash, and as they didn't have coin car washes in England like in the US, I thought, *Let's go back to the car place where we got it. Godfrey Davis! Surely, they must wash their cars.*

We got there midafternoon, and the attractive lady offered to take the car downstairs and have it washed for us. While she was gone, I asked one of her associates if this beautiful woman was attached and was told no. OK, good so far! Then I asked if her friend might go out with me. The girl said, "I don't know. You'll have to ask her yourself."

When the car came back up, I checked with her to make sure I wasn't missing anything, and then as we drove around the block, I saw a phone booth. I yelled, "Stop!" I got out, called the car rental place, and asked for this lady. She came on the phone with a beautiful, classy accent, and I introduced myself. Since John Osbourne was the credit card I'd used, as directed by Sharon, I said I was John and asked her out for Wednesday. To my amazement, she said yes.

I suggested we maybe have dinner and go dancing, and I got her phone number. This was a good sign, although I'd forgotten about the royalty or financial needs I was after.

I picked Vivienne up in a taxi, and we went to Mr. Chow on Knightsbridge. (You who know Mr. Chow will know it's the best place to go in LA, New York, or London.) Then after a great meal and nice conversation, we headed to Stringfellows Covent Garden, the most happening disco in town in those days. After a few dances—which neither of us were too fond of, I later discovered—we hailed a cab to take her home. On the way back,

I asked her out for Friday night and suggested we go somewhere she'd never been.

To my jaw-dropping amazement, Vivienne said, "I've never been to Paris." Oh, shit. Now I was in for it. But it could have been worse. She might have said no!

So on Friday, I took her to Paris, where we stayed at the Concorde La Fayette, a very nice hotel. I even got her a separate room. For two whole days, we walked the streets and held hands and fell madly in love. We even went to the Louvre Museum, and I think we passed the *Mona Lisa*, but we were more interested in each other. To make a great story even greater, when we married, we went to Rome on our honeymoon. It's been forty-one years, and Vivienne and I now have four grown children and four granddaughters.

After falling in love with both my lovely wife and Paris itself, it was back to Surrey, Ridge Farm, and recording the *Bark at the Moon* album. The band was Bob Daisley, who played bass and spent his days holed up writing lyrics, Tommy Aldridge on drums, Jake E. Lee the guitar player, and Don Airey on keyboards, in addition to Ozzy. I won't go into Bob's position in all this, but it was substantial. And he was a very nice fellow.

During that time spent recording, I stayed in the Granary, which was away from the main Ridge Farm house. It had two bedrooms, a large one for Ozzy and Sharon, who were newlyweds, and a small single bedroom for me. We ate most meals together, and there was a tennis court and a pool (but a bit too cold to swim). All in all, though somewhat run-down in appearance, the accommodations were nice. Even better, my English princess would come for visits, or I'd go into London to see her as often as possible.

I remember trying to go to sleep late at night, and in the studio across from the granary would be Jake playing guitar licks and often Ozzy singing. I wasn't getting much sleep as this would go on until the early hours of the morning. Jake and Ozzy would then sleep all day. I think Jake did this because he thought that's how you recorded an album—up all night.

One day I said something to him about the late-night noise, and suddenly he started screaming at me about he was the guitar player and that's when he played best. And besides, Ozzy liked it that way. I was put in my place by some young, smart-ass guitar player. Oh well, at least I was making ten or more times the money he was making, so his words didn't hurt too much.

Finally, summer came to an end, the recording was done, and Bobby was due to fly home to Los Angeles. Other than Billy Connolly, Bobby was the funniest Scotsman I knew. I got up early for some reason, went into the big house, and heard someone on the telephone. I rounded the corner and saw someone I did not recognize at first.

It was Bobby. His head had been mostly shaved, and his eyebrows were gone. Down the road was a pub where we'd often visit and have a pint or three, and he, Ozzy, and Jake went there the previous evening. It seems Ozzy or Jake had slipped a Valium or some downer into Bobby's beer, and while Bobby was passed out back at the studio, they shaved his head and eyebrows. Mind you, he hadn't seen his wife, who had stayed in LA, for three months. When he awoke, Bobby was so angry he wanted to choke the life out of both of them.

I got Bobby calmed down, helped him pack, and changed his flight to one leaving immediately for LA, so he could get out of there. I then gave him my Carrera sunglasses and drove him to Heathrow Airport. Ozzy, Sharon, and baby Amy were upstairs in the granary sleeping, and Jake . . . who cared where he was. Maybe I should have let Bobby throttle him?

I dropped Bobby off at Heathrow and drove back to the studio, where my princess was waiting. I said I was quitting, as you don't do that to your own. I then told Ozzy and Sharon. Ozzy reminded me that I helped shave promoter Erik Thomsen's hair once, but I always felt a huge guilt over participating in that. I said to Ozzy that I was wrong to do what I did, but I didn't do it to one of my own people and especially to one as kind and helpful as Bobby—and on the day he would see his wife after months away.

I packed my bags, left in the car with Vivienne, and got a hotel in London. I changed my flight for the next day and promised I'd send her a ticket to come to Dallas as soon as I was home. She probably didn't believe me and figured I was a typical male rat.

Despite all the turmoil, three interesting things happened. First and best, I found the woman with whom I'd spend the rest of my life and have a family. Secondly, Bobby Thompson ended up being apologized to and became Ozzy's tour manager. What? Though he deserved it since he didn't kill Ozzy. And finally, several years later, after being so mad at me for quitting when all that had happened, Sharon hired me to be the tour manager for one of the most fun and enjoyable bands I ever worked for. One that she managed—the Quireboys.

Ozzy Osbourne 1982-83 Speak of the Devil Tour Dates

September 26, 1982: The Ritz (New York, New York)

September 27, 1982: The Ritz (New York, New York)

December 10, 1982: Cornwall Coliseum (St. Austell, England)

December 12, 1982: Birmingham International Arena (Birmingham, England)

December 14, 1982: Wembley Arena (Wembley, England)

December 16, 1982: Queens Hall (Leeds, England)

December 18, 1982: Newcastle City Hall (Newcastle, England)

December 19, 1982: The Apollo (Glasgow, Scotland)

December 20, 1982: Royal Court Theatre (Liverpool, England)

January 12, 1983: Messukeskus Helsinki (Helsinki, Finland)

January 14, 1983: Johanneshovs Isstadion (Stockholm, Sweden)

January 16, 1983: Falconersalen (Copenhagen, Denmark)

January 18, 1983: Messehallen (Hamburg, Germany)

January 20, 1983: Stadthalle Offenbach (Offenbach, Germany)

January 21, 1983: Rhein-Neckar-Halle (Eppelheim, Germany)

January 22, 1983: Palais de Beaulieu (Lausanne, Switzerland)

January 23, 1983: Philipshalle (Düsseldorf, Germany)

January 25, 1983: Hemmerleinhalle (Neunkirchen am Brand, Germany)

January 26, 1983: Messehalle (Sindelfingen, Germany)

January 28, 1983: Hall Rhénus (Strasbourg, France)

January 29, 1983: Palais des Sports (Paris, France)

January 30, 1983: Forest National (Brussels, Belgium)

February 11, 1983: Onondaga County War Memorial (Syracuse, New York)

February 15, 1983: Huntington Civic Center (Huntington, West Virginia)

February 20, 1983: County Hall (Charleston, South Carolina)

February 22, 1983: Charlotte Coliseum (Charlotte, North Carolina)

February 23, 1983: Lakeland Civic Center (Lakeland, Florida)

February 25, 1983: Hollywood Sportatorium (Pembroke Pines, Florida)

February 28, 1983: Von Braun Center (Huntsville, Alabama)

March 1, 1983: Barton Coliseum (Little Rock, Arkansas)

March 5, 1983: Airline Highway Park (Baton Rouge, Louisiana)

March 9, 1983: Palmer Auditorium (Austin, Texas)

March 12, 1983: Pershing Center (Lincoln, Nebraska)

March 15, 1983: Palmer Auditorium (Davenport, Iowa)

March 16, 1983: Peoria Civic Center (Peoria, Illinois)

March 18, 1983: Kellogg Arena (Battle Creek, Michigan)

March 19, 1983: McMorran Arena (Port Huron, Michigan)

March 20, 1983: L. C. Walker Arena (Muskegon, Michigan)

March 22, 1983: Rockford MetroCentre (Rockford, Illinois)

March 27, 1983: London Gardens (London, Ontario)

March 28, 1983: Sudbury Community Arena (Sudbury, Ontario)

March 30, 1983: Colisée de Québec (Quebec City, Quebec)

April 1, 1983: Centrum in Worcester (Worcester, Massachusetts)

April 2, 1983: Historic Atlantic City Convention Hall (Atlantic City, New Jersey)

April 5, 1983: Glens Falls Civic Center (Glen Falls, New York)

May 29, 1983: US Festival, Glen Helen Regional Park (San Bernardino, California)

CHAPTER 15

Staying Home

A Rest Well-Deserved and Lots of Love.

After I left Ozzy's employ, as well as my beautiful British lady who wondered if she'd ever hear from me again, I arrived in Dallas, my real home. Looking back on it, I don't know why leaving was my first reaction or action because for almost all my career I had worked for British bands and companies. I knew London, liked the city, and even better, I had fallen madly in love with a beautiful woman who, like me, had been married before. But neither of us was attached now nor had children from previous relationships, and we enjoyed each other's company.

I realize I left without much of an explanation and doing so bothered me the whole way back to the US. Now that I'd gone and left the country, how must she be feeling after our summer together? I did say I'd get her over to America.

While I have no regrets moving back to Dallas after all these wonderful years, I do still occasionally think about what might have happened if I'd just stayed in London. I had plenty of money and could have easily gotten a work permit that would have allowed me to stay if I chose to. Alas, I didn't. Maybe I'd have ended up managing a big band or artist or been a quasi-celebrity myself, but that's not what I did.

However, you can never tell when or where cupid will shoot his arrow or where it will land. So almost as soon as I arrived in Texas, I got into my BMW and drove to a travel agency I knew in Snider Plaza, Mustang Travel. I bought this lovely lady a full-price, round-trip airline ticket to come to the US so she could return if she didn't find Dallas to her liking, which I hoped she would. I had it sent to her through special delivery, sparing no expense as I'd fallen completely in love . . . despite my promise to myself.

She was not royalty, a celebrity, or wealthy (not that I knew about), but she was gorgeous, extremely smart, and seemed to like being around me. We made a good team. I phoned and told her I'd sent her a ticket and that I would love for her to join me in Dallas. She said she'd be on the plane.

Excited, I hustled to find a nice apartment and bought some furniture and other necessities in preparation for her arrival. In the meantime, I visited with my family. My mom had remarried, which is a story for another time, and my older brother had divorced from his wife, with whom he had two children. He was a bachelor again and running his own accounting business. My younger brother had married and was leading the married couples' life. In fact, they are still married to this day, fifty years later. They all eventually met my new love and, like me, were taken by her. I was told I had made a good choice—I already knew that!

I had saved a sizeable amount of money and was in no great rush to go back on the road just yet, so I stayed at home, and together, she and I explored my old stomping grounds. We ate out often, saw movies almost daily, and enjoyed making the apartment our own. Thank goodness she felt the same about me as I did her. Life was beautiful.

One afternoon in our apartment, I surprised her. In a moment I'll never forget, I got down on one knee and proposed. She said yes. I knew this woman was someone who I could definitely say I wanted to spend the rest of my life with. I would never do anything to jeopardize our love.

I later threw a surprise party for her at Il Sorrento, a rather well-known Italian restaurant that is no longer in business. I invited about twenty guests, wanting them to meet my wife-to-be. While she enjoyed the evening, she asked me not to ever surprise her like that again. She did get me back years later, though.

However, after several months of having fun together, she wasn't bored, per se, but she wanted to find something to do, some kind of work just to keep her busy. She had met Stephanie and Lou Dickstein, who owned Rainbow Ticketmaster, the Dallas franchise of the burgeoning entertainment ticketing company owned by the Pritzker family of Chicago. Rainbow was a successful business, and Vivienne was hired as a part-time telephone ticketing operator. She worked a few days a week initially but went full-time in short order.

It wasn't long before she had made a group of friends at work and not much longer before she had climbed her way into a management position at the company. Vivienne and a girl named Debbie ran the growing telephone room, and with new technology developing all the time, both had to stay sharp. Together, the two of them (and Debbie's sister Louise) made a formidable team running the newest and what was quickly becoming the most popular way to purchase entertainment tickets.

I would take her to work and pick her up in the evenings, and then we'd play and have fun. I did actually attempt to work for the telephone order service as well under her supervision, but while I can assure you it wasn't because of her administrative abilities or fairness, that role in Rainbow just wasn't a good fit. Although I tried several other departments, thanks to the kindness of Stephanie, Lou, and Vivienne, the ticketing side of the business was not for me.

However, one great—no, magnificent—thing that came along because of our meeting and falling in love was me returning to my Christian roots and going back to church. You see, Vivienne grew up Catholic and was ushered away to a boarding school in England at eleven years old while her parents went abroad for executive civil-servant postings in Beirut and Lebanon. This was during the 1960s when the atmosphere in the Middle East was becoming extremely volatile.

It was when we were together at the Ridge Farm recording studio in Surrey that she asked me one Saturday evening if I would go with her to a local church nearby. I initially was taken aback by the question. Not because I wasn't a believer in Christ, but I just hadn't given anything like this a thought in many years. I agreed, and the next morning we attended a local Catholic service. I have to say it felt good being there, and even more so being there with her.

About seventeen years had passed since I'd been to church. I knew part of the reason my parents didn't press the issue of us attending church was that my older brother and I delivered the morning newspaper. We woke up at three o'clock every morning and weren't home until six thirty or seven, especially on Sundays. I'll have to give credit where credit is due, though, and say my mom often helped us when we were in our mid-teens because the papers were so large. We threw over 450 together, and my mother, God bless her, didn't want to have to wake us up at eight o'clock for church.

Before my mom died, I had a chance to ask her why we stopped going to church, other than the paper routes. She told me my father became disillusioned with the church because all they seemed to be asking for was money for Sunday School, and all he saw were the pictures we colored—no learning about the Bible. She said he didn't want to fund a day-care art class. My dad grew up going to Highland Park United Methodist Church in Dallas, which my grandfather helped build and served on the board.

You see, I grew up Methodist in Dallas, and my family was active in Northaven United Methodist Church. Even to the extent that my father was instrumental in the construction of a new campus building so we could move from my elementary school auditorium. My brother and I participated in Boy Scouts for many years (with my father as Scoutmaster), using the church's facilities for our weekly troop meetings. Then I discovered the appeal of the electric guitar, and I decided to wrap up my Scouting foray. Sadly and somewhat embarrassingly, I did so despite being just one merit short of my Eagle Scout badge, which my older brother had earned. That was a silly thing to not finish.

I have to take this time to say that, thanks to my lovely wife, I regained my faith and have not missed church more than a handful of times in forty years. We often go on other days or evenings now that retirement is in our vocabulary. In fact, all four of our children were raised in the church and served at the alter at different times. Unfortunately, when they went off to college, they lost their faith or hid it, as many of their college friends said things like, "You don't believe in that stuff, do you?" or something similar to deter them from attending to the faith and beliefs they were brought up with. I must say, it was a terrible byproduct of attending a larger college.

As far as work during this period of my life, I tried many scenarios that would allow me to stay in Dallas, but it was very difficult, especially after where I'd been and what I'd done for a living. I did help with a show on the Jacksons' Victory Tour after production manager Bugzee Houghdahl asked. I was doing some advance for the three Texas Stadium concerts that would be held in Dallas July 13–15, 1984. They had two teams leapfrogging across the country, and the one I was working with really did not have it together. At least our particular advance man working for the tour didn't. He figured the ten motor homes being used for offices and dressing rooms—with air conditioners running, mind you—could just be plugged into extension cords. That was about a $20,000 misjudgment. Of course, as always in the rock-and-roll business, the shows did go on and the stadium was packed.

After that I decided I'd stay home happily while our new family was being born and raised. I wanted to be there and be their dad. And Vivienne came home one day and announced she'd quit her job at Ticketmaster and wanted to homeschool the children. She wanted to be the one who saw the light go off in their heads when they learned something new.

Vivienne did a great job educating all four of our kids. They started dual-credit courses at an early age and received their associate degrees by age eighteen, leaving them technically with only two more years left to go at a four-year college to get a bachelor's degree. Though they called me the principal of Wildflower Academy Homeschool, my smart wife was who did all the teaching. I was there, but I was the one who cooked, washed, and ran errands so she could teach. I am so proud of her and the children.

In 1988, the call of the road returned to me, and Vivienne and I, after a long discussion, decided going back out and making some very good money so our comfortable lifestyle could continue would be a good thing for me. Being away from home, my wife, and the kids wasn't easy, but I phoned every day, and we got through it together. Again, another thing about them of which I am proud—being so strong and helpful while I was away.

My first foray back on the road was the Bee Gees' 1989 One for All world tour. I was gone nearly seventh months, and in the middle of that stretch, our daughter Paris was born on July 14. While that date marked the two hundredth anniversary of the Storming of the Bastille in Paris, she was so named because that was where her mother and I fell in love. That was rough only being home for two weeks when she was born.

I have never regretted giving up that time away from touring to stay home, start a family, and be with my lovely wife. It was invaluable, and I'd do it again without a moment's doubt. I owe so much to Vivienne and the love, understanding, and caring she showed for me and our family.

There was one strange thing that happened while I was off the road for a few years—the touring business changed. It seems that while I was maturing into a more settled person and lifestyle, so were many of my friends in the industry, musicians and crew alike. Putting my finger on what had changed was difficult at first, but then it became obvious that everyone had matured a bit as well, and no longer were things quite as wild and haphazard. Now, many people involved in keeping the show on the road, even down to the promoters, were taking things a bit slower and more seriously. There weren't so many late drunken nights or flying the next day hung over. The difference was very pleasant, I must say, and I personally enjoyed the change, both at home and on the road. The tours I did after that time were fun, although maybe not as innovative or surprising. They were mostly just day-to-day business.

I don't know what the scene is like now. It all may have reverted to the olden days, but touring has become such a huge money-making industry in all aspects of entertainment. Be it music, theatre, stage shows, etc., the amount of money being made each night is unbelievable. And the ticket prices are out of this world.

I don't envy those still in the business at all. I have a dwindling (due to age and illness, mostly) group of close friends and associates I keep in touch with who all worked during the same era as I did. There will never be another time like the 1960s, 1970s, and early 1980s as that was the real growth of the touring industry.

CHAPTER 16

Bee Gees One for All

All Around the World . . . and Back.

I had done a lifetime, so it seemed, with Ozzy and met the woman of my dreams, who I'd married and started a family with. But despite being off the road for a while, I still wanted to tour, although jobs were few and far between for some reason. Probably because I moved back to Dallas (I'd like to think not).

I was contacted in 1988 by Dick Ashby, my old friend from the Robert Stigwood Organization and the "real" Bee Gees manager, asking if I'd be interested in taking them out on the road with him one more time. And this tour would be going around the world—well, most of it anyway. I agreed happily as the money was good and the job was going to last most of the year. Of course, I was sad to leave my beautiful pregnant wife and growing family, but the offer was too good to turn down.

In mid-February 1989, I left for Florida. Rehearsals were at a club in a rather questionable part of Miami that they'd rented for several weeks. The band—most of whom I knew, aside from a couple of newcomers—and I were sequestered in a very posh rental estate on Biscayne Bay. I took the separate servants' accommodations so I could get away from the hubbub if I wanted. My temporary living quarters included one big room, a kitchenette, and a bathroom.

We would rehearse from early afternoon until early evening, but as these were professional musicians, everyone knew the songs so well that rehearsals went smoothly and quickly. Despite loud music blaring from inside this club, not many passersby were interested in what we were doing, except for a few who were ushered away by uniformed security.

The band consisted of Barry Gibb providing vocals and guitar, Robin Gibb with vocals, Maurice Gibb on vocals, keyboards, bass, and guitar, Alan Kendall playing lead guitar, Tim Cansfield on guitar as well, and Vic Martin and Gary Moberly working the keyboards and synthesizers. George Perry handled bass while Chester Thompson played drums on the first half of the tour with Mike Murphy taking over for the second half. Plus, Tampa Lann (Mike's future wife), Linda Harmon, and Phyllis St. James sang background vocals and added percussions. All in all, a darned good band.

I was fortunate I was able to bring my three-month pregnant wife to Miami for a long weekend to stay, see some rehearsals, and have a few nice meals. And she got to meet everyone I'd be spending the rest of the year with. I remember that fondly. When she returned to Dallas, our home in early March 1989, she was met with a late snow and ice storm. And she had two toddler boys, Ian and Simon, to deal with while growing our first daughter, Paris.

But soon the rehearsals were over, and it was time to hit the road. We were allowed to return home to regather our belongings for the first part of the tour, which would be in Europe. I packed, said some very sad goodbyes to my lovely wife and kids, and did probably the hardest thing I'd ever done. No, not the tour . . . leaving my family behind. At least they had a great mom to take care of them.

We were off to Germany to start the tour with a show in Dortmund on May 3. Touring in Germany in those days was always a treat as the audiences were good, and the hotels and food were nice as well. The sixth stop of the tour was in Zurich, where we stayed at a hotel just outside of town on a mountainside with a beautiful view. We were there for three or four nights, and I hadn't really noticed, but on the cattle farm next door to the hotel, every cow had a big bell around its neck. Although I was usually already awake, when they were let out in the early morning to feed, the clanging of the bells would wake a lot of other people up. The brothers traditionally slept late and were quite perturbed by the noise.

Our tour security fellow, Derek Kozlowski, spoke to the front desk to see what could be done, even if it meant bribery. The hotel assured him they and many other bands and celebrities had tried to get the farmer to quiet the cows and the obnoxious bells but to no avail. All they could do was offer an apology to Derek and the Bee Gees.

Well, not one to be told, "No, it can't happen," Derek somehow was able to convince the farmer to take all the bells off the cows for the remainder of our stay. All slept well from then on. What he accomplished was so amazing that we were compelled to give Derek the "No Bell Peace Prize" of Zurich, 1989.

While in Zurich, I wanted to buy a Swiss alphorn, like in the Ricola commercials. I took a taxi into town to a music store, and sure enough, they had them for sale. The instrument could come apart in about five-foot sections, and it even had a carrying bag. Then I asked the price and, well, let's just say the alphorn is still in Switzerland. However, later during the tour I did buy something even better with the per diem money I had saved up, but I'll wait until we get to Brussels to tell you about it.

While taking a taxi through Zurich—I think to the music store—I noticed something that gave me an odd feeling. Something in Switzerland was different than most places we'd visited. Then I saw a man walking down the sidewalk with a broom and a large dustpan, and suddenly I realized what the feeling was. The streets and sidewalks were spotless. No trash or cigarette butts, crumpled paper, or anything. Everywhere I looked was free of litter and trash, unlike many, or even most, cities I'd been to, although I had not yet been to Singapore. It was interesting in a nice sort of way but odd that I noticed the difference subtlety and didn't identify it immediately.

We did a date in Austria on May 21 and a couple of shows in Germany before then heading to Berlin for a pair of concerts on May 27–28. Mind you, this was when the Berlin Wall was still in place. I had been there several times prior, but on this trip we were playing a venue I'd never seen or even heard of, the Waldbühne in the middle of Olympiapark. When our bus with all the band and staff arrived, we drove around until finally turning into a gate. We were about two hundred yards from the outdoor amphitheater that seated more than twenty thousand, and they had dressing room trailers and catering, all the usual trappings of a traditional backstage area.

The interesting thing was you got to the stage by going through a long, lighted cement tunnel that ran under the stage. There, you would take a circular stairway up to the backstage wings. The promoter said this was where Hitler and other self-important Nazis would give speeches, and the tunnel was for their safety, so they never had to go anywhere near the crowds. That added a new dimension of interest to the venue.

That evening, seeing all those people singing and dancing along to the brothers was an incredible sight. It was magical, and I think the Waldbühne may have been one of my favorite venues we played. We went back two more times over the next month on that tour. The stadiums were huge with a lot of people, but for some reason this place just had something special about it.

We had played Nuremberg May 11 and 13, where the Evil One also gave speeches, his podium specially situated where the sun was behind him and shining into the eyes of the gathered crowd. They say he used that setup to give him an air of godliness in the audience's minds.

We popped off to play Wembley Arena in London for two dates, June 1–2, then went back to the continent to perform concerts in Berlin again and Paris. After being out on the street to do something, I came back to the hotel, and as I got on the elevator, there were two other people already in there. One was Yoko Ono and the other her male companion, I expect. On the ride up, I introduced myself and invited them to the show that evening, but they had to decline as they had previous obligations. She was very polite and nice and even seemed sad she couldn't come.

From Paris we went to Brussels, where I had already planned to meet a man I'd met several times before and, coincidently, was the show's promoter. I had told him I was interested in buying a diamond for my wife, as I'd been saving all my per-diem money, and I suggested I might be able to get the brothers' wives to come see his wares. Seems his family was in the diamond business as well as him being a concert promoter.

Well, when I told Linda, Dwina, and Yvonne—the wives of Barry, Robin, and Maurice, respectively—who was coming to my room and what he was bringing, they all quickly agreed. My friend brought along a briefcase of diamonds, and we had a great time looking. In the end, Linda bought a very large, high-quality diamond to be made into something when she got back to Miami while Dwina bought a sizeable uncut diamond and, likewise, spent a pretty Belgian franc. Yvonne decided she didn't need a diamond but had fun looking.

Once the ladies left, I reminded my friend that he had agreed if the wives bought some of his diamonds, he'd make me a very good deal on a stone that I could take back to my wife in Dallas. He had already picked out a nice one-and-a-half carat diamond for me, and knowing how much I had to spend, he said it was worth twice the amount that I paid him. But he was very pleased all went so well.

I remember the rest of the trip I was nervous traveling and leaving my hotel room for fear of having the diamond stolen. Or getting caught crossing a boarder and not declaring it, especially going back in the US.

After the last European date on July 1 in Hanover, Germany, we flew back to the States and to our respective homes for a two-week break. This was a good thing as my lovely wife gave birth to Paris on July 14. We loved being together as a family, but all too soon it was time for me to leave again for the road and the rest of the Bee Gees tour.

We would start the next leg with a show in St. Paul, Minnesota, on July 29, but took a day or two beforehand to rehearse at Paisley Park Studios, Prince's compound. Although we never saw him, every once in a while someone would whisper, "Shh," and point upward to the ceiling grid where Prince was said to lurk and watch everything without he himself being seen. Oooooooooo!

The shows were running well, but at home things were not going as smoothly as hoped. Vivienne developed a case of the postpartum blues, and it was terrible. I made the biggest mistake of my life by not running to her side to help. Instead, I tried to comfort her by calling often for lengthy conversations. She did go see a doctor and a counselor because she felt depressed and didn't know what was happening to her. This went on for a couple of months, and me, like the moron I am, thought it would be all right if I just called enough. Remember, we did not have FaceTime or even cell phones then.

I will always regret not being with her when she needed me. In fact, when I did return home, there was a definite chill in the air, and I couldn't blame her. I put the band and job ahead of her—a big mistake. But I happened to marry one of the most loving and forgiving women in the world and consider myself the most fortunate man alive. Especially with four beautiful children.

On August 4, while we were in Philadelphia, I felt very ill and run-down. I called a doctor to come see me, and it turned out I again had walking pneumonia. He put me to bed and gave me plenty of medicine. I missed one show but after that was better and got back on my feet. I still wasn't completely well, but I carried on as best I could.

A couple of days later, we were in New York City to play at Radio City Music Hall on August 9–10. This was going to be fun as I had never done a show there before. Having recently had a birthday, I was surprised when Linda, Dwina, and Yvonne brought a gift to my room, a solid gold, chain-link bracelet. I was floored they had done this and was thrilled.

However, while the bracelet was nice, it wasn't me, so to speak. It took some courage and maybe was the wrong thing to do, but I asked if they would mind if I exchanged it for a new watch. Since they'd bought the piece just down the street from our hotel, we all went there, and they helped me pick out a nice Seiko watch, which I wore for over twenty years before it finally gave up. I still keep it in my safe, though, as a token of their thoughtfulness. Several others gave me birthday gifts as well, including the three backup singers who surprised me with an African djembe drum. That, too, still sits proudly in my home.

We did the two nights at Radio City, and other than peeing next to actor Paul Sorvino, not a lot happened out of the ordinary—just good shows with good music. Having them perform in such a prestigious theatre was nice, and I got to wander around and see all the history.

Less than a week later, we popped into Canada for sold-out shows in Montreal and Toronto, August 15–16. The Canadian audiences loved the Bee Gees!

From there we came back to the States and made our way quickly westward to Las Vegas, which was always fun. The theater was inside the Aladdin hotel, then one of the larger casinos on the Strip. After leaving some money in a machine, it was off to Los Angeles, where we did two nights, August 30–31, at the Universal Amphitheatre, an enclosed venue. The last time we were in LA, we played Dodger Stadium. This was fun but different. The scene was much smaller and more friendly and intimate. I had a few guests come to the shows since I had a great number of friends in LA and luckily still do to this day.

Following our time in Southern California, we headed north toward San Francisco for a show on September 2 at the Shoreline Amphitheatre. Our final concert in the States went very well, except I sprained my ankle and had to go to an emergency room for X-rays. Fortunately, it wasn't broken. I had tried to wake up our overly zealous accountant, who'd had way too much to drink the evening before. When knocking on his hotel room door didn't work, I kicked the door a few times and hurt myself in the process. We ended up leaving him behind, only for him to catch up later with his tail between his legs.

Following our successful US leg of the tour, it was off to Australia and Japan. Now this was going to be fun—except I still felt bad I would even be farther away from Vivienne.

After a day or two of rest in Sydney, we started on November 7 in Canberra, the capitol of Australia, which was followed by shows in Adelaide and Melbourne. During this time, I had picked up a bacteria, which kept my stomach in a bad way. We stayed at a hotel on the Gold Coast, and I was too ill to go out. I guess this may have been my own conscious paying me back for my ignorance to not go home when I should have. However, a doctor came to the hotel, checked me over, gave me some antibiotics, and in twelve hours I was feeling much better. At least we still had Japan to go.

And in Japan, the time spent went as usual—great. We were met at the airport by cars and guides provided by the promoter. Everything was first class and taken care of. We booked rooms at a hotel a bit away from the hot spot district of Roppongi in Tokyo, where the backing band wanted to stay and party. I sort of overruled them, and we stayed in a five-star hotel instead of a smaller place in Roppongi.

This was a move that would come back to haunt me; a time when I discovered who my real friends were. When the Bee Gees went on tour again a couple of years later, Alan Kendall, as spokesman for the rhythm section, told Dick not to hire me as the tour manager because I wouldn't let them stay in Roppongi. Dick said he was sorry, but he didn't want to start an argument with the brothers, so he let it go. I was out! At least I really did nothing wrong. I was only trying to keep everyone together. But it caused the loss of an old friendship.

The shows in Yokohama and Matsuyama went well, and we did have fun. Well, I did, even if the band did not. Then it was time for the long journey back, which I was looking forward to with trepidation. I desperately wanted to go home, but I knew I deserved a real small doghouse when I arrived—if I was even let in the door.

As I've talked about previously, leaving a tour when it's finished is always a very hard and mind-numbing thing to do. You've been on the road with the same one hundred or so people for months, living in each other's pockets, always together. Then, suddenly, everyone goes their separate ways back to their own homes. And most of these people you know you'll probably never see again. It's an odd, sad feeling.

Then walking into your own house, after a brief "Oh, hi!" and a kiss or hug from the wife and kids, it's life as usual for them. The person coming home feels like the odd one out. They'd had to keep up their lives while I was away, and all I wanted to do was tell them my stories. "No time now," was usually the response. Plus, this time I was feeling pretty low already. I knew Vivienne was not pleased with me. God bless her for sticking it out with me when she could have so easily told me to go find a hotel room.

Still, I must reiterate that the Bee Gees were the most enjoyable band I ever toured with, and I will always be grateful to Dick Ashby for including me.

Bee Gees 1989 One for All Tour Dates

May 3, 1989: Westfalenhalle (Dortmund, Germany)

May 5, 1989: Ahoy Rotterdam (Rotterdam, Netherlands)

May 7, 1989: Ahoy Rotterdam (Rotterdam, Netherlands)

May 9, 1989: Valby-Hallen (Copenhagen, Denmark)

May 11, 1989: Frankenhalle (Nuremberg, Germany)

May 13, 1989: Frankenhalle (Nuremberg, Germany)

May 16, 1989: Festhalle Frankfurt (Frankfurt, Germany)

May 17, 1989: Festhalle Frankfurt (Frankfurt, Germany)

May 19, 1989: Hallenstadion (Zürich, Switzerland)

May 20, 1989: Hallenstadion (Zürich, Switzerland)

May 21, 1989: Wiener Stadthalle (Vienna, Austria)

May 24, 1989: Eisstadion am Friedrichspark (Mannheim, Germany)

May 25, 1989: Eisstadion am Friedrichspark (Mannheim, Germany)

May 27, 1989: Waldbühne (Berlin, Germany)

May 28, 1989: Eisstadion am Friedrichspark (Mannheim, Germany)

June 1, 1989: Wembley Arena (London, England)

June 2, 1989: Wembley Arena (London, England)

June 3, 1989: Waldbühne (Berlin, Germany)

June 8, 1989: Palais Omnisports de Paris-Bercy (Paris, France)

June 10, 1989: Cinquantenaire (Brussels, Belgium)

June 15, 1989: Wembley Arena (London, England)

June 17, 1989: Edinburgh Playhouse (Edinburgh, Scotland)

June 22, 1989: National Exhibition Centre (Marston Green, England)

June 26, 1989: Ahoy Rotterdam (Rotterdam, Netherlands)

June 28, 1989: Waldbühne (Berlin, Germany)

June 30, 1989: Freilichtbühne Loreley (St. Goarshausen, Germany)

July 1, 1989: Niedersachsenstadion (Hanover, Germany)

July 15, 1989: Wembley Arena (London, England)

July 29, 1989: Harriet Island Pavilion (St. Paul, Minnesota)

July 31, 1989: Poplar Creek Music Theater (Hoffman Estates, Illinois)

August 1, 1989: Pine Knob Music Theatre (Clarkston, Michigan)

August 3, 1989: Merriweather Post Pavilion (Columbia, Maryland)

August 4, 1989: Mann Center (Philadelphia, Pennsylvania)

August 6, 1989: Garden State Arts Center (Holmdel, New Jersey)

August 9, 1989: Radio City Music Hall (New York, New York)

August 10, 1989: Radio City Music Hall (New York, New York)

August 12, 1989: Great Woods Center (Mansfield, Massachusetts)

August 13, 1989: Saratoga Performing Arts Center (Saratoga Springs, New York)

August 15, 1989: Montreal Forum (Montreal, Quebec)

August 16, 1989: CNE Grandstand (Toronto, Ontario)

August 19, 1989: Jones Beach Marine Theater (Wantagh, New York)

August 21, 1989: Blossom Music Center (Cuyahoga Falls, Ohio)

August 23, 1989: Lakewood Amphitheatre (Atlanta, Georgia)

August 26, 1989: Aladdin Theatre (Las Vegas, Nevada)

August 30, 1989: Universal Amphitheatre (Los Angeles, California)

August 31, 1989: Universal Amphitheatre (Los Angeles, California)

September 2, 1989: Shoreline Amphitheatre (Mountain View, California)

November 7, 1989: National Indoor Sports Centre (Canberra, Australia)

November 9, 1989: Apollo Entertainment Centre (Adelaide, Australia)

November 17, 1989: National Tennes Centre at Finders Park (Melbourne, Australia)

November 18, 1989: National Tennes Centre at Finders Park (Melbourne, Australia)

November 28, 1989: Yokohama Arena (Yokohama, Japan)

December 7, 1989: Kenmin Bunka Kaikan (Matsuyama, Japan)

C. J. Snare (RIP) and Bill Leverty of FireHouse in Indonesia on a boat filming a video. Courtesy of L. McNeny.

Debbie Gibson Possibilities Tour laminated pass. Courtesy of L. McNeny.

FireHouse tour laminated pass. Courtesy of L. McNeny.

I was president of Borealis LED and helped design and sell these before LEDs took over the lighting industry. Courtesy of L. McNeny.

Eric Clapton and Jamie Oldaker (his longtime drummer) onstage during a Crossroads festival. Courtesy of Mary Oldaker and the Oldaker Estate.

Keyboard tech extraordinaire Rocky Morley (AKA the funniest guy in the touring business during the early Clapton/Jack Bruce era). Courtesy of Mary Oldaker and the Oldaker Estate.

Larry McNeny and a now grown-up Stephen Gibb, circa 2013. Courtesy of L. McNeny.

Larry McNeny riding an elephant in the Thailand jungle traveling with FireHouse. Courtesy of L. McNeny.

Clapton laminated backstage pass signed by his manager Roger Forrester. Courtesy of R. Forrester.

Larry McNeny waiting for the band, as always! Courtesy of L. McNeny.

Linda Ronstadt itinerary with Marvin Hamlisch and the Pittsburg Symphony. Courtesy of L. McNeny.

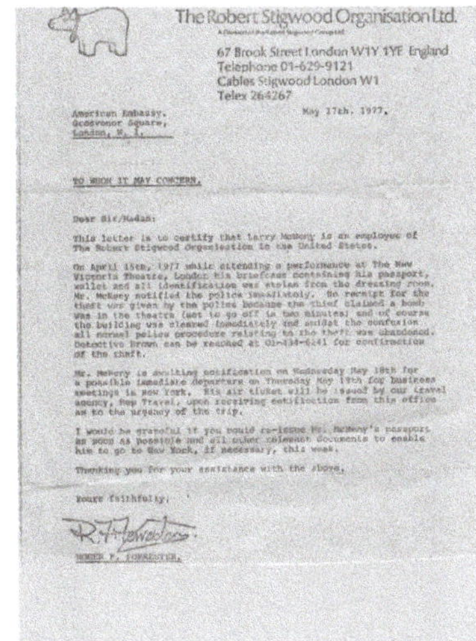

The Robert Stigwood Organisation Ltd.

67 Brook Street London W1Y 1YF England
Telephone 01-629-9121
Cables Stigwood London W1
Telex 264267

American Embassy,
Grosvenor Square,
London, W. 1.

May 17th, 1977.

TO WHOM IT MAY CONCERN,

Dear Sir/Madam:

This letter is to certify that Larry McNeny is an employee of The Robert Stigwood Organisation in the United States.

On April 15th, 1977 while attending a performance at The New Victoria Theatre, London his briefcase containing his passport, wallet and all identification was stolen from the dressing room. Mr. McNeny notified the police immediately. No receipt for the theft was given by the police because the thief claimed a bomb was in the theatre (set to go off in two minutes) and of course the building was cleared immediately and amidst the confusion all normal police procedure relating to the theft was abandoned. Detective Brown can be reached at 01-434-6241 for confirmation of the theft.

Mr. McNeny is awaiting notification on Wednesday May 18th for a possible immediate departure on Thursday May 19th for business meetings in New York. His air ticket will be issued by our travel agency, [illegible] Travel, upon receiving notification from this office as to the urgency of the trip.

I would be grateful if you would re-issue Mr. McNeny's passport as soon as possible and all other relevant documents to enable him to go to New York, if necessary, this week.

Thanking you for your assistance with the above,

Yours faithfully,

R. F. Forrester

ROGER F. FORRESTER.

Letter to the American Embassy after my briefcase was stolen and cash, passports, and car keys were taken during Jack Bruce's final show in the UK at the New Vic Theatre. I was trying to get a new passport to travel on. Courtesy of R. Forrester.

Linda Ronstadt
with

The Pittsburgh Symphony
conducted by
Marvin Hamlisch

July 10 - August 4, 1996

Another version of the Linda Ronstadt itinerary with orchestra (65 piece). Courtesy of L. McNeny.

Linda Ronstadt laminated backstage pass. Courtesy of L. McNeny.

Another Linda Ronstadt laminated backstage pass. Courtesy of L. McNeny.

Larry McNeny's band, the Stix and Stonz, in our soul era of music. Courtesy of L. McNeny.

The Stix and Stonz opening for the Mamas & the Papas in Dallas. Courtesy of L. McNeny.

Larry McNeny at work. Courtesy of L. McNeny.

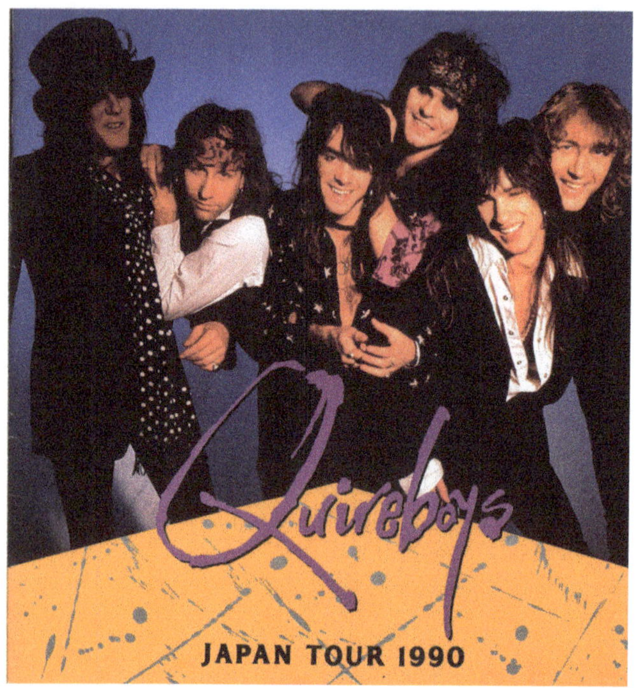

Courtesy of Sharon Osbourne.

Larry McNeny on our private plane. Courtesy of L. McNeny.

Jay Hagerman of Concerts West, promoter for many Clapton and Bee Gees shows. Courtesy of L. McNeny.

Quireboys laminated backstage pass. Courtesy of L. McNeny.

Quireboys promo photo. Courtesy of Sharon Osbourne.

Photo of the Quireboys' last show in Europe, including the crew and me. Courtesy of Sharon Osbourne, Manager for the Quireboys. Courtesy of L. McNeny.

Alan Rogan (guitar tech to the stars) with Ron Wood. Courtesy of Mary Oldaker and the Oldaker Estate.

Rocky Morley, great organ technician. Looking good in a suit, Rocky! Courtesy of L. McNeny.

The case for my first guitar. Courtesy of L. McNeny.

My first guitar, a Sears Silvertone with an amp built into the case, which I originally bought for $64.00. Courtesy of Silvertone.

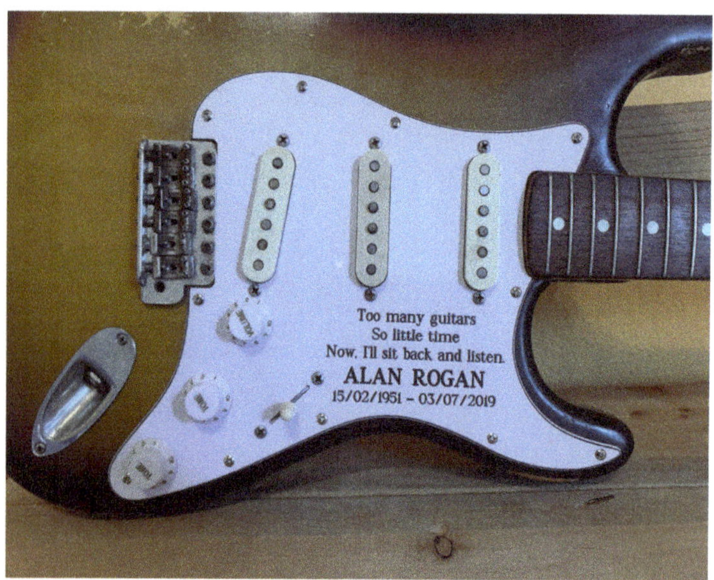

Strat dedicated to guitar tech to the stars and my good friend, Alan Rogan. Courtesy of L. McNeny.

Watching a sumo match with Mr. Udo, esteemed promoter in Japan. Courtesy of L. McNeny.

The Roamers, Larry McNeny's first real band, 1965. Courtesy of L. McNeny.

The program for the very first Prince's Trust British Invasion at the Royal Albert Hall. Courtesy of H. Goldsmith.

Ed Sheeran and Taylor, a cancer patient and friend of Teen Cancer America. Courtesy of Taylor's family.

CHAPTER 17

Yo Ho Ho and the Quireboys

How Mistaken Could I Have Been?

I was at home with my wife and children in Dallas one evening when the phone rang. If I'm not mistaken, it was after dinner, the dishes were done, and the kids were in bed. I answered it in the kitchen, and it was, to my surprise, Sharon Osbourne!

We caught up briefly before she told me why she'd called. She said, "What are you doing?" I told her I was currently off the road and looking for work, and she then asked if I could leave for Switzerland the following day. I said yes, of course, and asked for the reason. Sharon explained that she was managing a band who had produced several hit records, but their current tour manager was finding it hard to keep up with the confusion of their success. I said it sounded great, and I was on board.

She told me the name of the band was the Quireboys, who were formerly the Queerboys before making the change due to losing some opportunities to play shows because of the controversial name. This would be a tour of Europe and the UK and maybe some in Asia. She added I'd have to stop in London and come by her office to pick up some cash to take to Switzerland. That, too, was fine.

While I hated leaving my wife and children, this was what I did for a living and had for the last twenty years. And the money was excellent! So we had to get into the swing of things quickly. I took a town car from my house, waving a sad goodbye to my lovely family as I left for goodness knows how long.

I caught a flight from Dallas to London, took a taxi to Sharon's office, and was led in to see her immediately. We chatted and then she pointed to a life-sized cardboard-cutout photograph of the Quireboys, which I must say scared me. I immediately thought, *What have I got myself into?* They looked like pirates from Johnny Depp's movie, *Pirates of the Caribbean*. All six looked like pirates—filthy, loathsome pirates!

I sucked it up, smiled, and said to myself, "Well, how bad could it be compared to some of Jack Bruce's antics and fights?"

I returned to Heathrow Airport and flew to Zurich, where I was to meet the band. I got to the hotel, and within a short time we were all gathered in the bar chatting and having a great time. I realized that although they looked dastardly, they really were nice guys. One of my close friends from my days with Ozzy, Bob Thompson, was also on the crew for the Quireboys and that made it easier to fit in. He helped pave the way that I was an all right guy.

Now, could they play? I'd still not heard them play yet. We went that night to do the first gig and, wow, they were great. Three-bar blues and rock and roll, sort of like the Rolling Stones. The crowds (in the large clubs we played) loved them, and I enjoyed each song. Not often did I like every song a band played. Well, I lie. Eric Clapton and the Bee Gees were always spot on.

As the tour moved along, each day I got to be better friends with the band and crew. Jonathan "Spike" Gray handled the vocals, Guy Bailey and Guy Griffin played guitars, Nigel Mogg was on bass, and Rudy Richman played the drums. All of them were from England, except for Rudy, who was originally from Los Angeles. Everyone was nice and polite, and while a lot of alcohol was consumed, especially by several members of the band, they were always on time, and the shows were solid.

I remember one time we were headed to Berlin, and a couple of days ahead, I noticed the itinerary said we were staying at a hotel in East Berlin. The Berlin Wall had come down in 1989, but I still was not exactly comfortable with the accommodations, having been to West Berlin several times previously while the wall was still in place. It was a scary-looking deal by my thinking, so I called Steve Payne, who was the promotions manager for Whitesnake when Ozzy toured with them back in 1983. I didn't get on with him too well then; mind you, we were just the opening act. Today, though, I can call Steve a good and very fine friend of mine.

I questioned him on the choice of hotels. He said it was May Day weekend, a holiday in Germany, so we didn't have much choice. But he had it from good sources that it was a top-of-the-line hotel, only on the eastern side of where the wall once stood. Now that the wall was down and everything was open, it was going to be all right. I agreed to give it a try and thanked Steve.

When we did arrive, passing through what was once Checkpoint Charlie, we didn't drive too far before coming to a very large, grand, and old hotel. We checked in, and all the rooms, while maybe bugged (just kidding, I think), were nice and sufficient. When I said an old hotel, I meant old in the way the Plaza hotel in New York is. A vintage classic.

The time had come to phone home to Dallas, and normally I was able to dial direct. But because the phone system there was still a bit behind the times, I had to go through an operator. I said I needed to call America, but the operator said she'd have to phone me back when she could get a line. And she said it could be up to two hours. Wow, talk about antiquated.

About an hour later, the phone rang, and I was able to place the call to my family. I found all was well there, and though I was missed, they were getting along fine. Of course, all my paychecks went to my home while I was away, so there was no shortage of money.

The next day I went outside the hotel on May Day and explored the streets behind the former Iron Curtain, which was cool. I was walking along with hundreds of other people, and seeing all the West Germans and other tourists out window-shopping on this holiday was interesting. Except the thing I noticed was there was nothing in the shop windows to gawk at. They were shops of some kind, I figured, not speaking German, but the windows didn't have bright attractive displays begging you to come in and spend deutsche marks. I found it all to be a bit surreal as it was once a no-man's-land, and now it was open to all.

We did the shows in Europe and then went back to the UK for a run of dates, which were also popular since the band's hits had been just as equally successful there. The only sad thing was the Quireboys didn't have the same success in the United States. I attribute that to the fact that the Black Crows, a US band that played a very similar style (and equally as good), had already captured the American market for that retro R&R sound. But the Quireboys did tour the US eventually.

The UK leg was fun, although touring in the UK always was. Then we were off to Japan to do some dates as their record had also done well there.

I remember we flew from Heathrow to Tokyo on a route I'd never taken before. Instead of flying eastward, as it was shorter, we flew over the North Pole and had to make a fuel stop in Moscow.

I remember we landed there, my first time in the Soviet Union, and most of us deplaned. But when we did there was nothing to do inside the terminal, and we were not allowed outside the gated area, so we had to sit for a couple of hours until we could depart again. Being trapped there was somewhat disappointing. At lease no one was arrested for being a suspected spy.

We flew on to Tokyo and, as always in Japan, were warmly greeted by our promoter. We went to a well-known hotel in the Roppongi area of the city. It was sort of a round hotel with small rooms, as most are in Japan compared to many Western hotels, and per usual, CNN was the only English-speaking TV channel. On the ground floor was a restaurant that faced a center pool that had clear walls.

The band and crew got along well except for a petty jealously here and there, which usually surfaced after a round or two in the bar. One member of the band had a more concerning drinking problem than the others, and his attitude was what usually started things.

As I did with someone in almost every band I ever worked with, I tried to help him not drink so much. I wanted him to understand that he had it good and that he should enjoy the experience now and wait until a better time came along to make his ideas and problems known. This worked sometimes for a few minutes or an hour, but unless someone wants to really get it together, you can't talk them into it. No one can.

The drinking wasn't nearly as bad with these guys as it had been with others I'd toured with, but nevertheless, it was that same old angst and anger of one band member thinking he wasn't getting a fair shake.

The tour of Japan went smoothly, the band was well-received, and everyone seemed pleased. However, one morning I came down to breakfast to find a couple of the band guys having breakfast. They invited me to join them, and I agreed. Then they told me that during the previous night, Spike had enjoyed one too many drinks and decided it was time for a swim. Thank goodness someone was nearby because apparently he somehow ended up face down in the water, quasi-unconscious and ready to drown. Not on purpose, mind you, but due to the alcohol.

Fortunately, one of the band members or crew found him and pulled him out of the water, made sure he was all right, and helped him up to his room and to bed. I knew nothing of this, but it scared the heck out of me. What if he had had drowned? Not only would the band be done, but I suspect my career would be as well.

Later that day, I had a severe talk with him, and he was most apologetic and promised not to drink so much in the future or go swimming. It was a close call.

We flew back for more dates in the UK and Germany and were knocking those off one by one. I really enjoyed the band's music and stage presence, so overall the experience was nice, except the part where I missed my family.

During the UK jaunt, Sharon told me backstage that a US tour was being set up for the band, but they would be traveling by bus with the crew on the same bus as the band gear. Very compact. That didn't seem too bad until she said there was no particular itinerary yet. The agent would book shows when and where he could, but a tour schedule had not been laid out. The band needed to play anywhere and everywhere as much as they could.

I told her that due to the nature of having no fixed dates and with plans to be on the road in the US for months on end, I wasn't going to be able to do the job any longer. The decision was hard, but I couldn't do that to my wife and kids. Sharon said she understood.

Around that same time, a good friend of mine, and former Led Zeppelin tour manager, Richard Cole, was acting as Ozzy's minder in an attempt to keep him out of trouble and off alcohol (or anything illicit, for that matter). He was actually at the Quireboys show that evening with Ozzy, and Sharon asked him if he'd like to take over the tour manager position as I had to move on. Richard spoke to me and asked why I wasn't doing it. I explained my situation, and he understood, but since he was available, he said he would love to take over, with my best wishes.

After the tour finished, I said my goodbyes to the band, and I was sincere when I said I was sorry I could not carry on. They, too, understood. With that, I returned to Dallas and my loved ones at home.

The next time I saw the band, they were playing in Dallas, and I went to see them. They were great as usual, but the audience had come to see this UK band more out of curiosity, I suspect, than because they were fans of their music. They were probably fans when they left the club, however.

It was about eighteen years later that I took my wife and youngest (now grown) daughter to see the Quireboys at the 100 Club on Oxford Street in London. The band all greeted me warmly, as if no time had passed. The troubled member of the group had left but was still a friend, they said, and they had a new drummer. But they were good, and my wife and daughter had a great time. Loud rock and roll!

To this day, the Quireboys continue to record and perform all over the world. Spike left the band in 2022 with Guy Griffin, the lead guitar player, taking on the singing duties as well. Shortly after Guy Bailey died in 2023, Spike announced he was reconnecting with Nigel and Rudy to reunite the original Quireboys while Griffin later renamed his group Black Eyed Sons. I hope they all have continued success.

Although this tour was not as flush with money, it also wasn't flush with aggravation either. It was great, and I always remember that time fondly.

Quireboys 1990 *A Bit of What You Fancy* Tour Dates

April 6, 1990: (Zürich, Switzerland)

April 7, 1990: Élysée Montmartre (Paris, France)

April 8, 1990: Paradiso (Amsterdam, Netherlands)

April 12–22, 1990: Promotional Tour (Tokyo and Osaka, Japan)

April 26, 1990: Nottingham Royal Concert Hall (Nottingham, England)

April 27, 1990: Royal Court Theatre (Liverpool, England)

April 28, 1990: Hammersmith Odeon (London, England)

April 30, 1990: Huxleys Neue Welt (Berlin, Germany)

May 1, 1990: Glen Pavilion (Dunfermline, Scotland)

May 2, 1990: Tor 3 (Düsseldorf, Germany)

May 3, 1990: Westfalenpark (Dortmund, Germany)

May 5, 1990: Große Freiheit 36 (Hamburg, Germany)

CHAPTER 18

Debbie Gibson and Mom

Not Everything Is Possible!

Once again, I was back in my hometown of Dallas—off the road from a lengthy tour and enjoying, I felt, some deserved rest and relaxation—when the phone rang. The call was from a Diane Gibson, who said she was the mother and manager for the pop-singing sensation Debbie Gibson. Debbie was well-known and had a few moderate hits for her record company, and a tour was being planned to coordinate with the release of a new album she'd recently completed.

Diane asked if I'd be available to fly to New York for a meeting, and I said yes, if she was paying for the ticket. We met at their agent's office or the accountant's or maybe it was the record company's office, I can't remember. I was ushered in, where I was introduced to Diane and a fellow near my age named Omar Abderrahman, who said he had been Debbie's production manager on a previous tour and was hoping this would be number two.

Diane took the floor and told us about the new album, titled *Anything Is Possible,* and that she managed Debbie's career from out of their home on Long Island. She also stated Debbie, now old enough, was prepared to be the next Janet Jackson or Madonna and that her album would be a smash. Needless to say, they had big plans. She asked if I was interested, which I was, and we spoke about dates, salaries, number of employees, and band and crew. Within a couple of hours, the deal was done, and I was in a taxi on my way back to LaGuardia Airport.

I was pleased to have another gig and arrived back in Dallas with news of more income and more time on the road. This always was a sweet-and-sour announcement.

The plan was we'd spend a couple of weeks in Burbank, California, at an unused airport hangar where we would rehearse with her band. Against my advice to not build a $300,000 professionally designed stage until at least some dates had been booked, they did so anyway. The stage, though, was spectacular and resembled a diner from Anywhere, USA. It had an oversized toaster and a food counter with spinning stools and lots of chrome, just like a real diner. Sadly, this would be the only time that stage was assembled and performed on as after the rehearsals it was packed up and shipped to a storage boneyard for rock and roll sets somewhere outside Las Vegas. The stage was great, but the venues she was scheduled to play couldn't come close to accommodating a setup that size or such a huge production.

However, the saving grace in the whole Debbie universe was the band. She had hired the best she could, including guitarist Carlos Alomar and drummer Alan Childs, who were in David Bowie's band for his *Glass Spiders* Tour, and a keyboard player who called himself Atticus Finch (yeah, I know).

I remember once during the two or so weeks of rehearsals, I was awake all night with a fever of 102 degrees, sick as a dog. We were staying at the then-in-need-of-upgrading Sunset Marquis hotel in West Hollywood, and I phoned Diane in her room that morning. I said I was unable to go to rehearsal and asked if someone else could drive the band over to the hanger. I assured her that if I rested, I'd be better the next day.

The next thing I heard coming across the phone line was, "Oh, come on, Larry. Don't be so weak. Get up, get dressed, and get on with it!" I was incensed and disappointed, but that still didn't take away from the fact that I was seriously feeling bad. And I did not want to spread this virus. She obviously didn't care.

I didn't go and instead slept. Once the crew returned, Omar, who I had grown close to as a good friend, came by to check on me. Despite being somewhat better, I still took it easy for the rest of the day. Not only is it tough getting ill on the road with no family to help pamper you or get you medicine but added to that was Mrs. Gibson's helpful tidings. The other big feather in her pointed hat was due to come a number of weeks later.

We wrapped up rehearsals in Burbank, Omar's crew packed all the gear up, and we were off to perform at the Rock in Rio 2 festival, held at Maracanã Stadium in January 1991. We flew into Rio de Janeiro, Brazil, and took taxis to our hotel, which seemed a long way from the venue but had a great view of the ocean and Rio. I'd never been there before so I was excited to go, and I enjoyed every minute of it, except for when Debbie and her team were on stage—that was an embarrassment.

While there, I saw that the swimwear in Brazil was, well, let's just say skimpier than in the US, so clever me, I decided to go to a street vendor and buy my beautiful wife several Rio bikinis. I must say she rocked them! Enough of that . . . and she'd agree.

The city itself was very different. Some of it seemed very nice and posh while in other parts you could see the cardboard slum houses of the poor people. From just about everywhere, you could see the Cristo Redentor statue (or in English Christ the Redeemer), which is nearly one hundred years old and is designated as one of the new Seven Wonders of the World. I didn't go up there on that visit, but I did make the trek on another trip a few years later.

We were all carted in cars to the Maracanã, a vast football-type stadium. At that time, the venue could seat up to 150,000 people, although it has seated nearly 200,000 for a World Cup game. Since the stadium was renovated in 2013, it now seats just over 73,000, which is still a lot of people.

It was dusk when we got there for the January 26 show. As I was walking around, I noticed how old and cracked the stadium looked and was not confident it could withstand much more of these rowdy rock festivals without collapsing. The structure looked scary.

Debbie and her band were one of the opening acts for the sold-out show with the headliner for the evening being, wait for it, A-ha, the Norwegian band with one hit song, "Take On Me." Debbie had produced numerous quasi-hits in the US, but I guess A-ha was a big deal in Rio.

Regardless, Debbie's band took the stage for their first real performance in front of an audience, and while I was confident in the band and the dancers—six, I believe there were, all around Debbie's age with some being her friends—I was curious how the show would all come together. The crowd roared with screams and applause, and the band launched into the first song of about a forty-five-minute set.

And the first song went well, but then it suddenly became obvious that Debbie was in trouble in front of this large of an audience. She said thank you for the applause and then proceeded to ramble on about something. At one point, she handed the microphone to her lead dancer, who was scared shitless and didn't know what to say either.

The band started the next song, and for the rest of the set, the music went well, but it was obvious that Debbie and her dancers were in very uncharted waters performing for this many people, which I must agree was intimidating. All of the crew and many of the band members caught my eye and rolled theirs, meaning this was a disaster. *Get me out of here*, they all seemed to be telling me silently.

The music was good as Diane had hired a great band, but the show itself and the performance by the star and her dancers certainly wasn't one to write home about. Once the set ended and everyone was off the stage and back in the dressing room, there was a lot of silence and cautious glances at each other. I expect so no one would break out laughing at how bad it really was.

The only people I ever spoke to about it were some of the crew and band members who were mortified Debbie had performed so unprofessionally and poorly. They were just hoping no one caught their name as the band was introduced. As we left the stadium, I could hear the headliners singing their one hit, "Take On Me." *Let's get out of here*, I remember thinking, *before this stadium collapses.*

Omar and I spent the next several weeks advancing the rest of the tour and securing the hotels, trucks, and general travel logistics. In May, we all met up for rehearsals in New York before heading to Japan and Southeast Asia for some shows, which were likely subsidized by Debbie's record company. When we got back together, though, the band lineup had changed somewhat. We had a new guitar player—I guess Carlos didn't want that embarrassment to happen to him ever again—so as usual, Diane hired a great guitar player named Pat Buchanan, who was himself an aspiring singer-songwriter. In fact, I thought Pat was great, and to this day I have the demo cassettes he gave me of some of his songs. One titled "Don't Push the River" still stands out in my mind. I believe after Debbie's tour, Pat and his wife moved to Nashville, but we lost touch, as so often happens.

After a two-week break, I believe we then met up at the airport in Los Angeles and boarded our plane for foreign lands. While Debbie and her mom flew first class, the staff and band were booked in business and the crew in coach. My deal when I went on tour was anything over three hours was always business or first class, and another codicil was all my laundry and telephone calls were paid for. Flying business class to Asia was a great deal more comfortable than coach, I can attest.

Our first stop was in Tokyo, Japan, where we had a day off to catch up from the jet lag and, as always, have some fun, Japanese-style. The following day we took a train to Osaka for a 6:30 p.m. show. The concerts in Japan were always early because they tried to bring people in as they were getting off work and before they boarded trains to their homes. That was a lot of folks since many couldn't afford to live in expensive Tokyo.

After the show, the band did what was called "a runner." We left the stage and went straight into awaiting cars and then right to the train station, where we took a fairly brief ride (only a couple of hours on the bullet train) back to our hotel as we were playing the Budokan arena in Tokyo for the next two nights, June 13–14.

The Budokan is a famous Tokyo venue, and many bands have recorded albums there. There is nothing amazing about the place itself, and the arena only holds about fourteen thousand seats. I don't remember the shows being sold out, but then I really didn't care once the band was on stage and performing. In a way, especially with Debbie, it was just another concert, and not a great one at that.

We did the two shows, our last in Japan, although we did have a couple of days off in Tokyo. It was on one of those days when I and a couple of others went to a large park, as we'd been told it was fun to walk around and see all the sights. When we got there, we found the park's paved walking area was jammed with people (obviously, mostly Japanese), and there were vans and trucks of all kinds with generators powering PA systems and amplifiers. We soon discovered that every one of the three dozen or more performers were, believe it or not, Elvis impersonators! It was the most fun and ludicrous thing I have ever witnessed. While the majority were very mediocre and some quite bad, there were a few who were pretty darn good and even resembled the King. It really was a sight to see.

The other thing about our time in Japan was having to depend on per diems to eat daily, which was Diane's deal (this wasn't Eric Clapton). Dining in Tokyo can be very expensive, so except for the occasional jaunt to the Hard Rock Cafe for some better burgers, most people—band, crew, and dancers—ate at the nearby McDonald's or a local Japanese restaurant. One meal could easily take up almost an entire day's per diem, and that was not good.

We were due next to play two shows in Quezon City, part of Metropolitan Manila, but because of the 1991 eruption of Mount Pinatubo in the Philippines' Luzon Volcanic Arc, we had to change our schedule and put Manila at the end of the itinerary, if the city was lucky enough to still be there. This was the second-largest volcanic eruption of the twentieth century. Little did I know then that I'd not be able to buy my own Ferdinand Marcos shirts while there. That would have to wait until later.

We had a whole week off due to Mother Nature wanting to release some energy (or perhaps wanting to postpone a Debbie Gibson show for as long as possible), so we eventually traveled to Singapore, where we stayed at a nice hotel and had a day of rest before the show. I remember the city seemed like a poor man's Fifth Avenue with electronic shops everywhere, and I do mean everywhere. Shopping was like a hobby for these people.

A couple of us took the subway and were told to never, under any circumstances, chew gum or we'd get arrested. It seems they had built this new expensive, albeit short, subway system and immediately upon going into service, people were spitting gum on the trains' floors and carpets. In response, the government was cracking down on chewing gum on the subway and streets. It seems this was their rather effective way of keeping the city clean of ugly blotches of sticky, dirty gum. If you were caught, the punishment usually meant a big fine or jail time, so they were not kidding. This kind of made one pucker for fear of someone thinking you were chewing gum, or even worse, spitting on the sidewalk or street.

Later that same evening, Omar, the promoter's representative, and I went to the venue, a rather traditional western-looking auditorium that held maybe six or seven thousand people. When we got there and went in the back door, we realized that a show had only just finished, and low and behold, it was a *Sesame Street* touring show. *How cool is that?* I remembered thinking, as I had four little kids at home by now, along with my lovely wife.

I asked the promoter's representative if he could arrange a photo with Omar, me, and a few of the costumed characters before they changed into their street clothes. Within a few minutes, there on stage we stood, surrounded by the Count, Cookie Monster, Bert and Ernie, and Grover.

I thought, *Wow! I'm going to be a big hit with the kids when I get home. Me and the Muppets. I bet none of their friends' fathers know Grover or the Count.*

This was also when I discovered that once cigarette advertising was banned in the US, Salem and other brands had taken their money and gone to Southeast Asia to promote their product and sponsor concerts, trying to get more young people hooked on smoking. I remember the promoter coming to me and saying that if he could get Madonna to come do a show there, he'd get Salem (he said) to pay her one million dollars. This was at a time when Madonna was still in her hottest prime. I didn't know Madonna and certainly had no intention of getting that message to her. Wrong union, so to speak.

That night during the show, Omar, Diane, and I sat in the production office while the band was onstage and discussed the planned upcoming US tour for Debbie, in particular the upper Northeast. We talked at length about using station wagons and driving ourselves back and forth to the gigs as the drives were not particularly long. However, Omar and I had an extreme amount of experience touring, and we convinced Diane it would be safer for the band and crew to travel to these shows via tour coach buses. The kinds with bunks and a designated driver. We ran some numbers, and while a bit more expensive, she agreed the idea sounded like the best thing to do, and she told us to start planning.

The concert the next night was at that same venue but at a more reasonable time, with an opening act at 8:30 p.m. and Debbie going on at 9:00. The show went as usual, the band was great, and the rest, well, it happened. The audience seemed pleased, although they more or less may have been starved for entertainment.

We had a day off in Singapore, and I lazed around by the pool doing nothing but drinking cocktails with umbrellas in them before it was late enough to head to the bar to do some real drinking. Diane had left for New York that day.

We then flew to Kuala Lumpur, Malaysia, for another day off before our next concert, which was at the Putra World Trade Centre. It was an all-right venue, fairly new, but something didn't seem right, and it took me a while to figure out what it was. I was walking around, looking at the kids in the crowd waiting for the show, when it hit me. Or rather scared me as a German Shepherd lunged at me while still tethered to his military-uniformed keeper. There must have been over twenty of these guards inside the auditorium, all with dangerous-looking dogs. I even saw one dog bite a girl's wrist, causing her to scream. And she was only walking close by the dog on her way into the venue.

I went to the promoter and said we were not going on until all the dogs had been extracted from inside the venue. No show until the dogs were gone. Unfortunately, the promoter had me accompany him to the Big Cheese in the Big Cheese uniform (lots of badges and ribbons etc.). He then told me to tell this fellow my problem with the dogs and that we were not playing until they had left the auditorium. We just wanted the kids to have a fun time at the concert. The promoter translated in Malaysian, but I don't think that was necessary as he understood every word I said.

He was angry. I could see his face getting red and him looking at me very agitated. I told him that I had informed the crew that we would not start the show until all the dogs had left the auditorium. Admittedly, I did have a brief moment of clarity when I realized that I could well be arrested or become food for the dog that was standing with the guard next to him. Probably not one of the most intelligent things I have ever done. Still, I just knew that once the music started and the dogs were bombarded with the loud booming bass and drums, the activity on the stage, and the audience wanting to dance and have a good time, some kids that evening were going to get hurt.

This standoff went on for a while, and he stood his ground saying they wouldn't leave. I stood mine as well, returning to the stage, standing in the middle of it, and telling everyone not to start the show. It was now past the scheduled time to begin, and he gave me some *I'm going to kill you!* looks from where he was standing while speaking into a radio periodically and listening. So we all just stood there. The crowd was getting anxious for the show to start, but he could tell I was serious. I wanted to close my eyes and disappear since I could end up in a lot of trouble . . . or worse.

Finally, I saw him speak firmly into his radio, and within seconds I noticed all of the guards with dogs heading to the foyer and shutting the door to the main theater behind them. He gave me one last look of *This is not over* and left. I then told Omar, "Let's start the show."

Fortunately, everything went fine. The show was, well, the show, and the audience was great. And no one got hurt. We—and by we, I mean me—got out of the auditorium and back to the hotel safely and with no other threats. Unfortunately, the next day we again had off, and I wondered if this guard fellow might show up at our hotel to pay me a visit. I think I was being dramatic as he never came.

But if that situation were to ever come up again, I'd do the same thing. I was trying to protect the audience, and those guards didn't have good control over the dogs. People would have definitely gotten hurt. I'm just grateful I was not the target of his ire.

Next, we were off to Jakarta, Indonesia, the home of "no car is allowed a muffler," and the school that teaches "everybody drive as crazy as you can." The country was very, very different. Not only did getting from the airport to our hotel take a long time, but it was hot, and the smog and air were extremely dense.

On the way to the outdoor venue the next day, we passed some rivers in town that were cluttered with trash and human waste and were hardly flowing in any direction. In fact, I saw numerous people relieving themselves of urine and excrement in the rivers, or bogs as they should have been called. It was definitely an eye-opener.

I didn't know it then, but I'd get back to Jakarta a couple of more times and would have a much better, and not so shocking, experience.

We arrived at the venue, a huge field of at least one hundred acres and completely fenced in. We drove to the back and were shown to our dressing rooms and trailers, which were situated in an open-ended rectangle and kitted out in the best possible way. They did a good job of making the accommodations comfortable.

As always, I first went and checked that the stage was built well and would be sturdy for the concert, although I would have heard from the crew or Omar earlier if there was a question. And while it was fine, I did notice about seventy-five soldiers standing around the perimeter inside the gated area, all with automatic weapons. This was not a fight I was going to get into because the scene felt more controlled than the dogs. So in my mind, all was good. When the band finally took the stage with about fifteen thousand people in the audience, I felt it was going to be a good show.

Mind you, I had noticed that the tablecloths on the catering tables in the dressing room, situated with platters of cheese, fruit, and drinks, were made of an attractive Indonesian batik fabric. I did, in fact, purloin a couple of the more attractive ones and even had one made into a sport-coat-like jacket for my wife. It turned out even better than I had expected.

We went on to Bangkok, Thailand, for a concert on July 3. By now, Debbie was actually getting better at managing the crowds, and the show went fairly well. After Thailand, we headed to Taiwan, which I was excited about. Actually, of all the cities we were visiting, Taiwan sounded the most exotic, for some reason.

After checking into our hotel, several of us went to the Black Market or some name like that. It wasn't an illegal place but rather just an outdoor area with shops selling everything you could imagine. One in particular caught my eye—a fellow selling cobra elixir, which they said was supposed to make you a more manly man.

I stood watching the guy, sort of like a carnival barker, hustling in front of his store. A bored (or drugged or very old) orangutan would reach into a burlap sack, extract a turtle, and slap it down on the counter. The man would then start to take it apart with his very sharp knife. The object was to extract the penis of the turtle and its reproductive organs. Behind him was a small shop with a few tables where people were drinking something. There were bottles of liquid lining the shelves on the wall. I guess the turtles had magical powers as well.

A Taiwanese lady and her little three-year-old son were standing next to me, and we were no more than eighteen inches from the table where all of this was taking place. On another table next to the man, there was a stuffed cobra standing partially erect, as if he was getting ready to strike. We were casually watching the curious goings-on when suddenly the stuffed cobra readjusted itself, and we realized it was not a stuffed cobra but a real live cobra! The lady grabbed her son and took several steps back—back to where I had magically and immediately moved to get clear as well. I must admit that it did rather scare the heck out of me.

Regardless, I and whoever was with me bought a small bottle of the liquid and were told we were supposed to take a shot daily. The potion had vodka or some liquor in it as well as the excretion of the male cobra. We were assured this concoction would make us more virile.

After making the rounds of the other booths and not buying much of anything other than some boxing puppets, we went back to the hotel with the intention of trying some of the elixir. We gathered the crew at the bar and several of us took a sip and, well, I don't think anyone ever felt a thing.

We had another day off and then two concerts in a row at the original Taipei Municipal Stadium on July 6–7. During the day of the first show, I decided to buy a nice jewel with all of the per diem money I had saved to take home to my wife. I wanted a heart-shaped sapphire because I knew she liked sapphires. I walked to several shops recommended by the concierge of the hotel, and it was in the third store that I found what I was looking for. It was a heart-shaped sapphire, but it was mounted in a bracelet. I asked if they would sell me the stone by itself, and surprisingly, the salesman said yes. And the price was right. Could not have been better.

Within about twenty minutes, I was on my way back to the hotel with the stone, a bit nervous to be carrying such a valuable (well, for me) gem in my pocket. I was a good target waiting to get robbed.

To wrap up this snippet of the sapphire experience, that Christmas I gave my wife a custom-made gold cross with a small diamond set in each of the four ends, representing our four children, with the beautiful blue sapphire mounted at the juncture of the cross, representing our love. I designed it and had the piece made by a jeweler at NorthPark Center in Dallas. It turned out perfect. Vivienne was taken aback when she opened the gift, and she has worn it every day since she received it. It looks as beautiful on her as I had imagined.

Upon returning to the hotel after the first show, I realized I had some bug or food poisoning and was going to be in for a long night of driving the porcelain bus. Most everyone had been ill at some point during the tour, but I had been lucky until now. So for the rest of the dark hours of the night, I traipsed between the bed and the toilet. It was a particularly terrible experience, as I recall, and I felt like I wanted to lay down and die right there. I'm sure most people know this terrible feeling.

Finally, at about six o'clock in the morning, I fell asleep. My body was exhausted, and I simply had nothing left in me to come out. However, it wasn't too long before my hotel-room phone rang. I answered groggily, "Hello?"

On the other end of the phone, I could hear some angry voice saying it was Diane calling from New York, and what the hell did I think I was doing putting three buses on reserve for the potential US tour in the fall?

I was stunned by what was happening. I felt like it was some sort of nightmare caused by the illness, but then she repeated herself even louder. I replied that, along with Omar, we had met backstage in Singapore and had gone over the upcoming schedule, and in particular the travel plans for the Northeastern leg. We all agreed buses were what was best for good shows and safety.

Then what Diane said next was the most ludicrous thing I have ever heard in my life. She said she'd never okayed renting buses, and she continued by claiming she was not in attendance at any meeting with me and Omar in Singapore.

I asked her point blank, "Diane, are you calling me a liar?" She responded that she was, in fact, saying I was lying about her being in any such meeting or that she'd agreed rock-and-roll tour buses were the most logical way to travel for these designated shows. I think the rest of the conversation went something like this:

"Diane, if anyone is lying it's you, and furthermore, I quit as of right now!"

And I hung up the phone. I think the phone rang several times, but I didn't answer it and went back to sleep for an hour or so. They still had two more concerts to do, which was to make up for the canceled shows in the Philippines. Seems the smoke from the volcano had cleared enough for planes to fly into Manila. Sadly, I wouldn't go, but I wasn't going to have some inexperienced mother of some mall pop star call me liar.

Upon arising and showering—still a bit weak after an all-nighter of screaming at the ants—I packed my suitcase and called both Omar and Debbie, who had already heard from her mom. I made arrangements for my flight back to Dallas from Taipei, and before I left got to visit with some of the band and crew, who were sorry I was leaving but agreed with my point. However, the dancers and Debbie did not speak to me if we passed in the hall or lobby. Later that day, I took a taxi to the airport, checked in, and after phoning my wife to give her the not-so-welcome news, boarded the plane home.

While I have never wanted to speak with Diane or her daughter again, I have talked to some of the band here and there, and to this day Omar remains one of my closest friends. He is still one of the top production managers in the world, working with some of the biggest names in the entertainment business.

But I was just glad to get home to my family.

Debbie Gibson 1991 One Step Ahead Tour Dates

January 26, 1991: Maracanã Stadium (Rio de Janeiro, Brazil)

June 12, 1991: Osaka Castle Hall (Osaka, Japan)

June 13, 1991: Budokan (Tokyo, Japan)

June 14, 1991: Budokan (Tokyo, Japan)

June 22, 1991: Araneta Coliseum—canceled (Manila, Philippines)

June 23, 1991: Araneta Coliseum—canceled (Manila, Philippines)

June 25, 1991: Singapore Indoor Stadium (Kallang, Singapore)

June 27, 1991: Putra Centre (Kuala Lumpur, Malaysia)

June 29, 1991: San Pelita (Jakarta, Indonesia)

July 3, 1991: MBK Hall (Bangkok, Thailand)

July 6, 1991: Taipei Municipal Stadium (Taipei, Taiwan)

July 7, 1991: Taipei Municipal Stadium (Taipei, Taiwan)

I left the tour after the second Taipei date, which was my choice!

CHAPTER 19

FireHouse on Fire

On Fire with No Support!

My friend Tommy Booth, a travel agent based in New York City, had been wanting to get me paired up with this power-ballad rock band who had produced numerous hits in the late 1980s and early 1990s. But for some reason, our timing just never worked out. That is until 1995.

FireHouse had released its third album in April 1995 on Epic Records and was now planning a promotional tour through Steve Barnett and Hard to Handle Management. And guess what, I was available for the days the group needed a tour manager. Finally! I was technically working for the record company because Epic was footing the bill and paying my substantial salary. The people there had obviously heard I was good at my job as I was treated very well.

The first show on the tour was going to be in Kuala Lumpur, Malaysia, on June 17. After the deal was done and all was in order, I flew to Newark Airport in New Jersey to meet up with the band and hop on a plane for the *long* flight to Southeast Asia.

C. J. Snare was the vocalist and played keyboards, Bill Leverty was on guitar, the drummer was Michael Foster, and Perry Richardson handled bass. We all met in the concourse of the airport on June 12, and immediately I knew we'd get along well as we had a good laugh about who was going to sit next to the sumo wrestler-sized fellow in line ahead of us. He was massive.

We flew at least in business class for what seemed like forever and finally arrived in Malaysia, made it through passport control, and gathered our luggage. I was stiff but excited to be back in this exotic country with hopes that our hotel was going to be nice. From the look of the drive in, it was questionable.

Once we got into the city, though, there were some modern buildings that looked better and offered more promise of a good room. Mind you, this was when construction was happening on the Petronas Twin Towers, the tallest buildings being built in the world at the time. More about that later.

We stayed at the InterContinental hotel, which was beautiful. It had a great restaurant, and to make things even better, the Hard Rock Cafe, where we were to perform, was seventy-five yards down a hallway, so we didn't even have to leave the building if we didn't want to.

However, after arriving and noticing the band had gone off to catch up on sleep, I grabbed a cab. Thinking I'd be clever, I explained to the concierge that I wanted to go to an antique mall or shop. He signaled for a cab, spoke to the driver, and then, zoom, we were off. Next thing I knew, I was on a freeway full of whizzing traffic and within a few minutes noticed we were headed away from town. I did my best to remain calm, all the while thinking that my body might never be found.

I told myself I was worried for no reason and said to the driver, "Antique." He nodded as if to conform he knew just where we were headed. After traveling about twenty more minutes, with no Kuala Lumpur in sight, we pulled off the freeway and headed down a narrow cement street before turning onto a dirt road. It was quasi-jungle-looking with a few buildings scattered about—old buildings, not fancy city ones. The driver pulled into a dirt parking slot in front of one of them and then turned around to me, smiled, and said, "Batik!"

He had taken me to a local place where they made batik material, which was very prominent over there. Wow, did we get this one wrong. He signaled he'd wait while I went in—an offer I was grateful for—and I entered the scraggly building.

Inside, a lady met me, and sure enough, it was a small but efficient batik factory with finely made batik stamps hanging from the walls and printed and colorful material strung up everywhere there was a spot, drying. There were a dozen large cement vats, which looked like oversized bathtubs, and each was filled with a different color of dyed liquid. I walked around as the scene was sort of interesting, but once I'd had my fill of batik making, I asked the lady if she knew where I might find Malaysian antiques. Using my pidgin English and hand signals as best I could, she finally got what I was trying to ask. Antiques! She then told me the antique shops were in the city. Wow! A fifty-dollar cab ride to see how batik was made was just what I needed after twenty-three hours on a plane.

Back at the hotel, I heard there was a pool on the mezzanine floor, so on the first evening I thought I'd go for a swim since the weather was warm. The pool was beautiful, and the lights were on. It was fabulous. Then, to my surprise, out came Charlie Buster and Scott Hyman, the two technicians who were traveling with us.

It was a good end to a rather hectic day, and I got to know them both pretty well by the time our swim was over. Being friends with everyone on the tour is always a good thing because you never know when you're going to need something or someone's help. The band members never materialized, though, as I suspect they were upstairs still sound asleep.

Upon awakening the next morning, I went downstairs to have breakfast. Again, I usually chose to not use room service (as did most of the band). Instead, I wanted to be a part of the culture wherever we were visiting, even in the US.

The restaurant was full of people, and it had a buffet that was amazing. Western foods and Asian foods and foods for different religions, there was something for everyone. I played it safe and had some cereal (probably with donkey milk, who knows?) and eggs and toast. I was cautious, not wanting to get Montezuma's revenge. Then as the band came in to eat breakfast, I had company, and my table was filled, although instead of playing it safe, several of them just ate bits of everything being served. A habit that later during the Southeast Asian jaunt would come back to haunt them.

Now it was back to work. Along with our record-company hosts, I took the band on a number of interviews over the next two days. There were a couple by the hotel's pool and a few at radio stations or elsewhere. I even went out and bought a bag of freshly fried bugs to liven up one interview, but no one ate any. Meanwhile, Scott and Charlie got all the gear set up for the concert. Even better, the Hard Rock gave us free food, which is always nice, especially when the burgers, fries, and nachos are great.

On the day of the show, I first did some shopping, which was interesting. I bartered on and off with one storekeeper for over two hours, meaning I'd leave and then return again, hoping to get a lower price for a Malaysian man's wedding hat made of silk. I collected interesting things wherever we went, and finally I talked the lady who ran the shop down enough to where I felt comfortable I could afford it. The hat sits in my home to this day.

Another great part of those numerous jaunts to Asia and South America was that I'd ask the record representative if they had any new CDs they could supply me with to listen to. Usually within a day or two, the person would come back to me with a stack of them. Most were UK or American bands, but once in a while there would be one released by a local group from that particular country. After several years of this, I had a massive CD collection at my home in Dallas. Once the children moved out and my wife and I finally sold our house, I gave all the CDs to Goodwill. Besides, MP3 players were now on the scene and easier to manage. But back then, I always carried an extra duffle bag for all the CDs I might bring back.

That evening we were taken through the rear entrance of the Hard Rock and to the dressing room. The opening act was from the Philippines and played all cover material. On each song, they sounded exactly like the original recording—note for note, vocals for vocals. Of course, you know where Journey's new singer, Arnel Pineda, hails from. They must have a special knack for duplicating someone's singing or someone's playing. The group that night was better than any cover band I had ever seen.

FireHouse came on the smallish stage to a packed Hard Rock, and the place went nuts with each song. It was amazing to watch, and the band and crew had a great time, I am sure. And this was only our first show of the tour. We still had Singapore, Thailand, Indonesia, and South Korea to go.

Singapore was fine. We took a tour of all the shopping there, and if you have ever been, you know it's one of the best knickknack shopping places in the world, or at least in Southeast Asia. I remember buying an ebony-wood antique abacus, which still hangs in my house (in case I ever forget how to add and subtract).

Then it was off to Bangkok, Thailand, where our hotel was spectacular with great rooms and a very nice restaurant. Next door, there was a shop that made some very beautiful Thai coffins. I wanted to buy one, but I feared getting it back to Dallas would be too hard.

We visited a fancy mall, which was very similar to all the shops in Singapore, but at night we went to the street market that sold all kinds of strange stuff. I bought some knockoff Polo dress shirts that were very well made, and one became my favorite traveling shirt. My kids will always remember it, I am certain.

The concert was at their local Hard Rock, and the night went well, although there was nothing particularly spectacular about it, show-wise. The band was as good as always, and the kids were excited.

The next day we were off to Jakarta, Indonesia, where we stayed in a very nice hotel that wasn't too far away from the venue, another Hard Rock. This one had a huge stained-glass mural of Elvis behind the band's setup, and the owner of the club gave me a leather Hard Rock jacket as a gift. During the band's set, I snuck next door to a department store and bought dozens of yards of Indonesian cotton fabric to take back to Dallas for curtains and other things my wife might want to make. Again, that extra duffle bag I always carried came in useful. It was an interesting trip but not nearly as much fun as Thailand.

The tour continued on to Seoul, South Korea, where there was a lot of poverty but also a lot of commerce going on. It was an odd mix of both. The band actually played on an outdoor stage at an intersection of cross streets while traffic was stopped. It was very odd that they'd inconvenience all these motorists so some band from the US could perform for a bunch of teens for half an hour or so. But we got through it, and all in all, it was a great visit to Southeast Asia.

After Seoul, we flew back to the States on July 1 for the US leg of the tour, which involved primarily opening for other artists since FireHouse had not produced a hit record since 1992. They were still a major draw but not always a headliner. We played Tampa, Florida, on July 4, where the band knew a lot of people. Brian Johnson from AC/DC also lived in the area and got on stage to sing one of their songs, which drove the crowd crazy.

We toured the country through early August before going off to South America for a promo tour. There were a few stops at radio stations for a song or two on acoustic guitars, but mostly they were just interviews.

We went to Rio de Janeiro, which was fun. We attended a fancy party on the top of a skyscraper where the band were the guests of honor. The view of Rio at night was incredible. However, it was somewhat tough as not everyone spoke English and none of us spoke Portuguese. We also went up the mountain to see the Christ the Redeemer statue, which was an amazing sight, although the cable car ride was a bit scary. I'll never forget looking up at that giant statue.

We went to São Paulo, Brazil, as well for some PR, and I discovered that was where all the Volkswagen Beetles went when they disappeared from the US. They were everywhere. We then traveled to Buenos Aires, Argentina, which was a modern city, except for the slums we saw on our way into town. That was a sad sight. We also passed several huge stadiums that were long and open at either end, similar to our football stadiums. But we found out that these were used for tango-dancing expositions, which were very big there. People packed these stadiums to watch people dance. Pretty impressive.

We did a day of interviews at TV and radio stations, and when we got back to the hotel in the late afternoon, the record fellow asked us to dinner, to which we agreed. As we exited the car, he said, "I'll pick you up at about ten (that evening)." Once he drove away, we all gasped audibly at the late hour before we remembered that's when they normally ate.

He took us to a wonderful and well-known Argentinian churrascaria, where we had drinks and proceeded to eat a large meal of salad, vegetables, and so much meat. I know we all went back to our hotel moaning about how full we were and thinking we wouldn't need to eat for a few days.

Following a nice week in South America, we flew back to the US and continued to do some dates with other bands. September in 1995 was a great time as FireHouse was so good, and the members were all very nice guys. I remember thinking it wasn't as much work as many of the bands I'd toured with because they were easy to get along with. It was always good traveling with bands as the money was great, and the per diems, if they were being paid, added to the benefits. We usually had crew meals as well, so I was able to save even more money.

In fact, my time with FireHouse in 1995 went so well that I wound up going back out with them for a short tour through Southeast Asia and

Japan in 1996. One stop in particular stands out. After playing a show in Bangkok, we flew to Chiang Mai, a college town in northern Thailand. We got there, checked into an OK hotel, and were immediately whisked away to a convertible that was waiting to drive the band and me slowly down a main thoroughfare. Along the way, the guys were supposed to wave to the crowds of fans, although they turned out to be few and far between. This was the record representative's idea of a great PR stunt. We ended up at a record shop where the band signed autographs for a while, and then it was back to the hotel.

After dinner, five of us went to a Thai massage parlor. Well, I have to say that I don't believe any of us ever laughed so hard once we got over the initial nervousness. We all went in together, which we thought was a bit off, and were told to strip to our underwear. On the floor were about six thin mattresses placed side by side in a row. We were instructed to lie down, and as we were all making sarcastic comments and having a good laugh, these five ladies proceeded to maneuver our bodies into angles and bends and painful positions that we had never experienced before. Legs were squished up to your shoulder, and then they'd sit on your knees to flatten them. It was painful at the time, and all of us were moaning and cursing in a funny way, having never expected such rough treatment. But evidently this was a real Thai massage. I must admit it was great, and my body felt relaxed and limber, despite all the hilarious laughing as we moaned and groaned.

The following morning, I had committed to getting up and going with the band on a jaunt up into the mountains with the record rep. The time was way too early, but I made it. We stopped for lunch at a beautiful open-aired restaurant overlooking a tropical valley that was gorgeous. The food was good, and on our way back to the car, we stopped and rode elephants in the jungle for about forty-five minutes, which was cool. And for just five dollars, I was able to purchase the elephant hook—a small leader they used to guide the elephant—from the boy who led me. I then bought a wooden elephant bell that the animals wear so they can be found and heard in the jungle easily. It was a great memory.

We eventually wrapped the tour up in Japan, which was always fun. We played Nagoya, Osaka, and two shows in Tokyo. But even though we were only there for a week, when we flew back to our homes in the US, I now also had a new and well-paying job, which you'll read about in the next chapter.

FireHouse is still touring to this day, although without Snare, who unfortunately died in April 2024. C.J. was a great singer. He always warmed up before a show and was dedicated to keeping his voice healthy. And he was such a nice guy.

I do sometimes miss those days, and I still often communicate with Bill Leverty, the guitar player. What a life and experience it was. And I got paid to do it!

FireHouse 1995 Tour Dates

June 15–16, 1995: Malaysia Promotional Tour

June 17, 1995: Hard Rock Cafe (Kuala Lumpur, Malaysia)

June 19, 1995: Hard Rock Cafe (Singapore)

June 21, 1995: Hard Rock Cafe (Bangkok, Thailand)

June 23, 1995: Indonesia Promotional Tour

June 24, 1995: Hard Rock Cafe (Bali, Indonesia)

June 26, 1995: Indonesia Promotional Tour

June 29–30, 1995: South Korea Promotional Tour

July 3, 1995: Pine Knob Music Theatre (Clarkston, Michigan)

July 4, 1995: July 4 Celebration (Tampa, Florida)

July 15, 1995: Outagamie County Fair (Seymour, Wisconsin)

July 16, 1995: The Mirage (Minneapolis, Minnesota)

July 19, 1995: Waukesha County Fair (Waukesha, Wisconsin)

July 21, 1995: Acoustic Radio Performance (Costa Mesa, California)

July 22, 1995: Pacific Amphitheatre (Costa Mesa, California)

July 28, 1995: Head of the Lakes Fairgrounds (Superior, Wisconsin)

July 29, 1995: North Dakota State Fair Grandstand
(Minot, North Dakota)

August 2, 1995: Wisconsin Valley Fair, Marathon Park (Wausau, Wisconsin)

August 4, 1995: Monroe County Fair Arena (Monroe, Michigan)

August 6–15, 1995: South American Promotional Tour

August 17, 1995: State Fair of West Virginia (Lewisburg, West Virginia)

August 18, 1995: The Silo (Reading, Pennsylvania)

August 19, 1995: Bud Light Amphitheatre (Harveys Lake, Pennsylvania)

August 22, 1995: The Chance (Poughkeepsie, New York)

August 25, 1995: Birch Hill Nightclub (Old Bridge Township, New Jersey)

August 26, 1995: Mann Music Center (Philadelphia, Pennsylvania)

August 27, 1995: Merriweather Post Pavilion (Columbia, Maryland)

August 29, 1995: Beacon Theatre (New York, New York)

August 30, 1995: Beacon Theatre (New York, New York)

September 2, 1995: Acoustic Radio Performance (Louisville, Kentucky)

September 7, 1995: Acoustic Radio Performance (Hartford, Connecticut)

September 8, 1995: Ritz Theater (Charlotte, North Carolina)

September 12, 1995: York State Fair (York, Pennsylvania)

September 20, 1995: Club Quattro (Nagoya, Japan)

September 22, 1995: Club Quattro (Osaka, Japan)

September 23, 1995: Shibuya Kokaido (Tokyo, Japan)

September 24, 1995: Liquidroom (Tokyo, Japan)

CHAPTER 20

SHIPS

Six Hundred Fifty Japanese and One Gaijin.

It was fall 1995, and after touring again for a few years—on some very enjoyable tours, I must say—the time had come for me to hang up my suitcases again and be a dad. The kids were growing up, and we decided seeing them through the teenage years would take two of us.

The last time I found myself in this situation, though, the job I accepted was anything but enjoyable. One Sunday, while reading the Dallas paper, I spotted an ad for a company desiring a manager of operations. I got the position, but after a mere eighteen months it had turned out to be one of the worst experiences of my life. Not just touring life, but life in general. I won't even mention the name of the company.

They were Dallas-based and were impressed with my touring know-how, but their forte was sports, which wasn't all that different from music touring. They had several sporting events they'd take to cities around the world. They'd set up in various locations and then conduct a weekend of amateur competitions for whichever sport it was. On Monday, they were off to another city.

The office had a great number of employees, and most were young, paid very little, and worked very hard, long hours. I was one of the four oldest people in the company. The job started off seemingly fine, but before long I heard off-color jokes being told in mixed (male and female) company, and people were talked about behind their backs, often openly with no regard to who was listening. I quickly found out the atmosphere was not good. In fact, many young employees often passed comments to me about working nearly one hundred hours a week.

However, they were in the sporting business and hired straight out of college with a sports marketing degree, so they figured this was a great break. The boss and the top department heads, of which I was supposedly one, were not particularly nice people. If you weren't in their exclusive club, you didn't get noticed unless you did something wrong. The environment was caustic. I could only confide in one or two people and my wife.

Having said that, I've wasted enough space on this terrible experience and horrible group of people. Time to move on to the more enjoyable part of this chapter.

Fortunately, during my job search this time around, I discovered a Japanese event production company that had an office in Dallas, although most of its work took place in Japan. The group in Texas served as a liaison for all that went on abroad, especially events having to do with the entertainment industry.

I wrote the gentleman, Yoichi Aoki, asked for an interview, and sent my credentials for his perusal. Within a few days, he responded, and I was set up with a face-to-face interview at his office, a massive space on Luna Road and Royal Lane in northwest Dallas. The interview went well, and Yoichi hired me on the spot with a suitable salary and title. I was made a vice president of Shimizu International Production Services (SHIPS), the Dallas-based office of Shimizu Octo, Inc. I had been to Japan on several occasions and always had a great time and liked the Japanese people, so I was looking forward to this. So, too, was my wife.

I had one more touring obligation to perform before I could join Shimizu, and that was the Asian tour with FireHouse in 1996, which, as mentioned in the previous chapter, took me back to Japan. Yoichi decided that while I was there, it might be a good time to meet the CEO of the company, Mr. Takuji Shimizu. Sounded good to me, and off I went on tour with FireHouse, who turned out to be a favorite band of mine.

Since I had been to Southeast Asia before, I was aware of the custom-made suits that could be had for very little money. I found a reputable tailor in Thailand and made a deal that if I brought in customers and sold a certain number of custom suits, they would make me one or two for free.

And it turned out that the band members and a couple of their wives traveling with us all bought suits, so I was set. I had a beautiful double-breasted dark-green suit made for me. It fit perfectly, so I figured at least I'd look pretty good for my upcoming meeting with Mr. Shimizu.

Following FireHouse's last show in Tokyo, I was supposed to meet my future boss. He was taking me to dinner. I knew he didn't speak English well, or so he said, but his secretary came along to translate. I wore my suit to the gig and was sort of out of place with everyone else so casual, but all the same, being dressed up felt nice.

After the concert, the band knew what I was doing, so I said goodbye to them and waited a few minutes before a car pulled up at the back of the venue with a driver in front and Mr. Shimizu in back. I must say that being in a group of people where you don't speak the language is usually a bit uncomfortable, but this felt natural. The translator proved very useful, and Mr. Shimizu and I seemed to get along well at dinner. He said he was grateful I was joining their team. I was the only American out of some 650 Japanese employees.

The car dropped me off at the Capitol Hotel Tokyu, where the band had already turned in for the night, so it wasn't until the next day that I told them I had taken the job with Shimizu. As much as I wanted to stay with them as their tour manager or possibly even their manager, knowing they didn't have the income source of their earlier years, I had to take the position with Shimizu.

We finished the Asian dates and promo tour, and once again I was headed across the Pacific on my way back to Dallas. The flight was long, but I had learned how to sleep on a plane at the drop of a hat!

Upon my return, it was only a week or so before I was installed behind a temporary desk at Shimizu's Dallas office. It was very large with a low-ceilinged administrative area covering a portion of the space with the rest being a proper storage warehouse. Yoichi had leased space to another production company, which kept their equipment there and had a smaller office as well.

There was a receptionist, Cindy, who fielded calls, and Masumi Komatsu, who dealt with the Japanese translations and our clients in Japan. In addition, there was an office for Hisashi Takashi, who ran Aerial US, a recording company Yoichi had set up for his nephew to run, and he did a good job. I was at one end of the vast lobby area, although there were sofas and chairs grouped about. There was also a kitchen with a refrigerator and then a hallway that led to Yoichi's office.

In his office was a corner desk with a computer for Mary McCullough, his assistant who he had known for several decades going back to, I believe, his days at the Dallas Theater Center, where he was a set designer and builder. Yoichi had a large dining table as a desk that was always neat but covered with papers of projects he was working on. He always had his hands in something productive.

One day while looking for a better desk at a business supply place, I discovered glass panels about ten feet high that all connected. With these, we could turn our vast open lobby into a smaller lobby, a conference room, and two offices on the side—a larger one, which I would claim, and a smaller space in case it was needed. With some help, they were assembled, and it looked nice and office-like.

It wasn't much longer before Yoichi told me I was going to get an assistant named Kayoko Loucks, who lived in the Dallas suburb of Richardson but was, in fact, the daughter of Mr. Shimizu, the chairman of the company. Yikes! What would this be like? She was married to a fellow from Kansas, an English/Japanese translator, and they had three children.

Kayoko was very shy and reluctant at first when she came to the office. Not because she was an assistant to me, but because she had not been in that type of office setting in a while, if ever, and she didn't want to cause any waves. But we always discussed ideas, how to entice new customers or attractions, and what we could do to increase company business. That was a good time.

Shortly after joining Shimizu, I received a phone call from a fellow with a company who was promoting a tour with Linda Ronstadt for the summer of 1996 that would include Marvin Hamlisch and the Pittsburgh Symphony Orchestra for the first leg. He was looking for a tour manager to handle road details and primarily assist the symphony as Linda and Marvin had their own minders. This was going to be a tour through about twenty-five or so cities, performing mostly in amphitheaters. Linda would be primarily singing her ballads with a few of her key band members playing on stage while Marvin would conduct the seventy-five-piece orchestra.

I spoke to Yoichi, and he agreed it would be a good thing to do as I'd be on loan from Shimizu, so to speak. I would take no salary from Shimizu, though, because I was being paid very well by the tour. Unfortunately, I once again had to say goodbye to my lovely family; this was always the toughest part.

The touring party and orchestra would fly on a large privately charted jet. One of the main things I'd have to keep up with was the labor union hours and breaks for the symphony players who had certain restrictions concerning travel on performing days, travel on nonperforming days, rehearsal days, sound checks, etc. It sounded more complex than it turned out to be.

We rehearsed in Pittsburgh for less than a week with mostly just Marvin and the orchestra. I can't remember if Linda and her band even attended these rehearsals as one of the first places I met Linda was on the chartered plane to Michigan. The first show we performed was on July 15, 1996, at the Kresge Auditorium in Interlochen. The hotel was on the water, and with my experience and good people skills, checking in wasn't too difficult. We had a few hours before leaving for the venue, which gave me a chance to socialize with the touring group. It seemed like it would be a good summer and a nice way to spend the evenings, even if I did have to be away from home.

When the concert was going on, I was able to relax and walk around or listen. Basically, once I got my advance work taken care of, I could mostly do as I wished. There was no opening act, so the show was about two hours in length, including a brief intermission. The orchestra was great and seeing Marvin conducting was cool. And, of course, hearing Linda sing nightly was also nice. All in all, the experience was extremely pleasant. In fact, I cannot think of any incident that caused friction or problems.

However, I did notice something odd about ten days into the tour. Several times a night, Marvin would reach into his tuxedo pocket and extract something small, look down at it, and then return the item to his pocket. I noticed this happening on a few occasions, often several times in one evening, and even while the show was going on.

One day I saw a quiet moment with Marvin and asked him just what was he doing on stage each time he pulled something out of his pocket? Marvin looked at me and glanced around coyly, as if he didn't want anyone to hear, and whispered to me, "I'm checking the Yankees score." Not much I could say to that.

Linda toured for three weeks with the Pittsburgh Symphony before taking two weeks off. The break was appreciated as we all enjoyed a few days at home. When we regrouped, we picked up where we left off, although now she was making a swing through California and areas west, and she had other symphonies backing her.

We were based in LA at the Four Seasons Hotel during this portion of the tour. I have a friend who is an incredible songwriter and singer who has never made it as a star in his own right, but he has written songs for other celebrities and even produced their records. His name is Andy Parks, although he goes by the stage name of John Andrew Parkes. He is my age, and to be honest, I think he would agree that he'll probably never have a hit record or a following much bigger than what he claims now, which saddens me. Anyhow, all those years ago, when we were a bit younger but not spring chickens, I had Andy come by the Four Seasons and play three songs in a vacant suite for Linda's tour producer.

The producer and I sat and listened to Andy play on the piano and sing with no microphone. When he stopped and looked over toward us sitting on a sofa, the producer said how incredible he was. The songs had even made him well up with tears and very emotional. That was a good start.

Then he said, "I'd love to put you out on tour with any number of stars, opening their shows. But the only problem, and I know what will happen, is the headline artist will not allow you to play more than one night. You're too good. You would intimidate them right off the stage. They wouldn't want to follow you."

He apologized and said he thought Andy was one of the most talented singers, storytellers, and writers he had ever heard, but there was nothing he could think of to do with such abundant talent all in one person. Later, Andy and I commiserated over coffee in the cafe, where he said, "That's been my problem all along in too many cases." Andy was my close friend. He lived in South Texas, and we spoke often. I always told him, "You're the best!" And he was. Andy died unexpectedly in October 2024

We opened the second leg of Linda's tour with a pair of shows in Seattle, August 17–18, and worked our way down the coast, playing the Universal Amphitheatre on August 24. After a stop in San Bernardino, we were then off to play at San Diego's Hospitality Point on August 26, which was a great facility right on the water. To make a promising night even better, I was asked if I would host Bob Hope, his wife, and their friends by taking them to their seats, helping them if they needed anything, and returning them to the VIP area at intermission and after the show.

I had worked with, well, around Bob Hope before when I was with Andy Gibb. This was when Andy performed for his seventy-seventh birthday TV special, which was called *Bob Hope's All-Star Comedy Birthday Party* and was filmed at the Air Force Academy in Colorado Springs. Needless to say, I was thrilled to be asked to host him. However, it seems that time had taken its toll on Mr. Hope since I'd last seen him in 1980. He was nearly blind or had severe sight problems and seemed much frailer. I did introduce myself and explained that I was with Andy at his seventy-seventh birthday, and I reminded him how we stayed with the base generals and that ice skaters Tai Babilonia and Randy Gardner were there. To my surprise, he remembered, or at least said he did, and he greeted me kindly as he did all of his guests.

We played three more shows, moving eastward to Las Vegas and then down to Arizona, and then suddenly the tour was over. Within a number of hours, everyone was saying their goodbyes and were on their way home.

I have to say, at my age then, that was a perfect tour to wrap up my long career on the road. Polite people, great songs, a calm scene, and a great deal of prestige. All in all, it was a happy way to close my lonely suitcase for good. Plus, I'd usually have to then look for more work, but I already had a job back at home that I was thoroughly enjoying.

My position at Shimizu was to primarily be a liaison between western entertainment acts going into Japan and my counterparts abroad, detailing what production needs would be required during their tours through Asia. Additionally, I sought companies in the US, Canada, the UK, and Europe who might be heading to Japan.

Shimizu did production services for a large part of the entertainment industry in Japan. We worked for the Tokyo Dome and the Osaka Dome, furnishing crews, ticket takers, and portable toilets and providing clean up. The company also built structures, had a sizable vinyl-sign business, a restaurant-fabricating division, and at one point had more Columbus McKinnon electric chain hoist motors than any other production company in the world. We were among Tomcat Global's biggest truss customers and worked closely with Atomic Design and Vari-Lite.

One of Yoichi's aces, Mark Fisher, was a well-known British stage designer for the Rolling Stones and U2, among many others. Yoichi would bring Mark in often when big-named Japanese bands wanted a sizable and unique stage to tour their country with. Although they never toured outside of Japan—well, not to the West, at least—there were some major stages designed and built, some of which toured with their bands for up to a year.

Obviously, Shimizu and the bands would benefit more by prebuilding the staging and effects in Japan, so in a town outside of Tokyo called Chiba, we had a massive warehouse facility and a large soundstage available. It was perfect for bands to rehearse in and even shoot a video or live show if they wanted.

I would often be asked to get involved in one of Yoichi's directed projects and so would travel to Japan, which was always fun. Except I never got to take my wife along, sadly.

It was somewhat frustrating trying to scrape up business, though, because I was used to being handed a business (a tour as it were), taking the reins, and running with it. I tried not to let it bother me, but it did.

I thoroughly enjoyed my associates in Japan and Dallas, and Kayoko and I got along well, but it wasn't the active business I was used to. I guess part of the attraction of touring was that every day was completely different. That is, everything but the show, usually. However, the primary benefit of this job was that I got to spend almost every night and morning with my family and be in their lives, whether they liked it or not (just kidding).

Sometime during the late 1990s, I was contacted out of the blue by a representative from Nike in Oregon, asking if we did production for events in Japan. Of course, my attention was piqued, and I said, "Yes, how can we help you?" A couple of their designers had come up with what they called an interactive miniature golf course that was scheduled to be built on Odaiba, a man-made island next to the impressive multistory Fuji Broadcasting Center. This was to run the same weekend as a big golf tournament in Japan.

Excitedly, I told Yoichi about the call, and we discussed how to handle the inquiry. It could be a big deal. I called Nike back and told them some of the preliminary things we needed to know: size of venue, time frame for construction, equipment and materials anticipated, personnel, just basic things. We were able to give them a ballpark quote for the building of this design, and they invited Yoichi and me up to their corporate offices.

We flew to Oregon to meet with them, and in addition to enjoying the Nike campus, we had a productive meeting. We listened to their presentation on what they envisioned in Japan for this event. They were expecting over ten thousand people per day (paying attendees) to this miniature golf course, which would be spread over five acres of what had once been basically a landfill. When it was our turn to speak, I talked about our company's abilities to handle all they needed, and then they asked for a cost. At that, Yoichi said he had been consulting with our Japanese associates, getting estimates for the materials and the type of work Nike needed, and he gave them a figure of $250,000.

Mind you, this event had nothing to do with the actual golf tournament going on with Tiger Woods and other famous golfers. It was separate yet still associated remotely. But Nike's feeling was that since everyone couldn't go to the golf tournament, they would go to the Nike interactive course and have a golf outing of sorts. In the car with Yoichi on the way to our hotel for the night, my cell phone (an early flip-phone model) rang, and it was one of the executives from Nike saying they would agree to our quote. When we got back to Dallas, we would iron out a contract and all the necessary details for this event.

Over the next month, I worked with Yoichi, Masumi, and Kayoko, coordinating everything Nike wanted, and left the contract to Yoichi, Mary, and the Japanese office to sort out. This was a large coup for me, I believed.

The time came for us to fly to Japan for the event. Yoichi was already there, as he often went early, so only Masumi and I were on the flight. Again, my wife couldn't attend as we had four kiddos at home. We arrived in Japan and went to a hotel Nike had arranged for us, which lasted all of two nights. It was too far from the event site and the hotel next door where all the Nike people were staying.

The first day we went across the Rainbow Bridge to Odaiba and found the site was a bare field. We had several work trailers set up, and during one of several meetings, we were introduced to a production manager Nike had hired to look after their side of things. Some top executives and producers from Fuji Television and Japan Airlines (JAL) were in the meeting as well, and we discussed plans on how often we'd meet to keep everyone coordinated and on the same page. The language difference made things a bit difficult, but there were interpreters for the Yanks, which was helpful.

This miniature golf course, though, was not like a miniature golf course you and I would think of. It wasn't nine or eighteen small holes, but rather large and extremely odd ideas of what these designers thought would attract Japanese fans. Oh boy, were they mistaken. *Had they ever been to Japan?* I wondered.

One of the holes was a giant step-up grass-covered platform (in fact many of these holes were step-up affairs) with maybe eight steel golf bags that had TV screens showing loops of Tiger Woods and other golfers playing in various tournaments. Another hole was a towering fifteen-foot-tall and twenty-foot-long sand trap that the attendees were supposed to walk through so they could get a feel of what it would be like in a sand trap. What? I believe there were maybe three holes where a person could actually putt a golf ball into a cup, but this was someone's bizarre idea of what would sell to the Japanese audience and get them to fork over hard-earned yen to enter the facility.

Each day many Shimizu workers would come out and build the course according to the plans Nike had supplied. Meanwhile, Masumi and I would spend our days putting out fires as problems arose. Usually things would be settled in time for our production meeting, which always included the corporate executives and totaled about twenty people. And almost every day, without fail, the fellow Nike hired to represent their interests would say something out of order or that something couldn't happen in a certain way and, once translated, would raise the ire of the executives. A couple of times they were close to pulling their funding on the project, as they did not like his attitude or the way he was addressing them.

Fortunately, with Masumi's help, I was able to jump in, calm the situation, and get everyone to agree to continue moving forward. I'd convince the sponsorship executives not to withdraw their support and let us trudge on despite their disdain for the Nike production manager's attitude and disrespectful manner.

Despite arriving in Japan early, Yoichi finally made his appearance at the job site around two weeks into the build. He was baffled about all that Nike had designed as well, although he was more familiar with the plans going into it than I was, having detailed the costs for the quote. However, he didn't think it was going to be a success either. A few of us knew it, mostly those of us from Shimizu, but we kept it to ourselves and especially did not say anything to the sponsors.

After nearly four weeks of building and transitioning this bare land into an impressive-looking event site—complete with banners, ticket booths, trash receptacles, snack facilities, and big screens that would broadcast the actual tournament—one of the last things to do was put in actual live grass all over the five-acre site. I arrived one day, and there were large pallets of green turf laid out with about a dozen ladies of various ages, dressed in white- or cream-colored outfits, laying the grass side by side so it would look naturally grown. These ladies, I soon realized, were permanently stooped over from laying grass as this is what they did for a living. Their backs were permanently arched from constantly being bent over laying grass. It took several days, but they worked fast.

Then it happened, and with only two days to go before the grand opening. During the production meeting, the Nike fellow said that the grass was drying and curling up on the edges and was unacceptable. Everyone in that trailer was floored and sat aghast, staring at him. He said it had to be redone. I again calmed the situation, at least temporarily, and asked Masumi to see if Yoichi could get over there quickly. He did and a closed-door meeting was held that resulted in Shimizu agreeing to have all the grass scooted together and painted. Yoichi sent me for a loop when he said that Shimizu would pay for all of this, even though I didn't feel it was our fault.

I was angry, but the ladies and painters got busy, fixed all the grass, and sprayed it a nice green, so all was acceptable. As we were two days to the start, all the Nike people were there, even the two young designers whose silly idea this whole thing was. After having us deliver some greenery in the form of potted plants and shrubs, they signed off on our agreement, and technically, other than administering the affair for the weekend, we had done our job.

Later that day, I was with Yoichi, and he knew I was not pleased about the grass situation (or other technical difficulties, for that matter), but he told me that I shouldn't worry. Shimizu would still make a sizable amount of money from this event as not only was Nike paying for the building costs, but there were also dismantling costs and the scrapping of the used materials, of which we'd keep all the plywood for other projects. And believe me, there was a lot of plywood—a lot!

In addition, he informed me that Nike had been given a choice on the grass, knowing that since this was taking place in November, it was not prime grass-growing season. They could either pay a premium price for guaranteed green grass that would not shrink or buy a cheaper version and hope for the best. You can guess what they chose by the outcome of the shifting and painting exercises those poor ladies had to endure. Yoichi was always very calm and reassuring,

The following morning, we all met at the site for the grand opening. There were TV cameras and the sponsor executives and even Tiger Woods came, if I remember correctly. The event was to run through Sunday evening while the real golf tournament was being played at a prestigious Japanese golf course.

Once all the cameras and executives had departed, it was time now for the public, but they were scarce. When people found out this wasn't a normal, albeit fancier, miniature golf course, they didn't want to pay the high price to attend. They wanted to putt the ball not walk around looking at things some designers had imagined would be of interest. In the end, instead of getting nearly forty thousand attendees over the weekend, I believe we had less than five thousand. It was a big flop for Nike and the sponsors, to whom the Nike executives had sold the concept and its potential for success.

On Sunday evening, when it came time for the event to close, not a single Nike person could be found anywhere on site. We closed the gates, locked up, and turned off the lights. Yoichi and the executives from Fuji and JAL suggested our immediate Shimizu team of about five people and their group of four all go have dinner at a nearby Korean BBQ place. That worked for me.

We went and sat on the floor, as expected, and I sat sort of in the middle but across from Masumi while Yoichi sat at one end with the executives. We had a great meal, especially since I didn't have to do the ordering. We ate and chatted and scratched our heads at how Nike could have thought this event would be a good idea, as they evidently didn't know the Japanese people well. Then suddenly the table went quiet, and I noticed everyone was looking at me. Great, now what had I done?

I looked at Masumi, my friend, workmate, and reliable interpreter. I must have had a worried look on my face because she said something to the effect of, "Oh, Larry, don't worry. They were talking down there about you, and the executives with Fuji and JAL told Yoichi that had it not been for your intervention and calm at every meeting, especially the ones with the Nike production manager, they would have scrapped the project and taken their losses and never dealt with Nike again." They raised their sake cups to me in salute, and I was extremely humbled and thrilled on the inside. I glanced at Yoichi down the table, and he had a big smile on his face—I am hoping from pride.

Despite missing my family for a month, the best thing about the whole experience was the hotel. It was spectacular, and the meals I ate while there were all wonderful. And I made new Japanese friends and had a unique experience, one not many will ever have. Japan is a wonderful place, and the people are great. Several years have passed since I worked for Shimizu, but I still keep in touch with some of my associates in Japan and even some from Yamaha and other companies I dealt with during my rock-and-roll touring days.

I carried on with Shimizu and Yoichi for a while longer and even started an LED lighting business with him before LEDs were everywhere, which I will tell you more about in the next chapter. I will always look back on my time there as being very special, and I worked with some very special people, including Jean, Yoichi's wife.

Now here we are, a few years down the road—OK, a good number of years down the road—and Yoichi has sadly passed away and so has Mary while Masumi and Hisashi got married. Unfortunately, I don't know where Cindy is. Mr. Takuji Shimizu died in December 2024 in his early nineties, and his son Taro Shimizu is the current president and CEO of the company.

Once we were back in Dallas after our trip to Japan for the Nike event, Kayoko Shimizu soon announced that since her husband was spending so much time in Japan for work, they had decided to sell their home in Texas and relocate there. The move didn't take long to happen, and whoosh, she was gone. Changes, always changes!

Today, Kayoko, my one-time shy assistant, is now the executive vice president of Shimizu Octo, the largest entertainment production company in Asia. I am very proud of what she has accomplished, and I believe her father is as well.

Thank you to all of you, my Japanese friends and associates!

Linda Ronstadt 1996 *Dedicated to the One I Love* Tour Dates

July 15, 1996: Kresge Auditorium (Interlochen, Michigan)

July 16, 1996: Fraze Pavilion (Kettering, Ohio)

July 17, 1996: Gund Arena (Cleveland, Ohio)

July 19, 1996: Garden State Arts Center (Holmdel, New Jersey)

July 20, 1996: Jones Beach Theater (Wantagh, New York)

July 21, 1996: Great Woods Center (Mansfield, Massachusetts)

July 23, 1996: Merriweather Post Pavilion (Columbia, Maryland)

July 24, 1996: Fox Theatre (Mashantucket, Connecticut)

July 26, 1996: Etess Arena (Atlantic City, New Jersey)

July 27, 1996: Oakdale Theatre (Wallingford, Connecticut)

July 28, 1996: Saratoga Performing Arts Center (Saratoga Springs, New York)

July 31, 1996: Blockbuster Pavilion (Charlotte, North Carolina)

August 1, 1996: GTE Virginia Beach Amphitheater (Virginia Beach, Virginia)

August 2, 1996: Walnut Creek Amphitheatre (Raleigh, North Carolina)

August 3, 1996: Nissan Pavilion (Gainesville, Virginia)

August 5, 1996: Meadow Brook Music Festival (Rochester Hills, Michigan)

August 17, 1996: Pier 62/63 (Seattle, Washington)

August 18, 1996: Pier 62/63 (Seattle, Washington)

August 21, 1996: Concord Pavilion (Concord, California)

August 22, 1996: Reno Hilton Amphitheatre (Reno, Nevada)

August 24, 1996: Universal Amphitheatre (Universal City, California)

August 25, 1996: Blockbuster Pavilion (San Bernardino, California)

August 26, 1996: Hospitality Point (San Diego, California)

August 27, 1996: Aladdin Theatre (Las Vegas, Nevada)

August 29, 1996: Tucson Convention Center (Tucson, Arizona)

August 30, 1996: Blockbuster Desert Sky Pavilion (Phoenix, Arizona)

CHAPTER 21

Road Cases

On the Record.

In mid-2004, I was in my home office working, no, hustling some of my projects, as I always did. I had hopes one would receive a happy welcome, and I would be able to start a new profitable venture.

The streaming of TV shows was only in its infancy then but growing rapidly, and I came up with the idea for a series about what life on the road touring was like primarily in the late sixties and seventies. Each show would have a necessary celebrity participant, which the audience and a network would demand, I felt sure, but the idea was to gather a couple of band members or a popular star and surround them with a few of their former or current touring crew. They would sit together somewhere in a relaxing atmosphere with snacks and drinks, including liquor (not everyone was going to Alcoholics Anonymous yet), and with the help of a low-key but educated and experienced moderator, a conversation would be initiated. Everyone would then have an enjoyable few hours reliving old times touring together.

It just so happens, as you might imagine, that people remember the same event in different ways, despite the fact they were both there. Maybe one was drunk and the other sober, you get the idea. This same scenario had happened to me over the years in a variety of locations with different bands and people, and each time the experience was magical in that everyone usually had a good trip down memory lane. The interactions were usually very funny to watch or be a part of.

That, in a nutshell, was the idea—film these gatherings and edit them into a clever show. These would not be about the celebrities but instead would focus primarily on the people who helped the celebrities get on stage, make hit records, and gain stardom.

It is worth stating here that neither I nor any of the off stage people I can think of ever felt any jealously or bitterness toward the celebrity or band we worked for just because they were making much more money than most of us. We were usually paid well when working for a major artist.

I decided I needed someone in Los Angeles who I could work with, who had good connections like me, and who had been around long enough to want something like this to happen. So I phoned the old lighting designer from my days with Ozzy Osbourne, Paul Dexter. He was a good friend, easy to get along with, and thank goodness, loved the idea as soon as I mentioned it. In fact, he said he'd been wanting to do something about what all we had done and accomplished, including possibly writing a book about life on the road.

I told him I had a name for the series, *Road Cases*, a play on the word headcases, for which the industry is widely known to have had because of the way many acted. You may be too young to remember all those years in the sixties when it was a joke to say to parents, "Lock up your daughters" because such and such band or singer was coming to town. The reputation of the rock-and-roll industry preceded itself with the aid of celebrated talents who were often making bold front-page headlines through some antic on stage or off. Or due to their untimely deaths, usually from drug overdoses, like Jim Morrison, Janis Joplin, Jimi Hendrix, or any of the dozen other sad cases. In later years, it became the heavy metal bands that scared parents, especially the one I toured with, Ozzy.

However, all of this negative publicity, from way back in the sixties to Ozzy's exploits, only seemed to cause more people to want to go see rock-and-roll concerts. Like in the olden days of the circus coming to town.

Paul loved the name, and we agreed on an equal partnership if anything ever happened with this project. We then laid out a plan to move forward. One of the things we wanted to do was identify a video production company that would go along with this idea and do the filming and editing, which was out of our lane. We came across a company called Incue, which was owned by Scott and Dave McVeigh, brothers who had an office in the West Hollywood area. We spoke with them, and while they, too, said they had thought of similar ideas, they agreed the project was sound and would be worth trying. We agreed on an even partnership with Paul and me and that we should meet as soon as possible.

I arranged a flight to LA, and we met with them at their office. After watching a video résumé they had created for their company, we knew they were capable of doing what needed to be done and, in fact, had experience interviewing people and getting answers from guests who were normally camera-shy.

One of the Incue members had a friend at the William Morris talent agency, and within a few weeks we were contacted by two of their agents, one in Los Angeles and one in New York. They were interested in signing us to see if they could license the show. Personally, I was on cloud nine, but I think all four of us were quite pleased with such an early positive reception. They offered us a one-year exclusive-representation contract, which idiotically we all signed without proper thought. We had legal counsel, but our lawyers didn't know what was coming our way.

I then flew back to LA for a meeting with the four of us and the William Morris people. I remember seeing Dennis Quaid in the lobby heading upstairs to his agent's office, I suspect. Nevertheless, we finally were called up to a certain floor and shown into a conference room where a couple of younger agents sat. Introductions were made, and we began by presenting our ideas for *Road Cases* and how the show should be done.

When we'd finished, although they had seen our presentation, they came back with a completely different idea of what they wanted to sell. Their suggestion was for us to put a camera and cameraman (meaning Scott or Dave) on the bus with a band, the Foo Fighters being mentioned as an example. We would film six to eight weeks behind the scenes on the tour and then take the footage and edit that into a series. Their plan was nothing at all like what we had presented to them—nothing!

We all smiled and tried to find some common ground on the matter, but they seemed set on their vision for *Road Cases,* our show. This was not how it was meant to be projected to a viewing audience. Yes, you can say they were the agents and must have known what was best and what would sell and that we were silly for not just going along with their idea. But we had spent a great many years on the road in the entertainment and film industries, and we didn't just want to roll over like a dog wanting to be petted.

After the meeting ended, with smiles, handshakes, and promises to find a suitable solution, we four returned to the Incue office and discussed the ways it might work. In the end, we agreed the William Morris people were on a different page than we were. I believe we concocted a letter stating that, after thinking about it long and hard, we couldn't agree to let them represent us unless they would pitch the show as we had originally intended. We all signed the letter and sent it to them, knowing this could either backfire or help them see our point of view.

Well, it backfired big-time. They responded by saying we'd signed a one-year contract with them, and we could do nothing else without their participation and a percentage of profits being taken on the *Road Cases* concept until the year was over. So as angry as we were getting caught in such a trap, we decided to wait out the agreement until it expired, hoping the idea wouldn't be taken by someone else.

The four of us kept in touch and continued creating concepts for the show and how we'd proceed once the contract with William Morris expired. Using all of our contacts, we tried to keep the idea alive while at the same time trying to keep it under wraps. Some months later, as we continued to shuffle emails back and forth as to how to bring this all together, Paul announced that LDI, a lighting trade show, would allow us to attend the convention and do some film work while there.

I was very familiar with the annual LDI trade show because of the LED entertainment lighting company that Yoichi Aoki and I had owned called Borealis. Once LEDs appeared on the scene, we were all in for this new innovative technology. It was coming no matter what anyone did, so we jumped in feet first. Our idea was to alter stage lighting for the whole industry.

Through our distributor, we had shown these unique and innovative new lights successfully at the LDI show for several years, usually gaining new clients and a lot of interest. And after a lot of hard work and calling in favors and hustling, we did find a good amount of success, including putting our LED lighting on the world's largest cruise ship at the time. In fact, we were approached by the makeup company Sephora, as like them we had any color you could imagine. We were even hired by our competitor's biggest client to take over their needs. It was a Canadian company who eventually, after trials, gave us a half-a-million-dollar contract, which would have put us in business in a major way.

Unfortunately, we were instead put out of business by a patent that we and hundreds like us felt shouldn't have been issued. I remember the competitor being so very pleased to hand us (with their team of attorneys) their cease-and-desist letter once its patent was approved. I even notified the legal teams at GE and Philips about the patent being issued and what it would mean to the LED business eventually, but all they said was to keep them posted. We ran out of money, couldn't continue the legal fight, and had to close.

A few years later, I heard that Philips bought the patent from them for roughly half-a-billion dollars. Once again, it was one of those lessons learned, and I'm not bitter about it, except we believe that the patent shouldn't have been issued because the research and experimentation in the LED arena had been going on for at least a dozen years by the time they filed their patent. That should have made it null and void, but no one would listen. Can I prove anything? No. Would I change anything if I were able to? Maybe, but I'm not bothered by it any longer, and other than writing it down here, I have never given it much thought. I believe everyone will get their just reward in the end.

Sadly, and I do mean sadly, several weeks later Yoichi called me into his office and said he was forced to downsize the company after the Borealis loss and that I no longer had a job. I think he felt as bad as I did, but I know that wasn't possible.

Anyway, back to my new venture, *Road Cases*. It seemed Paul had contacted a friend high up with LDI, and she was able to arrange a room at the convention center in Las Vegas for us to set up cameras and a small set. We'd then be allowed to ask film-crew people and artists who would be attending LDI to stop by for an interview, if they signed a release.

We spent a month or so arranging things and determined it was going to cost Scott and Dave about ten thousand dollars to get their cameras and equipment there, but they agreed making the trip was worth it. Meanwhile, Paul and I spread the word about the interviews and the new TV show, trying to create some hype.

I also arranged to take my family (finally!), so my oldest son from his college in Santa Fe and my second son and our two daughters all converged on Las Vegas. While they knew I'd be busy all day and evening, they were all right with it. There were plenty of things for them to do and see, especially as none of them, including my wife, had been there previously. Our adjoining rooms at the Luxor Hotel were quite nice, and I could tell they were all excited we were getting a short vacation out of the blue. I was just thrilled we'd all get to go together, and I was happy I could spend some time with my son from college as I hadn't seen him since we dropped him off at the beginning of his junior year. Having my family there was the best part of that long weekend. I still have videotapes to refer to.

The day after arriving, I took a shuttle to the convention center, met the team, and we began setting up for the day's shoot. Within a couple of hours, we were ready, and like magic, a few friends and business associates started showing up. After getting each release signed and providing a brief explanation about the purpose of this exercise, the cameras would roll. Scott and Dave took turns prompting the subject to tell his story. Turns out, it wasn't too difficult once they got into the swing of it all. When necessary, whoever was in the interviewer's chair off camera would ask the person a question, which worked great because it would lead to an anecdote or story that usually lasted as long or longer than we'd imagined.

Over that day and the next, there were about thirty people who came to sit in the chair and tell their road tale. Some were more famous than others, but they were all valuable and useful stories. It was great! A few times when my family would stop by and someone was telling a randy story, I'd get embarrassed when foul words or inappropriate subjects were being discussed. Oh, well.

On the final day, the helpful LDI lady, who I will always be grateful to, arranged for us to transfer into a larger auditorium-like room that had a few hundred chairs set up and a stage area. All the cameras and equipment were moved, and we rented sofas, chairs, a carpet, and a coffee table to be used for a set. We also had thirty or more large road cases stacked up as a backdrop. The idea was to do a panel-type segment of the show with numerous guests joining in and Paul as the moderator.

Sadly, the idea was not well-publicized or attended. Maybe about thirty people, including my family, were in the audience, but I have to say it turned out to be one of the funniest hours of my life. About eight or so crew people showed up, and Paul was ready with his prompts. The panel discussion was hilarious, and the fact that more folks weren't there to see it or experience it was such a shame. Regardless, the weekend went as good or better than expected, and we felt we had good, usable material in the can.

Once back at our home bases, Scott and Dave edited the tapes into a pilot episode of sorts, and we used the show to shop our concept to other possible production sources. Doing so was not as easy as it would have been if an agency had been behind us, but we kept on knocking on doors.

After a few months, we received a call from Scott and Dave telling us they were going to have to move on. But they were not going to relinquish any of their financial percentage rights to the material they had shot in Las Vegas. That was fair because we didn't know when or how or if we would ever be using any of this footage again. We said a bitterly sad goodbye but agreed we all still thought the concept had strong legs—if done the right way.

While I was basically off the road, Paul was still touring with a well-known and long-surviving band, REO Speedwagon. Doing so kept him liquid in expensive LA and allowed him to keep his finger on the pulse of what was happening on things I didn't hear about through my network. It was, I believe, a pleasing situation for the both of us.

One day I got a call from Paul, who said he had talked to an associate he'd met on the set of the moderately budgeted 2001 movie *Rock Star,* which starred Mark Wahlberg. Paul was the lighting director for the rock-and-roll concept scenes in the movie while the other fellow was the production designer for the entire film. They had a conversation, and apparently the other guy loved the *Road Cases* idea so much that he wanted to get involved and help make it happen.

We all spoke, and while we were not happy with the terms this fellow laid out, we eventually agreed as he had great contacts. And since the Writers Guild of America (WGA) was on strike and nothing was being filmed, he felt confident he could get a crew together to shoot some footage. He even had an idea that allowed us to successfully acquire a largish amount of money to make this a reality.

It seems his daughter and the daughter of a friend who was a TV executive went to the same private school in LA. The friend was the head of Cablevision (owned by a conglomerate in New York) that had a music station within its network called Fuse. We spoke with the station's executive and attorney to work out the details and the transfer of money as well as the timing of the filming and editing to take place.

In this instance, they wanted *Road Cases Shorts*—a new name but the same idea as ours—with no music overlaid. They were planning on playing these thirty- to ninety-second clips of interviews and scenes between the concert footage their network was principally known for.

Getting a deal done took a few weeks and several phone calls, but in the end the station gave us its whole interstitial budget for the year to make our show. We were suddenly ready to push "lift off" on *Road Cases*. While giving this fellow his large percentage was not one of our most cherished moments of the affair, we were at least seeing some light at the end of the camera lens.

Arrangements were made for a month hence to use the two-hundred-and-fifty-seat auditorium on the grounds of the Getty Villa off the Malibu Coast. The fellow was going to call in as many favors as he could from cameramen, grips, makeup people, and caterers to make it a bit easier. And though all would be paid, the crew wasn't totally happy with the amount, I feel certain, but it was at least a little bit of money coming in during the strike, and they were able to do their craft.

Paul and I notified all of our industry friends, many of whom knew about *Road Cases* already and were happy to attend. Paul was also able to get Def Leppard's old fake Marshall stacks to use as set pieces, and with a set of drums featuring a *Road Cases* logo on the front, we were ready. I flew out to Los Angeles with my son Ian, who had graduated from college by then and was often working wherever the film, TV, or commercial business would take him. He was happy to come.

On the first day, during the setup before any of the interviews, we gathered and laid out our plans. It seems someone thought it would be a good idea to have two attractive young ladies doing the interviews. While they were in makeup and people were getting ready, Ian was asked by Paul's associate, the now producer, to film and document the entire affair. It was all being filmed in HD, and he was fine with that. Ian had the freedom to film as much or as little as he wanted, and, well, I think he just liked being there.

The filming and interviews began, and the set looked good, but the ladies were terrible as they didn't have a clue about anything regarding the music industry, except who their favorite band or song of the week was. We all recognized it immediately, and within an hour or less they were quietly given a few dollars and the old heave-ho.

Now we were back to Paul and a grouping of people just sitting around chatting and having fun. There was some alcohol available to anyone who needed a little Dutch courage to get going, but most were happy to open right up, talk, and laugh. All of these people knew each other and had not been together in a while, so it was fun for them to reminisce.

I must say that during some of our conversations before gathering in Malibu, the producer friend had mentioned he was close with the owner of a deli in the Valley and that it was a hangout for rock stars who wanted a late bite to eat. While I was out of the main filming auditorium, where we had no audience anyway, an interview started with a few people on stage. As I came back inside, I noticed that a young man wearing a T-shirt from the deli was sitting on stage trying to join in but looking out of place. The producer had slipped him in for what I am sure would have been weeks of free Reuben sandwiches for himself. It didn't take long until he was ejected, as he had nothing to do with anything at all in the industry. I'm sure he was embarrassed, and I wonder if the producer was ever allowed to eat at the deli again.

Another stupid thing that happened was the producer had a friend who owned a DeLorean like the one in *Back to the Future*. He thought it would be cool to do an interview in the car, filming from the outside. Why? Well, wouldn't you know it, while we weren't looking, he had grabbed a cameraman and an interview subject, and they were outside somewhere doing a show in the DeLorean. We didn't want to make a big deal about it, so we let it slide, but none of the footage was ever used, I don't believe.

All the while, the executive from New York was in attendance, watching from the darkened auditorium. He would come up to me, knowing I had originally created this with Paul, and make comments quietly in my ear, such as "Good call," or "Glad you got rid of those two." He was a nice guy, and I'm sorry we didn't get to do more business together.

Finally, at the end of the second day when everyone was done and tired, we struck the set and headed our separate ways. Ian and I went for a celebratory meal on the way back to the hotel room we shared. The next day, we were on an American Airlines plane homeward bound to Dallas.

A month or so later, the producer friend of Paul's, who had been designated to do the editing, was working with a lady engineer at a studio in New York, then one of the two best HD editing facilities in the US (or so I was told). They were having to do the editing over a condensed period of time because overall Cablevision had, I believe, twenty-eight stations they owned and had to prepare shows for. A few were music-based, but many were not. Needless to say, studio time was in high demand. However, the word I was receiving was that all was going well, the editing would be done in a couple of days, and "By the way, it looks great!"

We were all pleased until we got a phone call saying the conglomerate who owned the network had just lost a lawsuit to a major internet outfit, and not only did it have to pay a large fine, but it also had to sell about half its stations, including, yes, the one that had backed us and we were counting on. Son of a gun! Lightening does strike in the same place as often as it wants.

In the end, the station gave us all the tapes that were edited (sixty or more) and all the raw footage, wished us luck, and sent us on our way. It wasn't long until the producer decided he had to go back to work to make a living for his family and basically left Paul and I with the tapes, many of which can still be seen on YouTube.

Eventually, after probably five years of work, Paul told me he had to drop out and could no longer work on *Road Cases.* It was all mine now. That was a while ago, and a few celebrities have done something similar, interviewing artists or people in the industry (Sammy Hagar, for one, and also a well-known soundman we once filmed). But to this day, no one has done *Road Cases* as it was intended to be. The show, which is still viable and important, may never get done, but it should.

Road Cases will tell stories of what it was like touring . . . the way they should be told!

CHAPTER 22
Additional Happenings

Exceptional Moments.

In this final chapter, I need to write down some of the things that may not have fit easily or flowed correctly into one of the earlier chapters, so I opted to take a final stab at some "outtakes" of a few events, which I think you might enjoy. Mind you, this is by no means all of them, but rather some that immediately come to mind.

Eric Clapton Era

Money was no object when touring with Eric Clapton during the Roger Forrester/Robert Stigwood Organization Brook Street days. Of course, Robert was not around the offices much and seldom did he ever make an appearance at a concert, but his penchant for first-class living was immersed in the company and the overall way we carried on daily business while touring.

The expression is an old one, but when it came to making sure EC and his band were happy, Roger made sure Eric lacked for nothing. The same went for any of the staff and crew. Rarely was there ever anything to complain about, as I saw it. Eric and the band didn't require special treatment or much in the way of frivolities, but they had the comfort of knowing that whatever they wanted would be taken care of, thanks to the hard work of Roger, me, or someone we paid.

A small example of going to extreme lengths to accommodate Eric's needs or wants came during an early tour. We'd stayed at a hotel in

Mobile, Alabama, where they had a talkative parrot that would converse with patrons at the bar. Eric loved this bird, and next thing we knew, he had his own parrot. He named him Bomber, I guess because he'd fly over and often the bombs would drop.

At the end of the US tour, during which we traveled on our own private plane, Eric found out that Bomber could not travel with him in first class back to England, no matter how much he offered to pay British Airways for a ticket. The bird would have to ride in the cargo hold and then go into quarantine as all normal animals do—even if they traveled on the Concorde.

So what did Roger do for Eric's beloved parrot of a few weeks? He chartered the private plane we were using, which was based on the West Coast, to fly Roger, Alphi, Eric, and Bomber to the UK, via Greenland and all stops in between for fuel. I am sure the bird had to be quarantined, but the restrictions were lighter than if he'd flown on a commercial flight. I even think Bomber may have quarantined at Eric's house.

I don't believe Pattie was too fond of Bomber nor was Eric after he really got to know him. And with the amount of time and training required to get a parrot to talk and be social, it just wasn't going to happen. Imagine how much the charter flight for the parrot was and how many people could have been fed with the money spent. That's how I thought of it.

Another Shot of EC

During my first tour with Eric, he was drinking at least a fifth of Courvoisier brandy a day mixed with 7UP and maybe an ice cube or two, although the British usually shun ice in their drinks. We ran out of brandy often and many times had to buy a bottle from the hotel bar, which if you've ever tried to buy a bottle from a nice hotel bar you know it's very expensive. Normally at least double the liquor-store price.

Roger asked me to find a way to keep our own supply stocked up. We both eyed the free Courvoisier in the dressing room each night and realized it mostly went untouched and left behind. No longer.

So there I was, huddled in my hotel room like some secret agent, with my black leather pilot's briefcase that opened flat at the top. I had bought some dense foam and set about creating a case for Eric's beverages. I cut the foam in such shapes where the case held two bottles of Courvoisier upright, two quart-sized bottles of 7UP, and Eric's appropriate glass. Very compact. I believe we even bought a case of Courvoisier to keep in the belly of the plane as our refill stash.

For a while, this portable liquor cabinet became an extension of my arm whenever we moved from one place to another. When we were stationary, it usually stayed in EC's room or in Rogers's suite.

Backstage, the rider always had liquor listed, so we confiscated the extra bottles of brandy and quickly built up quite a stash. Initially, the briefcase was a curiosity, but then it became a sad burden. I often wondered how Eric could play so well under such a heavy cloud. Of course, if anyone out there knows about Winston Churchill, the great British statesman, they say he drank from the time he woke up until the time he went to bed. But he was apparently a very effective, high-functioning acholic. What did I know?

Eric played some amazing shows while I was with him, and I was always amazed at his talent. Being a guitar player not anywhere close to his ability, I could barely drink a beer without thinking I sounded out of tune.

Lots of people at that time, including me, drank in excess on the road, but not the quantities Eric was downing. Eric was a good drunk, though, if there is such a thing. By good drunk, I mean he was a calm, peaceful, even polite drunk. Whereas some others I worked for turned violent and angry, Eric just mellowed out and went with the flow.

Obviously, people knew this was a road to physical ruin, but no one was doing anything to help Eric at the time. I guess they figured alcohol was much better than heroin. I often wondered why Roger or Pattie didn't voice their concerns, but I then wondered if they did so in the privacy of their own suites. I never saw them voice or express any worry, except when Roger would ask me or whoever was making Eric a drink before a show to go light on the hard stuff. We were to wait until after the performance to make it stronger, if he asked.

Fortunately, Eric survived his time with the bottle and now has a beautiful family and life. He seems very happy. I'm proud and so glad he is no longer drinking.

Another Bad Day for a Bad Guy

Many of the UK band managers from the glorious 1960s often came from questionable backgrounds—the club life, bouncers, bodyguards, that sort of thing. Their reputation was well-known, and they really didn't care who you knew. However, not all were tough guys, like Roger and Dick Ashby, the Bee Gees actual manager, although I feel certain they knew the phone numbers to call when needed.

A story Roger told me is an incident which drove that point home.

While at home one evening with Pattie, Eric's former heroin drug dealer stopped by his house in Surrey to "say hello." He ended up staying through the night as he had made sure to bring his stash, assuring he would be a welcome guest. Evidently, they got high and eventually crashed at some point.

The next morning Eric awoke in his bed feeling frazzled and dragging—a drug-induced stupor. He then noticed a packet of smack on his bedside table that his so-called friend had left "just in case he needed more," hoping EC would maybe get hooked again. The dealer would have his best client back!

Eric thankfully realized he was being set up by this lowlife and phoned Roger and confessed it all. I am sure Roger spent some time thinking about what to do, but he came up with a plan.

Though I do not know the details of what exactly happened, the dealer was tracked down, and when the police arrived at his doorstep, he was found to have an illegal amount of heroin in his possession. He was sent to prison where he served, or maybe is still serving, a decent number of years behind bars.

Best Friends Are Where You Make Them

Alphi O'Leary was a wonderful man and someone whose friendship I will cherish forever. He was formerly the bouncer at the Speakeasy, a famous London nightspot. His brother Laurie O'Leary, an owner of the club, was more well-known for his relationship with the Kray Twins, the oft-celebrated bad boys of the city's East End.

The O'Leary boys grew up in the Bethnal Green area of the East End before it was as posh as it is now. I was told that Laurie had been a driver for the Krays and participated in a few of the gang's more successful getaways. I met Laurie and chatted with him a few times over the years. He was always a gentleman, and I liked him.

Alphi, too, was a gentleman and taught me much about life and living in London while Roger taught me about the music industry and dealing with a big star. When I knew Alphi, he was working for Roger and whoever Roger said was paying at the time. Did Alphi work for Eric, Jack Bruce, or Roger? He never questioned who but always did his job and did it well.

Alphi had worked for Marc Bolan of T. Rex fame, of the hit song "Bang A Gong (Get It On)," years before he worked for RSO. Late one afternoon, Alphi was taking Marc to a show in Birmingham, England, when there was a wreck. Though severe, they were in good enough shape to continue on to the event—or so they thought.

Once at the venue, Alphi was making sure Marc was all set in his dressing room when Alphi collapsed. It seems his neck had been broken in the wreck. He was immediately rushed to the hospital, where he spent a long recovery. He always, as I recall, had a stiff neck, and I am sure it caused him a lot of pain, although he never complained about it.

While in the hospital, Alphi wrote a book of poems, and they are wonderful. He didn't publish it, but he made copies for close friends, and I am privileged to be one friend of his who owns a copy. This gentle giant of a man had such a big heart.

He was a wonderful guy, and he sadly died of stomach cancer a few years after Eric (or Roger?) relieved him of his duties despite his nearly twenty years of service. From what Alphi told me, there was no reason given for his firing, except that we both knew Roger did shuffle personnel periodically to keep things fresh. Doing so had its good side for him and Eric, but it was an obvious downside for those being moved on.

Following his dismissal, Alphi's girlfriend of twenty-five years left him, which for all of us, it seemed as if she felt like, *If he is no longer with Eric, why should I stay with him?* Don't know if that was the case, but Alphi believed it, and I don't think he ever recovered from that.

I did get to spend a day with him at his home in Surrey where the railroad tracks ran down at the end of his garden, which Roger made light of. I will always treasure that day. As I left, he gave me a CD (yes, those days) that contained every Beatles album. Wow! I challenge anyone to find someone who'd say a negative word about Alphi O'Leary.

Eric's Balls

On June 20, 1977, there was a wonderful incident that happened at the Olympiahalle in Munich, a massive venue that had once hosted events during the 1972 Summer Olympics. It seems the road crew had been planning a surprise for the band (and crowd) to celebrate the last night of Eric's European tour, one of the biggest on the continent at the time. This was one of the first recorded tour pranks for what became a long tradition.

With Eric playing his usual set, everything went as normal for the first half of the show. Then casually, a Ping-Pong ball came bouncing across from stage left, bringing a curious glimpse from the band.

There was nothing for a song or two, but then two Ping-Pong balls crisscrossed the stage. This garnered a bit more attention and a few quizzical looks from the band and audience. After another song or two, the time had come for "Layla," which was the final song of the set.

As anticipated, the crowd went crazy with the opening notes of the great love song, and they danced and sang right along with the band. About halfway through the song, unbeknownst to the band, fans, and auditorium management, ten thousand Ping-Pong balls were simultaneously dropped from a catwalk some eighty feet above the stage. The spectacle was amazing, I must say, when all the balls hit the stage and band, bouncing every which way.

The band was really caught off guard, but professional to the end, they kept right on playing. The crew then began throwing Ping-Pong balls at the band as they ricocheted around, and the crowd joined in the festivities as well since there was no controlling where the balls bounced.

Somewhere there is a photo of the ten thousand balls about ten feet over the band members' heads just before they hit. I wish I had a copy. (If anyone has one, please send it to me!) This end-of-tour gag was perhaps the first of what would eventually catch on with many rock bands. Others would try to do something unique, but the Ping-Pong balls will always be the first and best.

Another end-of-tour crew prank occurred at a smaller venue in Guildford, Surrey, near Eric's hometown, I believe. The show went well, and the smaller crowd (smaller venue) loved it. But during the encore, which at the time was something wildly exciting like the song "Cocaine," the road crew slowly and calmly came on stage and started disassembling the amps, drums, and organ piece by piece. Everything.

The pace picked up, and it was soon noticeable in the sound of the song—no cymbals, no bass amp, Eric's amp was unplugged and taken away. The crowd quickly caught on, and the band, surprised, realized there was nothing they could do but just try to keep on playing as long as they could until the crew finally took the guitars and snare and drumsticks.

That signaled the end. Everyone had a good laugh, Eric and the band thanked the audience and road crew, and the event was over, albeit in a very unconventional and hilarious manner.

Walking the Plank at Eric's Home

As we were preparing for our last show of a Clapton UK tour, which would be at Cranleigh Village Hall in Surrey, I was working in the Brook Street office a few days before the concert, doing my accounts early, as I had learned. The phone rang, and I picked it up. It was Keith Bradley, the sound man and crew chief who was relied on heavily. As we were chatting about something, an odd thought came to my mind, and I went with it.

I told him there was a party being planned at Eric's place after the show since it was so nearby. I told Keith that all of the crew was invited, which they were, but I also maliciously added that it was going to be a fancy dress party (costume party). He said, "Yeah? What's the dress?" Off the top of my head, I responded, "Pirates!" I told him the band had rented costumes, and if they could, the crew was encouraged to do so as well.

I believe I told Roger and his secretary, Diana Snelling, what I'd done, which they loved, but we didn't say anything to anyone else.

After the show, the band all went back to Eric's house. George Harrison and Elton John were there, as they were neighbors, and a few dozen other people who I didn't know. There were people serving drinks and appetizers; the scene was all quite subdued then. The crew had not arrived because they had to take down the gear.

Finally, when they did show up, we saw them coming down Eric's drive, and they all were dressed like pirates. They had gone out and rented costumes, hats, hooks, parrots, eye patches, the lot. As they got closer to the house and realized no one else, including the band and Eric, were dressed as pirates, they realized they had been pranked.

Everyone had a great laugh, and the crew seemingly forgot whose silly idea this was as I was never attacked and didn't receive any retribution. Thank goodness. It could have been painful!

Buy Me a Heineken, Mate?

There was a crew fellow who I will have to say was the funniest guy I ever met. His name was Peter "Rocky" Morley. His mate, who made sure Rocky was always safe, was Bobby Richardson. Both were fine friends.

I worked with Rocky on the Jack Bruce tour and with Eric primarily. When I met him, he had already been married and divorced a number of times due to his traveling, I am sure. He got per diem money, and within twenty-four hours was usually empty of his funds. Such a kind person, Rocky was always buying a round at the bar, one for everyone and two for himself. He always had a good story to tell, though, and never ran out of funny ones, I can assure you.

It was always great seeing him backstage just to hear what he'd been up to that day. He was a close and good friend and, like Alphi, is someone I miss seeing. Last I heard, Rocky had several health issues with his heart but was living in Houston, Texas, with his wife and was doing well. We met for coffee in the South London area of Croydon in 2010 and had a wonderful visit. Touring would not have been nearly as fun if he had not been on the scene.

I could probably go on with stories for pages, but I have to stop somewhere. So this is where!

EPILOGUE

On and on in My Mind!

Since leaving the music business, I have pursued my creative side in earnest, writing as much and as often as I can. I've come up with concepts and stories of both fiction and nonfiction and have written treatments for old film remakes I wanted to see made. I even penned ideas for sequels to films I'd seen and enjoyed, including writing a sequel to *Casablanca* after watching the original Humphry Bogart movie during an overseas flight. My story took up where the original left off.

I have compiled a portfolio of more than forty original pieces. Some are completely original stories, but there are also a few sequels, a few prequels, stage musicals, children's books, rhyming books, and picture books. If nothing else, writing is a great way for me to release some of the constant barrage of mind-cluttering creative ideas that attack me seemingly every day. In fact, this attempt at a memoir, encapsulating my career, is just one more idea that I couldn't put down until I had written it. Whether a book got published or not wasn't the real object, though it was a bonus. I just can't ignore the urge to put my thoughts down on paper.

I married a wonderful woman four decades ago, and she has put up with so many of my hairbrained ideas and concepts—some work, some don't, but all stay in the portfolio. While she has always been encouraging, as I am aging, I have thought, *What is going to happen to all my ideas? Will one of my children take my portfolio and do something with it? Will it be put away in a file? Or in a dumpster?* Sort of like thinking, *What if Shakespeare's writings had all been destroyed before his work ever made it to the stage?*

Being creative is great, but you must have backers or producers who want to fund your work for it to be successful or for it to at least have a chance. And that is about as hard as trying to get a record deal in the olden days.

Because my wife is British and an American, and all four of our children have dual citizenship, we traveled to the UK often when they were young. That has allowed me to keep in touch with most of my friends and associates, although I lost touch with some. We still travel there about every eighteen months to see family and friends and to catch up. The trips are always fun.

However, where I live north of Dallas, we have many British friends nearby. I was recently doing an audio recording for a musical I created and wanted to tape a shortened version as a sample. For this, I wanted to use people with British accents, and coming up with enough Brits to fit the script was easy. Don't know why they've settled in this area, but seemingly a lot have.

Thanks to my brilliant wife, we are financially secure in our retirement years and can do as we please, but she has three part-time jobs (more to keep her active, not for the money), and I stay busy with our land; there's always mowing, repairs, and other projects. And now that we have four granddaughters, our kids seem to have us on speed dial as their most trusted (and cheapest) babysitters.

In looking back at my life touring, I believe these stories could go on and on as I keep coming up with more, but I will have to stop and let this be all for now. I had a magical and wonderful career. Being in the music industry wasn't always easy or secure, but when I was working and touring or in the studio, it was truly special.

That time was like nothing I have ever been a part of before or since, and I believe most who toured during the 1960s, 1970s, and early 1980s would agree. There are no words that can give my story the real justice it deserves, but I have tried to convey the magic as I experienced it.

I met many celebrities, made a lot of friends globally, and had opportunities no one could imagine. I ate at the best restaurants, rode elephants in the jungle in Thailand, listened to great music every night, traveled on the most exceptional private transports, and am now here to share my memories with you.

I don't believe for a second that money buys or brings happiness, and I never saw it that way with the artists. Sure, it made their lives easier to pay bills (although some didn't even know how to pay a bill) and buy any fancy car they wished, but I never saw the rock stars I worked with as anyone I'd have traded places with—not even for a moment.

I was treated kindly and am grateful for that, and I was paid handsomely to travel the world, a feat not many will ever accomplish. I wish everyone could see the world as I did or, heck, in any circumstance because there is so much to learn from so many different races and cultures. That was a major part of the magic.

Do I miss touring? Yes, sometimes I think what fun it would be to do again, but I don't honestly believe that in this current day and age the music business is anywhere near as magical and unique as it was during my time touring.

Thank you to all who made it happen, the celebrities, crew, managers, agents, technical companies, transportation companies, hotels, and the thousands of people I had the pleasure of working with. I pray I left as good an impression on you as you did on me.

By no means was this all that I experienced during my career, but for now, it's a good start—or ending!

Thank you!

ACKNOWLEDGMENTS

This book was within me a long time before I actually sat down to write it. Although my now-grown children knew what Dad did for a living, I wrote this memoir as a more detailed explanation of the job I loved for so long, not really planning on having it be published.

There were many years and many thousands of miles during my decades on the road, and remembering all that went on during that time would seem incomprehensible. But fortunately, I was a saver and kept all my itineraries and laminates. And thank God I have a pretty good memory. That plus the events, good and not so good, happened within a circus filled with celebrities. Their recognizable names and people wanting me to recount my stories of the road throughout most of my life helped keep a large majority of the facts within an easy mental grasp. To the best of my knowledge, the events, dates, names, and places are as accurate as I can remember them—at least that is my intention.

This book, if my children read it, will give them a better idea of what my life was like away from home, and whoever else reads it should get an idea of what life in the music-touring business was like for those of us who were out there feeling our way alone in the dark before the industry matured and high technology and huge arenas and stadiums became the norm.

It was a wild ride right from that first phone call in Tulsa, but there were even exciting times in my teen years being a musician touring the club and party circuit in Texas. There were many great garage bands with Jimmy, Tommy, Doyle, Jimmie, Seab, John, Rick, Larry, Jim, Lanny, and Dale playing clubs like Louann's, the Studio Club, Purple Onion, Club Saracen, the various fraternities and sororities, and Market Hall on New Years Eve. Wow, what a night!

Then there were the vehicles. A family station wagon, various trailers, the Singer sewing machine company's cast-off vans (circa 1962), the hearses, the school bus, and the unnamed business whose truck took us to Los Angeles and back twice with a not too reliable odometer cable.

I'd like to state here that most of us were very lucky young men and women back then to have survived it all.

Once the phone call came, though, my life changed into a much higher gear-ratio, which, for a change, included enough money to not have to worry about the things that hindered us during those formative years. Money is not what it's all about, I assure you, but it sure does help.

Along the way, even in my younger years, wonderful musicians would make the headlines, but not how they would have chosen. Those such as Buddy, Janis, Jimi, Jim, Brian, Keith, and so many more left the industry and their loved ones far too soon.

However, I can't forget losing those in the business who were closer to me, like Jack, Gary, Carl, Dick, Jamie, C.J., Guy, Tom, Ronnie, Maurice, Robin, Alphi, Lorrie, Willie, Di, Jack C., Joe C., and John Andrew Parks. My goodness, there are too many to remember them all, and I can tell you it does hurt a bit even writing their names. I am glad to still have so many of my music associates and friends still on this mortal coil and mostly in good enough shape to hopefully last a few more years.

In trying to be someone's savior at times, I did discover something I really *had* to learn, and that was you cannot convince a person not to drink too much or do too many drugs no matter how often you talk to them until the sun comes up. They have to decide themselves that there is a better way than the damaging road, both physically and mentally, they are currently on. If they don't decide for themselves, they won't change. I'm not saying don't try to help, but doing so is usually futile, and with that often comes a sad ending.

I want to thank my publishing company, TCU Press, Dan Williams for putting up with all my novice mistakes and questions, Marco Roc, Adrienne Martinez, and the rest of Dan's team who had a part in making me sound better. Also thanks to my editor, Kurt Daniels, who showed great patience with me and kept me in the right year and city and with the right band.

Also many thanks to Roger Forrester, Dick Ashby, Robert Stigwood, Tony Hymas, Hugh Burns, Simon Phillips, Marcy Levy, Bill Oakes,

Yvonne Elliman, Rob Cowlyn, Bugzee Hougdahl, Sharon Osbourne, Pete Mertons, Bobby Thompson, Lee Dixon, Bob Richardson, Rocky Morley, Omar Abderrahman, Keith Bradley, Jeff Bradley, Mary Oldaker, Harvey Goldsmith, Michael Eaton, Colin Newman and all at SLRV in London, Jay Hagerman, Sims Hinds, Ed Skillman, Don Airey, Brad Gillis, Rudy Sarzo, Kayoko Loucks, Taro Shimizu, Mr. Takuji Shimizu, Yoichi Aoki, Hisashi Takashi, Masumi Komatsu, John Meglan, Simon Davies, Daniel Flannery, Jonathan Barnes, Bill Leverty, Michael Foster, Perry Richardson, Lanny Lander, Larry Meletio, Jim McClellan, Jimmy Vaughn, Mickey Raphael, Rick Zelazny, Herman Drees, Patty Granville, Buff Shurr, Len, Kay, Vincent, Tony Baggarley, and Jacob Barnes.

I could not have done this without the love and patience of my wonderful wife of over forty years, who, while I was out somewhere in the world, kept our home running, had a full-time job, and eventually homeschooled our four children, Ian, Simon, Paris, and Malia, up to college. She also had her own podcast, *The Sociable Homeschooler*, before podcasting was the "in" thing. I don't know how she did it. No, I do know how she did it—with God's help each and every day.

A special thank you to my parents, who were the coolest parents for a person like me to have. They were always supportive and loving, no matter what.

I could probably go on and on, but if you and I crossed paths on the road somewhere during our time in the music business, thank you for all your help, time, commitment, patience, and understanding. It was great, and if I could do it all over again, well, I would.

On top of the others I have acknowledged, I give all credit for my life, blessings, abundance, and this book to my Lord and Savior, Jesus!

ABOUT THE AUTHOR

Larry was born in Dallas and as most young kids, he played intramural sports at elementary school. Then, after a painful "face plant" in the dirt, he realized, "no girls chased football or baseball players like they did the Beatles" in the early '60s, so Larry calmly decided that he'd learn the guitar and be a famous rock star—forget sports! After nearly eight years playing at clubs and dances on the local Texas, Oklahoma, and Louisiana circuit, spending a couple years in LA trying to get a record deal, having won almost every Battle of The Bands in Southern California, and still ending up with no record deal, Larry decided he needed to find a new angle to the music business where he might have a better chance at succeeding. Realizing he was the one who booked the band, rented the van, booked the cheap motels, collected the money, and distributed it, he thought the business/management part of the business seemed ideal. The rest, as they say, is history, or in this case, his story!

www.ingramcontent.com/pod-product-compliance
Lightning Source LLC
LaVergne TN
LVHW051937100826
845154LV00002B/13
9780875659596